First World War
and Army of Occupation
War Diary
France, Belgium and Germany

9 DIVISION
Headquarters, Branches and Services
General Staff
1 August 1916 - 30 September 1916

WO95/1736

The Naval & Military Press Ltd
www.nmarchive.com
Published in association with The National Archives

Published by

The Naval & Military Press Ltd

Unit 10 Ridgewood Industrial Park,

Uckfield, East Sussex,

TN22 5QE England

Tel: +44 (0) 1825 749494

www.naval-military-press.com

www.nmarchive.com

This diary has been reprinted in facsimile from the original. Any imperfections are inevitably reproduced and the quality may fall short of modern type and cartographic standards.

© **Crown Copyright**
Images reproduced by permission of The National Archives, London, England, 2015.

Contents

Document type	Place/Title	Date From	Date To
Heading	9th Division Gen. Staff Aug-Sep 1916		
Heading	General Staff. 9th Division, August, 1916. Sept. 1916		
Heading	9th (Scottish) Division. General Staff War Diary, August, 1916. Vol 15		
War Diary	Bruay	01/08/1916	14/08/1916
War Diary	Camblain L'Abbe	15/08/1916	31/08/1916
Operation(al) Order(s)	9th Division Operation Order No. 71. Appx 1	10/08/1916	10/08/1916
Miscellaneous	March Table.		
Miscellaneous	Reference 9th Division Operation Order No. 71 Para. 4. Appx: 2	10/08/1916	10/08/1916
Miscellaneous	Recipients of Operation Order No. 71. Appx: 3	11/08/1916	11/08/1916
Miscellaneous	26th Inf. Brigade. Appx: 4	16/08/1916	16/08/1916
Miscellaneous	Proposals For Night Operation To Be Carried Out By The 9th Division. Appx: 5	18/08/1916	18/08/1916
Miscellaneous	Proposed Artillery Action No Z Day Appendix A.		
Operation(al) Order(s)	9th Division Operation Order No. 72 Appx. 6	20/08/1916	20/08/1916
Miscellaneous			
Miscellaneous	IVth Corps	21/08/1916	21/08/1916
Miscellaneous	IV Corps No. 1714 (G).	17/08/1916	17/08/1916
Miscellaneous	First Army No. 812 (G).	03/08/1916	03/08/1916
Heading	General Staff. 9th Division. September, 1916.		
Heading	General Staff 9th Scottish Division. War Diary. September, 1916. Vol 16.		
War Diary	Camblain L'Abbe	01/09/1916	26/09/1916
War Diary	Cauroy	27/09/1916	30/09/1916
Miscellaneous	Appendices.		
Operation(al) Order(s)	9th Division Operation Order No. 73.	01/09/1916	01/09/1916
Operation(al) Order(s)	9th Division Operation Order No. 74.	01/09/1916	01/09/1916
Operation(al) Order(s)	9th Division Operation Order No. 75.	04/09/1916	04/09/1916
Miscellaneous	9th Division Instructions No. 29 (G).	02/09/1916	02/09/1916
Miscellaneous	26th Infantry Brigade	09/09/1916	09/09/1916
Operation(al) Order(s)	9th (Scottish) Division, Operation Order No. 76.	13/09/1916	13/09/1916
Miscellaneous	Table A.		
Miscellaneous	Table B. Accommodation Available For Brigades On Completion of Relief.		
Miscellaneous	1st South African Brigade.	14/09/1916	14/09/1916
Miscellaneous	1st South African Infantry Brigade. Headquarters.	15/09/1916	15/09/1916
Miscellaneous	9th Division.	14/09/1916	14/09/1916
Miscellaneous	2nd Regiment South African Infantry. South African Brigade.	14/09/1916	14/09/1916
Miscellaneous	The Adjutant, 2nd S.A.I.	14/09/1916	14/09/1916
Miscellaneous	4th Corps.	17/09/1916	17/09/1916
Miscellaneous	Recipients of Operation Order 76.	16/09/1916	16/09/1916
Miscellaneous	A Form Messages And Signals.		
Operation(al) Order(s)	9th Division Operation Order No. 77.	17/09/1916	17/09/1916
Operation(al) Order(s)	9th Division Operation Order No. 78.	20/09/1916	20/09/1916
Miscellaneous	Table A.		
Operation(al) Order(s)	9th Division Operation Order No. 79.	22/09/1916	22/09/1916
Miscellaneous	March Table.		
Miscellaneous	9th (Scottish) Division. Dispositions of Units.	27/09/1916	27/09/1916

Type	Description	Date 1	Date 2
Miscellaneous	B.M. 2/290. 27th. Infantry Brigade. To, 9th. (Scottish) Division.	08/09/1916	08/09/1916
Miscellaneous	27th Infantry Brigade.	07/09/1916	07/09/1916
Miscellaneous	9th Division.	07/09/1916	07/09/1916
Miscellaneous	9th (Scottish) Division. Intelligence Summary.	17/09/1916	17/09/1916
Miscellaneous	9th (Scottish) Division. Intelligence Summary.	18/09/1916	18/09/1916
Miscellaneous	9th (Scottish) Division. Intelligence Summary.	20/09/1916	20/09/1916
Map	No Man's Land, Berthonval Section.		
Miscellaneous	For War Diary		
Map	Edition 7A		
Miscellaneous	War Diary		
Map			
Diagram etc	France. Sheet 36C		
Miscellaneous	France. Sheet 36B.		
Miscellaneous	Central Registry. Subject, And Office of Origin. Minor Operation-Raid	25/09/1916	25/09/1916
Miscellaneous	IV Corps No. H.R.S. 641.	19/09/1916	19/09/1916
Miscellaneous	IV Corps. 27th Infantry Brigade, 1st S. African Brigade	19/09/1916	19/09/1916
Miscellaneous	IVth Corps. 27th Infantry Brigade, 1st S. African Brigade,	19/09/1916	19/09/1916
Miscellaneous	9th Division.	17/09/1916	17/09/1916
Miscellaneous	1st Army.	18/09/1916	18/09/1916
Miscellaneous	4th Corps.	17/09/1916	17/09/1916
Operation(al) Order(s)	26th Infantry Brigade, Operation Order No. 39.	11/09/1916	11/09/1916
Miscellaneous	. Barrages Appendix I.		
Map			
Miscellaneous	Operation Order. 8th Bn. The Black Watch.	13/09/1916	13/09/1916
Miscellaneous	No. 2.		
Miscellaneous	Para. 3. Object.		
Miscellaneous	Operation Order. 5th Cameron Highlanders. General Idea.	12/09/1916	12/09/1916
Miscellaneous	Amendment To 9th Divisional Artillery Operation order No. 59.	13/09/1916	13/09/1916
Operation(al) Order(s)	9th Divisional Artillery. Operation Order No. 59	10/09/1916	10/09/1916
Miscellaneous	Not To Be Written On.		
Miscellaneous	Central Registry. Subject, And Office of Origin.	13/09/1916	13/09/1916
Miscellaneous	IVth Corps No. 1701/10 (G)	16/09/1916	16/09/1916
Miscellaneous	4th Corps.	15/09/1916	15/09/1916
Miscellaneous	1st South African Brigade.	14/09/1916	14/09/1916
Miscellaneous	1st South African Infantry Brigade. Headquarters.	15/09/1916	15/09/1916
Miscellaneous	9th Division.	14/09/1916	14/09/1916
Miscellaneous	2nd Regiment South African Infantry. South African Brigade.	14/09/1916	14/09/1916
Miscellaneous	The Adjutant, 2nd S.A.I.	14/09/1916	14/09/1916
Miscellaneous	Not To Be Written On.		
Miscellaneous	Scheme J. AA Bde. Operation Orders.		
Operation(al) Order(s)	Operation Order No. 66.	11/10/1916	11/10/1916
Map			
Operation(al) Order(s)	1st S.A. Infantry Brigade. Operation Order No. 67.	15/10/1916	15/10/1916
Operation(al) Order(s)	H.Q., 1st South African Infantry Brigade. Operation Order No 68.	17/10/1916	17/10/1916
Map	SAI Bde	17/10/1916	17/10/1916
Operation(al) Order(s)	H.Q. 1st S.A.I. Brigade. Operation Order No. 69.	18/10/1916	18/10/1916
Miscellaneous	Schedule Accompanying Operation Order No. 69.		
Miscellaneous	Scheme J. 27th Bde. Operation Orders		
Miscellaneous	B.M. 2/971. Headquarters, 27th. Inf. Brigade.	17/10/1916	17/10/1916

Type	Description	Date 1	Date 2
Operation(al) Order(s)	27th. Infantry Brigade Operation Order No. 101.	17/10/1916	17/10/1916
Miscellaneous	Scheme J Special Co P.E. Operation Orders.		
Operation(al) Order(s)	Operation Order No 18 No 4 Special Company R.E.	17/10/1916	17/10/1916
Miscellaneous	C Form (Duplicate). Messages And Signals.		
Operation(al) Order(s)	Operation Order No. 17. No. 4. Special Company R.E.	11/10/1916	11/10/1916
Miscellaneous	Scheme J 47th and 9th Drive. Artillery Operation Orders		
Miscellaneous	Addendum No. 2 To 9th Divisional Artillery Operation Order No. 68	17/10/1916	17/10/1916
Miscellaneous	Addendum No. 1 To 9th Divisional Artillery Operation Order No. 86	17/10/1916	17/10/1916
Operation(al) Order(s)	9th Divisional Artillery Operation Order No. 68.	17/10/1916	17/10/1916
Miscellaneous	Distribution		
Miscellaneous	Addendum No. 1 To Right Divisional Artillery Group Operation Order No. 65.	11/10/1916	11/10/1916
Miscellaneous	Distribution		
Miscellaneous	Addendum No. 2 To Right Divisional Artillery Group Operation Order No. 65.	12/10/1916	12/10/1916
Operation(al) Order(s)	Right Divisional Artillery Group Operation Order No. 65.	11/10/1916	11/10/1916
Miscellaneous	Schedule of Fire--Table "A"--(To Accompany Right D.A. Group Op. Order No. 65). Creeping Barrage.		
Miscellaneous	Schedule of Fire--Table "B"--(To Accompany Right D.A. Group Op. Order No. 65). Stationary Barrage.		
Miscellaneous	Schedule of Fire--Table "C"--(To Accompany Right D.A. Group Op. Order No. 65).		
Miscellaneous	Addendum No. 1 To Right Divisional Artillery Group Operation Order No. 65.	11/10/1916	11/10/1916
Operation(al) Order(s)	Right Divisional Artillery Group Operation Order No. 65.	11/10/1916	11/10/1916
Miscellaneous	Schedule of Fire--Table "A"--(To Accompany Right D.A. Group Op. Order No. 65). Creeping Barrage.		
Miscellaneous	Schedule of Fire--Table "B"--(To Accompany Right D.A. Group Op. Order No. 65). Stationary Barrage.		
Miscellaneous	Schedule of Fire--Table "C"--(To Accompany Right D.A. Group Op. Order No. 65).		
Miscellaneous	Addendum No. 2 To Right Divisional Artillery Group Operation Order No. 65.	12/10/1916	12/10/1916
Miscellaneous	Scheme J. Operation Orders 9th Division		
Miscellaneous	Addendum No. 2 To 9th Division Operation Order No. 86.	17/10/1916	17/10/1916
Miscellaneous	A Form Messages And Signals.		
Operation(al) Order(s)	9th Division Operation Order No. 86.	16/10/1916	16/10/1916
Miscellaneous	A Form Messages And Signals.		
Operation(al) Order(s)	9th Division Operation Order No. 86.	16/10/1916	16/10/1916
Miscellaneous	A Form Messages And Signals.		
Operation(al) Order(s)	9th Division Operation Order No. 85.	11/10/1916	11/10/1916
Miscellaneous	Scheme J. 26th Bde. Operation Order		
Miscellaneous	C Form (Original). Messages And Signals.		
Operation(al) Order(s)	26th Infantry Brigade, Operation Order No. 49.	17/10/1916	17/10/1916
Operation(al) Order(s)	26th Infantry Brigade, Operation Order No. 48.	12/10/1916	12/10/1916
Miscellaneous	Cover For Documents. Nature of Enclosures. Scheme J		
Map			
Miscellaneous	15th Division No. 100 (1)/11 G.a.	15/10/1916	15/10/1916
Miscellaneous	9th Division Desert	15/10/1916	15/10/1916
Map	SAI Bde		

Type	Description	Date	Date
Miscellaneous	Addendum No. 1 To III Corps Operation Order No. 147.	17/10/1916	17/10/1916
Miscellaneous	No. 4. Special Company, R.E. Report On Operations 18.10.1916.	18/10/1916	18/10/1916
Miscellaneous	1st S. African Brigade.	17/10/1916	17/10/1916
Miscellaneous	26th Inf. Brigade. 1st S. African Bde. 15th Division 30th Division for information.	17/10/1916	17/10/1916
Miscellaneous	26th Inf. Brigade. 30th Division. C.R.A. For Information	17/10/1916	17/10/1916
Miscellaneous	26th Infantry Brigade.	17/10/1916	17/10/1916
Miscellaneous	26th Infantry Brigade, 1st S. African Brigade.	16/10/1916	16/10/1916
Miscellaneous	III Corps.	14/10/1916	14/10/1916
Miscellaneous	A Form Messages And Signals.		
Miscellaneous	C Form (Duplicate). Messages And Signals.		
Miscellaneous	C Form (Original). Messages And Signals.		
Miscellaneous	Conference. Held At S. African Bde. H.Q. At 9 a.m. On 15/10/16.	15/10/1916	15/10/1916
Miscellaneous	26th Infantry Brigade. 1st South African Brigade. C.R.E. 9th Seaforths.	14/10/1916	14/10/1916
Miscellaneous	No. 4. Special Company, R.E. Report On Operations 12.10.1916.	12/10/1916	12/10/1916
Miscellaneous	9th Division. Points Affecting The Attack On 12th October 1916.	13/10/1916	13/10/1916
Miscellaneous	26th Inf. Bde. 1st S. African Bde. C.R.A.	12/10/1916	12/10/1916
Miscellaneous	9th Division. 15th Division. Heavy Artillery. B.G., R.A. Air Report 3 P.M.-4 P.M. On "Chinese Attack" 11/10/16.	11/10/1916	11/10/1916
Miscellaneous	Recipients of 9th Division Operation Order No. 85.	11/10/1916	11/10/1916
Miscellaneous	1st S.A. Infantry Brigade.	10/10/1916	10/10/1916
Miscellaneous	Instructions Received By G.O.C. South African Infantry Brigade From Div. Commander 10/10/16.	10/10/1916	10/10/1916
Miscellaneous	A Form. Messages And Signals.		
Miscellaneous	26th Inf. Brigade. 27th Inf. Brigade. 1st S. African Bde. C.R.A. C.R.E. 9th Seaforths.	19/10/1916	19/10/1916
Miscellaneous	26th Inf. Brigade. 27th Inf. Brigade. 1st S. African Bde. C.R.A. C.R.E. 9th Seaforths.	10/10/1916	10/10/1916
Miscellaneous	26th Inf. Bde. 1st S. African Bde. C.R.E. 27th Inf. Bde. C.R.A. 9th Seaforths. For Information.	09/10/1916	09/10/1916
Miscellaneous	Cover For Documents. Nature of Enclosures. Scheme K.		
Miscellaneous	Messages And Signals.		
Miscellaneous	C.R.A.	23/10/1916	23/10/1916
Miscellaneous	26th Infantry Brigade.	22/10/1916	22/10/1916
Map	Map. C.		
Miscellaneous	S. African Brigade, C.R.A. C.R.E. 9th Seaforths, "Q" A.D.M.S.	22/10/1916	22/10/1916
Miscellaneous	Copies Taken To 26 to 27 Bdes Personally	22/10/1916	22/10/1916
Map	Amended Map.		
Map	Amended Map		
Miscellaneous	Scheme K 27th Bde Operation Orders		
Miscellaneous	Preliminary Orders.	22/10/1916	22/10/1916
Operation(al) Order(s)	27th. Infantry Brigade Operation Order No. 103.	22/10/1916	22/10/1916
Miscellaneous	Scheme K. 9th Divn Operation Order.		
Miscellaneous	Operation Orders In Connection With Scheme K.		
Miscellaneous	A Form. Messages And Signals.		
Operation(al) Order(s)	9th Division Operation Order No. 88.	22/10/1916	22/10/1916

Type	Description	Date	Date
Miscellaneous	Addendum No. 1 To 9th Division Operation Order No. 87	25/10/1916	25/10/1916
Operation(al) Order(s)	Correction No. 1 to 9th Division Operation Order No. 87.	21/10/1916	21/10/1916
Operation(al) Order(s)	9th Division Operation Order No. 87.	20/10/1916	20/10/1916
Map	Amended Map		
Miscellaneous	Scheme K. 3rd Corps Operation Order		
Miscellaneous	Addendum No. 5 To III Corps Operation Order No. 148.	26/10/1916	26/10/1916
Miscellaneous	C Form (Original). Messages And Signals.		
Operation(al) Order(s)	Correction No. 3 to III Corps Operation Order No. 148.	22/10/1916	22/10/1916
Operation(al) Order(s)	Correction No. 2 to III Corps Operation Order No. 148.	20/10/1916	20/10/1916
Miscellaneous	Identification Trace For Use With Artillery Maps.		
Miscellaneous	A Form. Messages And Signals.		
Miscellaneous	Addendum No. 1 To III Corps Operation Order No. 148.	22/10/1916	22/10/1916
Operation(al) Order(s)	Correction No. 1 to III Corps Operation Order No. 148.	19/10/1916	19/10/1916
Operation(al) Order(s)	III Corps Operation Order No. 148.	19/10/1916	19/10/1916
Map	Pys-Le Sars-Ligny-Thilloy		
Miscellaneous	9th Division	26/10/1916	26/10/1916
Miscellaneous	Addendum No. 4. To 15th Division Operation Order No. 105.	26/10/1916	26/10/1916

9TH DIVISION

GEN. STAFF
AUG - SEP 1916

GENERAL STAFF,

9th DIVISION,

AUGUST, 1916.

Sept - 1916

9th (SCOTTISH) DIVISION.

GENERAL STAFF WAR DIARY, AUGUST, 1916.

Army Form C. 2118

WAR DIARY
INTELLIGENCE SUMMARY
(Erase heading not required.)

Instructions regarding War Diaries and Intelligence Summaries are contained in F. S. Regs., Part II. and the Staff Manual respectively. Title Pages will be prepared in manuscript.

Place	Date	Hour	Summary of Events and Information	Remarks and references to Appendices
BRUAY	1/8		The 9th Div: Artillery continued its move by rail to 9th Div Area.	
"	2/8		The 9th Div. Artillery completed its concentration in the 9th Div. area. B.G.R.A. 4th Corps visit G.O.C and explains an operation to be undertaken by the 9th Division when it goes into the line – Probable date of going into line about Oct Aug. 12"	
"	3/8		G.O.C. held conference of its regulars and Machine Gun Officers at 27th Bde Head quarters on the subject of the booms on the employment of Machine Guns in the late operations. G.O.C. 26 Bde modified that ten Booms will be required to carry out the operation referred to above.	
	4/8 5/8 6/8		Nothing to record —	

Army Form C. 2118

WAR DIARY
INTELLIGENCE SUMMARY
(Erase heading not required.)

Instructions regarding War Diaries and Intelligence Summaries are contained in F.S. Regs., Part II. and the Staff Manual respectively. Title Pages will be prepared in manuscript.

Place	Date	Hour	Summary of Events and Information	Remarks and references to Appendices
BRUAY	7/8		Nothing to record	
"	8/8		G.O.C. attended a conference at Corps Headquarters –	
"	9/8		IV Corps Order No 121 received as to relief of 39th Division by 9th Div in BERTHONVAL and CARENCY Sections –	
"	"		9th Div O.O. No 91 issued as to relief of 37th Div by 9th Div in BERTHONVAL and CARENCY Sections – 26th Inf Bde to relieve 63rd Inf Bde on night Aug 12/13 in BERTHONVAL Section 27th Inf Bde to move to reserve area on Aug 13th 27th Inf Bde to relieve Composite Bde of 37th Div in CARENCY Section on night Aug 14/15 1st S.A.I. Bde to move to Reserve Area on Aug. 15th G.O.C. 9th Div to assume Command of front at 10.A.M. on Aug 15th	Appx. 1
"	10/8			

Army Form C. 2118

WAR DIARY
INTELLIGENCE SUMMARY
(Erase heading not required.)

Place	Date	Hour	Summary of Events and Information	Remarks and references to Appendices
BRUAY	11/8		9ᵗʰ Dn X4/1607/1 issued reference 9ᵗʰ Dn O.O. No 71 para 4. 64 & 63ʳᵈ Fᵈ Coys R.E. to relieve 152ⁿᵈ and 153ʳᵈ Fᵈ Coys R.E. respectively on Aug 12ᵗʰ. 90 Fᵈ Coy R.E to move to camp at BOIS DE LA HAIE on Aug 12ᵗʰ. Gun Field Companies of 37 Dn to be at disposal of 9 Dn when G.O.C. 9 Dn assumes Command of the Line. (i.e. 10AM on Aug 15ᵗʰ.)	appx. 2
"			9ᵗʰ Dn X4/1607/3 issued - 9ᵗʰ Dn Artillery to relieve 37 Dn Artillery on nights 13/14ᵗʰ and 14/15ᵗʰ Aug. 9ᵗʰ Dn Medium and Heavy Trench Mortars of 37 Dn to remain in the line - Note 9ᵗʰ Dn R.A and 37 Dn R.A to exchange guns -	appx. 3
"	12/8		3rd 26ᵗʰ Inf Bde relieved the 63ʳᵈ Inf Bde in the BERTHONVAL Section on the night Aug 12/13ᵗʰ.	
"	13/8		27 Inf Bde moved from DIEVAL-LE COMTE Area to Reserve Area.	

Army Form C. 2118

WAR DIARY / INTELLIGENCE SUMMARY

(Erase heading not required.)

Instructions regarding War Diaries and Intelligence Summaries are contained in F.S. Regs., Part II. and the Staff Manual respectively. Title Pages will be prepared in manuscript.

Place	Date	Hour	Summary of Events and Information	Remarks and references to Appendices
BRUAY	13/8		9'Dn. Artillery moved forward from DEVRES Area to 37'Dn. Area preparation to carrying out the relief of the 37 Div. Artillery.	
"	14/8		On the night Aug 13/14th the leading section of the 9'Dn. Artillery relieved the leading section of the 37 Div. R.A.	
CAMBLAIN L'ABBE	15/8		On the night Aug 14/15 the rear section of the 37'D.A. relieved the rear section of the 9'D.A. On this same night (Aug 14/15th) the 27'Inf. relieved the Composite Bde of the 37 Div. in the CARENCY section. At 10. A.M. 9'Div. Headquarters closed at BRUAY and opened at CAMBLAIN L'ABBE the G.O.C. 9'Div. assuming command of the right sector at the same hour. The G.O.C. attended a Conference at Arches 1st Army Headquarters at 11. A.M.	

WAR DIARY

INTELLIGENCE SUMMARY
(Erase heading not required.)

Army Form C. 2118

Instructions regarding War Diaries and Intelligence Summaries are contained in F.S. Regs., Part II. and the Staff Manual respectively. Title Pages will be prepared in manuscript.

Place	Date	Hour	Summary of Events and Information	Remarks and references to Appendices
CAMBLAIN L'ABBE	15/8		1st S.A.I. Bde moved to reserve area on the evening of Aug 15. relieving the composite Bde of the 37th Div. On the receipts of orders for the system	
"	16/8	5.30AM 5.30PM	Situation quiet. Orders received (4thDivn XS/1631/3) for 26th Inf. Bde. to extend its left on the night 17th/18th Aug. and relieve 87th Inf. Bde. as far north as TONCHET Trench	Appx. 4
"	17/8	5.30AM 5.30PM	Situation quiet 405 men of 1st S.A.I. Bde attached to C.R.A. for work on communications — 300 men of 1st S.A.I. Bde attached to 26' Bde for work in the line — The work of both (three parties in connection with the preparal operations of the 26' Inf. Bde.	
"	18/8		The enemy rather more active on this day with Artillery on ZOUAVE VALLEY and C.T.'s and with Trench Mortars — One Trench Mortar active	

Army Form C. 2118

WAR DIARY

INTELLIGENCE SUMMARY

(Erase heading not required.)

Place	Date	Hour	Summary of Events and Information	Remarks and references to Appendices
CAMBLAIN L'ABBÉ	18/8		Proposals for attack on enemy's front support line trenches on VIMY A.10.c.5 forwarded to 4th Corps ('G' D.n X 4/1584/9).	appx 5
"	19/8		Quiet day. Enemy blew a CAMOUFLET at IRISH CRATER at 10.15 A.M. Good deal of damage done to front trench and gallerier.	
"	20/8		4 Corps H.R.S. 609 received detaching one Inf. Bn. of 3rd Div. to relieve 1st S.A.I. Bde in Reserve Area on nights 23/24th Aug. 9th Div. O.O. 26 issued detailing relief of 26 Inf. Bde by 1st S.A.I. in BERTHONVAL Section on the night Aug 23/24th. On relief 26 Inf. Bde to proceed to Reserve Division Area.	
"	21/8		Quiet day.	
"	22/8		Quiet day. Orders received at 10 p.m. for 18th NORTH. FUSILIERS (PIONEERS) attached to 9th Div. to be withdrawn at once and despatched by road to 2nd Army Area.	

WAR DIARY
INTELLIGENCE SUMMARY
(Erase heading not required.)

Army Form C. 2118

Place	Date	Hour	Summary of Events and Information	Remarks and references to Appendices
CAMBLAIN L'ABBÉ	23/8		1st S.A.I. Bde relieved 26th Inf Bde in BERTHONVAL Section. Relief carried out by day. On relief 26th Inf Bde moved by bus to Reserve Div Area – Bde HQ FRESNICOURT. 1st S.A.I. Bde in Divisional Reserve. 63rd Inf Bde 37th Div. replaced under the orders of the 9th Div – also and came temporarily under the orders of the 9th Div – 9 N. STAFFORDS (PIONEERS) arrived at VILLARS-AU-BOIS and temporarily attached to the 9th Div.	
"	24/8		Quiet day.	
"	25/8 26/8		Quiet days. The left group assisted by French mortars commenced cutting wire in the left Section and continued this operation in the 26th Inf map.	

WAR DIARY

INTELLIGENCE SUMMARY

(Erase heading not required.)

Army Form C. 2118

Place	Date	Hour	Summary of Events and Information	Remarks and references to Appendices
CAMBLAIN L'ABBÉ	27/8		G.O.C. with G.S.O.1, C.R.A, & G.O.C. 26' Inf. Bde., attended a conference at Corps Headquarters at 10 A.m. in connection with the proposed operation of the 26' Inf. Bde. — Proposals for this Operation were submitted to the Corps during the afternoon. — 26' Inf. Bde. held a practice attack at CUVIGNY FARM at 6 p.m. and 9 p.m. —	
"	28/8		Quiet day. 26' Inf. Bde. held another practice attack at CUVIGNY Farm at 6 p.m. and 9 p.m.	
"	29/8		Quiet day.	

Army Form C. 2118

WAR DIARY
INTELLIGENCE SUMMARY
(Erase heading not required.)

Place	Date	Hour	Summary of Events and Information	Remarks and references to Appendices
CAMBLAIN L'ABBÉ	30/8	12 midnight 30/31st Inst.	Enemy fired a Camouflet at S of F3 S.15.a.1.7 at Heading of our gallery not destroyed and no casualties.	
		Aug 30 a quiet day – Very heavy rains which caused much damage to our trenches		
"	31/8		Quiet day	

URGENT.

SECRET.

Copy No 26

Appx 1

9th Division Operation Order No. 71.

10/8/16.

1. The 9th Division will relieve the 57th Division in the right sector in accordance with attached Table.

2. (a) Details of Infantry reliefs will be arranged direct between Brigade Commanders concerned.
   The command of each section will pass on completion of relief which will be reported by wire to Divisional H.Q.

   (b) Details as to the relief of Field Ambulances will be arranged direct between A.Ds.M.S. concerned and of Mobile Veterinary Sections between A.Ds.V.S. concerned.

3. The 9th Divisional Artillery will be prepared to relieve the 57th Divisional Artillery on the nights of 13th/14th and 14th/15th August. All details of relief to be arranged direct between B.Gs.R.A. concerned.

4. Further orders as to the relief of the Artillery (including Medium Trench Mortars) R.E. and 9th Seaforths (Pioneers) will be issued later.

5. The 27th Inf. Bde. and 1st S.African Bde. when moving forward to the Reserve Brigade area will move with not less than ten minutes between Battalions.

6. The command of the right sector will pass to G.O.C. 9th Division at 10 a.m. on August 15th, at which hour 9th Division Headquarters will close at BRUAY and open at CAMBLAIN L'ABBE.

7. PLEASE ACKNOWLEDGE BY WIRE.

a. E. M hamall W 4/or

for Lieutenant Colonel,
General Staff,
9th (Scottish) Division.

Issued at 4 p.m.

Copies to:-
No. 1 to 26th Inf. Bde.
2 to 27th Inf. Bde.
3 to 1st S.African Bde.
4 to C.R.A.
5 to 50th Bde. R.F.A.
6 to 51st Bde. R.F.A.
7 to 52nd Bde. R.F.A.
8 to 53rd Bde. R.F.A.
9 to Trench Mortars.
10 to Divisional Column.
11 to C.R.E.
12 to 9th Seaforths.
13 to 9th Div. Train
14 to 9th Signal Coy.
15 to A.A. & Q.M.G.
16 to A.D.M.S.
17 to A.D.V.S.
18 to A.P.M.
19 to 4th Corps
20 to 36th Div.
21 to 63rd Div.
22 to 60th Div.

23 76th Tun.Coy.R.E.
24 182nd Tun. Coy.R.E.
25 Special Battn. R.E.

MARCH TABLE.

Date	Unit	From	To	To relieve	Remarks.
11th Aug.	26th Bde. M.G. Coy.	CAMBLAIN L'ABBE	BERTHONVAL Sec.	63rd Bde. M.Gun Coy.	
Night 12th/13th.	26th Inf.Bde.	Reserve Bde. Area.	BERTHONVAL Sec.	63rd Inf. Bde.	63rd Bde. moves into Reserve Bde. area on relief.
13th	27th Inf. Bde.	DIEVAL – LA COMTE Area.	Reserve Brigade Area	63rd Inf. Bde.	To arrive at billets by 8.30 p.m.
	20th San. Sec.	BRUAY	CAMBLAIN L'ABBE	37th Div. Sanitary Section.	27th Bde. H.Q. to be established at CHATEAU de la HAIE at 7 p.m.
14th.	27th Fld.Amblce.	BRUAY	LES QUATRE VENTS.	49th F.Amblce.	
	28th Fld.Amblce.	DIVION & MAISNIL BOUCHE.	GRAND SERVINS	48th F.Amblce.	
	S.A.Fld.Amblce.	FRESNICOURT	ESTREE CAUCHIE and CAUCOURT.	50th F.Amblce.	
Night 14th/15th	27th Inf. Bde.	Reserve Brigade Area.	CARENCY Section	Composite Bde.	Composite Bde. move to Reserve Bde. area on relief.
15th.	1st S.African Brigade.	FRESNICOURT Area.	Reserve Bde. area.	Composite Bde.	To arrive in billets by 6.30 p.m. S.African Bde. H.Q. to be established at CHATEAU de la HAIE at 6 p.m.

Appx. 2

C.R.E.
37th Division.
26th Brigade.
27th Brigade.
1st S.A.Brigade.
Q.
9th Div. Train.
A.D.M.S.
A.P.M.
IV Corps.
9th Seaforths.

SECRET.

No.X.4/1607/1.   10th August,1916.

Reference 9th Division Operation Order No.71 Para.4.

1. The 64th and 63rd Field Companies R.E. will relieve the 152nd and 153rd Field Companies R.E. respectively at VILLERS AUX BOIS and Advanced Billets BERTHONVAL Section on the 12th August, for work in the right section.
   All details of relief to be arranged between C.R.E's concerned.

2. The 90th Field Company R.E. will march on the 12th August from LACOMTE to CHATEAU DE LA HAIE where it will be accommodated in tents. It will work in the left section.

3. The 154th Field Company R.E. will remain in its present billets and continue work in the left section.

4. When the G.O.C, 9th Division takes over command of the line one of the two remaining Field Companies (i.e.152nd or 153rd Field Company) and the 18th NORTHUMBERLAND FUSILIERS (Pioneers), of the 37th Division, will come under the orders of the 9th Division.

5. The Headquarters of the 9th Seaforths (Pioneers) will remain as at present.

Major,
General Staff,
9th (Scottish) Division.

appx. 3

To:-

Recipients of Operation Order No. 71.

No. X.4/1607/3.   11th August, 1916.

Reference 9th Division Operation Order No. 71 para 4.

1.   The 9th Divisional Artillery will relieve the 37th Divisional Artillery (less the Heavy and Medium Trench Mortar Batteries) on the nights 13th/14th and 14th/15th August.

2.   The hour at which the B.G.R.A. 9th Division assumes command of the Artillery of the Right Sector will be arranged between B.G.R.As. concerned and notified to Divisional Headquarters.

3.   PLEASE ACKNOWLEDGE RECEIPT.

A. E. M'Namee Major
for Lieutenant Colonel,
   General Staff,
9th (Scottish) Division.

appx: 4

26th Inf. Brigade.
27th Inf. Brigade.
1st S.African Bde.
C.R.A.
C.R.E.
9th Seaforths.
182nd Tunnelling Coy.
176th Tunnelling Coy.
"Q".

SECRET

No. X.5/1651/3.   16th August, 1916.

---

1.   The 26th Inf. Bde. will extend its left on the night August 17th/18th and relieve the 27th Inf. Bde. as far North as TONCHOT Trench.

2.   All details of relief to be arranged direct between Brigades concerned.

Completion of relief to be reported by wire to Divisional Headquarters.

3.   TONCHOT Trench and the group of Craters, LOVE, MOMBER and TWINS will be inclusive to the 27th Inf. Bde.

4.   Please acknowledge by wire.

Lieutenant Colonel,
General Staff,
9th (Scottish) Division.

SECRET.

IVth Corps.

No. X.4/1584/9.   18th August, 1916.

Proposals for night operation
to be carried out by
the 9th Division.

1.   The objective of the Division will be to seize and consolidate the enemy's front line from S.15.c.45.40 to S.15.c.25.95, and his front and support lines from S.15.c.25.95 to the southern lip of the crater at S.15.a.15.70.

The southern extremity of the captured line will be joined up with our present front line at S.21.a.65.70 by opening up an existing unused trench.

The junction of the Northern end of the captured line with our present front line will depend on the mining situation at the time.

2.   In addition to seizing and consolidating the line mentioned above it is intended to seize and hold temporarily as a covering line during the process of consolidation the enemy's support line from S.15.c.25.45 to S.15.c.35.95.

A suspected hostile mine shaft in the trench running N.E. from S.15.c.35.95. will also be destroyed if found.

3.   If I can be given 4 days latitude as to date I shall instal gas and make the attack on the first night on which the wind is favourable.

Without that latitude I prefer to trust to a short intense bombardment and possible assistance from mines, as the presence of unused cylinders in our trenches during the enemy's counter bombardment is a serious risk.

(4)

4. From now on, wire should be cut at various places along the fronts of the 17th, 4th and 1st Corps, and on the night of our attack a concentrated bombardment should be arranged if possible by the 17th Corps on the enemy's trenches and craters in S.21.b. and d. between the hours Zero minus 1 hour and Zero plus two hours, while similar demonstrations are made opposite the left of the 4th Corps line and the right of the 1st Corps front, in order to distract and disperse the fire of the hostile batteries opposite us.

5. (a) Appendix A. shows the proposed action of the artillery during the operations, if gas is used.

(b) If gas is not used, I shall eliminate the bombardment previous to Zero minus three minutes. At that hour I shall begin the intense 5 minutes bombardment as shown in Appendix A, and shall trust to the element of surprise and to the intensity of the artillery curtain.

(c) A Divisional Artillery in addition to the 9th will be required for the operation and it is hoped that no time will be lost in getting in the extra batteries as a lot of work will be necessary for digging in the batteries, command posts and communications.

I am also depending on reinforcements to the present Heavy Artillery of the Corps.

6. The operation will be carried out by the 26th Inf. Bde. assisted by such Pioneers and R.E.Field Companies as may be necessary.

A portion of the 1st S.African Bde. which will be holding the right of the Divisional line on the day of assault will be employed to cover the consolidation of the trench joining up the right of the captured line with our front line.

7. The Brigade will be distributed with three battalions in the front line, the fourth battalion being in Brigade Reserve.

Each battalion in the front line will employ 2 or 3 companies in the assault, the remaining companies being used as carriers and to man our original front line trench.

8. Stokes Mortars will co-operate by bombarding the enemy's front line during the last two minutes previous to the assault.

9. Five mines will be exploded at Zero under, or in close proximity to the enemy's front line and about 8 fronts of entry into the enemy's line will be made between these craters, the craters themselves being secured by parties specially detailed for the purpose.

10. If the wind is favourable gas and smoke will be used in accordance with the following time table:-

```
-65 to -45      White Star
-45 to - 5      Red Star and smoke.
- 5 to - 3      Smoke only.
 0 (Zero)       Assault.
```

The gas will be used along the whole front from about S.21.b.2.0. to about S.14.b.9.5.

Smoke will be used along the remainder of my front, and should be used similarly along the fronts of the Divisions on my flanks.

11. Communication to the captured line will be obtained by opening up 5 old communication trenches in prolongation of -

> VINCENT AVENUE
> INTERNATIONAL AVENUE
> GRANBY AVENUE
> BLUE BULL SAP.
> ERSATZ AVENUE.

and by connecting GOBRON AVENUE with one of the new craters.

12.   Anticipating the enemy's barrage on the ZOUAVE VALLEY I am taking steps to assemble all the troops necessary for the operation on the E. of the Valley.

                                        Major-General,
                        Commanding 9th (Scottish) Division.

SECRET

APPENDIX A.

PROPOSED ARTILLERY ACTION ON Z DAY.

Reference map 1/5,000
Sun-Print.

1. Wire cutting.

(a) 18-pounders of the 9th Division will cut wire in front of enemy front trench West of the PIMPLE.

(b) The 9th Divisional medium trench mortars will cut wire on the enemy front line from the TWINS CRATER to XXXXXXXXX S.15.c.4.5½.

The Trench Mortars of Divisions on either flank will be asked to cut wire on their fronts.

Wire should be cut on the whole of the IVth and 1st Corps fronts if possible during the next fortnight.

18-pounders of the 9th Division will keep enemy observing stations in squares S.15 and S.21 under fire to protect trench mortars while wire-cutting.

2. Heavy artillery to bombard deliberately the trenches and strong points in the following areas:-

(a) Northern Area.
Rectangle S.15.a.2.8. - S.15.a.1½.4.
S.15.a.5.7. - S.15.a.5.3½.

(b) Centre Area.
Trenches and craters in the rectangle -
S.15.c.5.9. - S.15.c.6.5.
S.15.a.6.1½. - S.15.d.0.8.
Also craters in S.15.d.

(c) Southern Area.
Trenches and craters in the rectangle -
S.21.b.4.4½. - S.21.d.6.8½.
S.22.a.1.5. - S.22.a.1.0.

The 4.5" howitzers of the 9th Division will assist in

the

the bombardment of the Northern and Southern Areas.

3. The Heavy Trench Mortars will bombard the craters in S.15.c.

4. **Bombardment at Zero - 1 Hour.**

(a) The Heavy Artillery to intensely bombard the same areas as in para 2.

At Zero the Heavies on the Northern and Centre Areas will lift to the line of craters S.15.a.5.1. to S.15.d.5.2: those on the Southern Area will remain and will stop fire at Zero + 2 Hours in the absence of further orders.

The 60 pounders to form a barrage on the general line S.9.d.6.5. - S.16.c.2.5. from Zero - 1 hour to Zero + 2 hours.

The Counter Battery Groups to engage hostile batteries.

(b) The Heavy Trench Mortars will bombard the craters in S.15.c. from Zero - 1 hour till Zero + 2 hours.

(c) The 9th Division Artillery (18 prs. and 4.5" Hows.) will bombard the enemy front line trenches from the TWINS Crater to S.15.c.4.3½ at normal rate till Zero - 50 minutes, then increase to intense rate; at Zero - 48 minutes all guns will lift to the line S.15.a.5.5. - S.15.d.1.6. along trench and craters, remaining on this line for two minutes firing at intense rate; at Zero - 46 minutes all guns will come back to the front line, fire for two minutes at intense rate, then drop down to normal rate.

At Zero - 25 minutes the rate of fire will be increased to intense; at Zero - 23 minutes all guns will lift as before on to the line S.15.a.5.5. - S.15.d.1.6. and fire for two minutes at intense rate; at Zero - 21 minutes all guns will come back to the front line and fire intense for two minutes, then drop down to normal rate.

(From

From Zero - 3 minutes to Zero plus 2 minutes the rate of fire will be intense, H.E. only being used for the last two minutes.

At Zero plus 2 minutes guns will lengthen 50 yards after each round until a box barrage is formed along the line S.15.a.3.6. - S.15.a.5.5. - S.15.a.5.1. - S.15.d.0.7. - S.15.c.7.6 - S.15.c.7.3. and remain on this barrage until Zero plus 2 hours. The rate of fire for the first five minutes after Zero plus 2 minutes will be intense, after this, normal.

An outer barrage will also be formed from S.15.d.5.5½ to S.21.b.1.6.

5. The Medium Trench Mortars will bombard the hostile front line from the TWINS CRATER to S.15.c. using Newton Fuzes so as not to do too much damage to the trenches.

Fire will open at Zero - 1 hour and cease at Zero plus 2 minutes.

6. On the S.O.S. Signal being given all guns and howitzers will at once re-open fire on the final barrage.

7. It is understood that the Divisions on our flanks will assist :-

(a) The Division on our Right by barraging in square S.21.b. from Zero to Zero plus 2 hours.

(b) The Division on our left by barraging on a line from KENNEDY CRATER to the East from Zero till Zero plus 2 hours

8. Ammunition. 1000 rounds per gun will be dumped by the 9th Division Artillery. 500 rounds per gun of this will be dumped in boxes.

50% H.E. and 50% Shrapnel will be used except during the Infantry assault from Zero to 0 plus 4 minutes when H.E. only will be used.

The/

The 4.5" Howitzers when firing on the front trenches and until the final barrage line is reached will only use ballistite cartridges.

9. Detailed Orders for liaison will be issued later.

Note. (a) The reinforcing Divisional Artillery is included when the 9th Divisional Artillery is referred to.

      (b) Normal rate of fire, one round per gun per minute.

          Intense rate of fire, 3 rounds per gun per minute.

Note. The Heavy and Medium Trench Mortars will commence their tasks of wire cutting and bombardment of craters, trenches etc. as soon as their emplacements are ready, and will not wait for "Z" Day.

appx. 6

URGENT.

SECRET.

Copy No 25

9th Division Operation Order No. 72.

20/8/16.

1. The 1st South African Brigade will relieve the 26th Inf. Bde. in the BERTHONVAL Section on the night August 23rd/24th.
All details of relief will be arranged direct between Brigades concerned.
Command will pass on completion of relief which will be reported by wire to Divisional Headquarters.

2. On relief the 26th Inf. Bde. will proceed by bus to the Reserve Division Area under orders which will be issued later.

3. A Brigade of the 37th Division will replace the 1st South African Brigade when that Brigade moves forward on the night August 23rd/24th.

A. E. M'Kharna Major
for Lieutenant Colonel,
General Staff,
9th (Scottish) Division.

Issued at 7 a.m.

Copies to:-

No. 1 to 26th Bde.
2 to 27th Bde.
3 to 1st S.A.Bde.
4 to C.R.A.
5 to 50th Bde. R.F.A.
6 to 51st Bde. R.F.A.
7 to 52nd Bde. R.F.A.
8 to 53rd Bde. R.F.A.
9 to Trench Mortars.
10 to Divisional Column.
11 to C.R.E.
12 to 9th Seaforths.
13 to 9th Div. Train.
14 to 9th Signal Coy.
15 to A.A. & Q.M.G.
16 to A.D.M.S.
17 to A.D.V.S.
18 to A.P.M.
19 to 4th Corps.
20 to 37th Division.
21 to 60th Division.
22 to 63rd Division.
23 to 176th Tunnelling Coy.
24 to 182nd Tunnelling Coy.
25 to War Diary.
26 to File.
27 to O.C. E. Coy. Special Battalion.

Spot at which Stokes mortars will be collected in event of an advance.

IVth Corps.

No. X.5/1652.   21st August, 1916.

      Reference IV Corps No. 1714 (G) of 17th inst.

      In the event of ~~an~~ advance, Stokes Mortars will be collected at cross roads S.8.b.1.4. and near the road S.14.b.5.8.

Major-General,
Commanding 9th (Scottish) Division.

IV Corps No. 1714 (G).

9th Division.
~~37th Division.~~
~~63rd Division.~~

~~G.O.C., R.A.~~) For Information.
~~D.A. & Q.M.G.~~)

    With reference to attached copy of First Army letter No. 812 (G). In the event of an advance, these* will be collected under divisional arrangements at points from which Ammunition Park would arrange to collect them. We could then guarantee having the Stokes Mortars at less than 24 hours notice.

    Will you please inform this Office of the spot which you select in your Divisional Area.

H.Q., IV Corps,
17th August, 1916.

Brigadier General,
General Staff, IV Corps.

* Stokes Mortars

<u>First Army No. 812 (G).</u>

IV Corps.

     Reference First Army No. 812 (G), sent to I and IV Corps only:-

     Information has now been received from G.H.Q. that it is not proposed to sanction any transport for Stokes' Mortars.

     The present policy, which is unlikely to be changed, is that these mortars shall be left behind, collected under arrangements to be made by the Q.M.G.'s staff and subsequently brought up to the Army should it have again to revert to trench warfare.

Adv. First Army.
3rd August, 1916.

(Sd.) O.H.L.Nicholson, Major, G.S.
for Major General,
General Staff, First Army.

GENERAL STAFF,

9th DIVISION,

SEPTEMBER, 1916.

GENERAL STAFF   9th SCOTTISH DIVISION.

WAR DIARY.

SEPTEMBER, 1916.

WAR DIARY
or
INTELLIGENCE SUMMARY

(Erase heading not required.)

Army Form C. 2118

Place	Date	Hour	Summary of Events and Information	Remarks and references to Appendices
CAMBLAIN L'ABBE	1/9		Quiet day. 9 Div. Op. Order No 93 issued directing relief of 63 Inf. Bde 37 Div. by 26 Inf. Bde in BOIS DE LA HAIE Area on Sept 2nd — On completion of relief 63 Inf. Bde to come under the orders of the 39 Div. — 9th working parties of 850 m. of 63 Div. working for the 9 Div. not to go back with their Brigade, but to remain with the 9 Div. LTM batteries to be attached to the 26 Inf Bde. 9th 63 and 111 L.T.M. batteries to be attached to the 26 Inf Bde. 9 Div. O.O. No. 94 issued directing relief of 1st S.A.I. Bde by the 26 Inf Bde in the BERTHONVAL Sector on Sept. 3rd. —	00 93 00 94
"	2/9		Quiet day. movements of 26 Inf. Bde & 63 Inf. Bde directed in O.O. 93 of Sept 1st carried out. —	
	3/9		Quiet day. 12 A. SCOTS carried out a raid on the enemy's front trench at S. 9. a. 1. 9½ at 12 midnight Sept 3/4: — Reaching Posts 9 & S.9.a.1.9½ at 12 midnight Sept 3/4 —	

Army Form C. 2118

WAR DIARY
or
INTELLIGENCE SUMMARY
(Erase heading not required.)

Instructions regarding War Diaries and Intelligence Summaries are contained in F. S. Regs., Part II. and the Staff Manual respectively. Title Pages will be prepared in manuscript.

Place	Date	Hour	Summary of Events and Information	Remarks and references to Appendices
CANBLAIN L'ABBÉ	3/4		into enemy's front line, but found many dead, and bush bombing fight ensued — Some GERMANS were killed and wounded, and our party had to retire without securing a prisoner. One Other Ranks wounded, and two O.R. Casualties. One Officer & four Other Ranks wounded, and two O.R. missing. 28 Inf. Bde relieved 1st S.A.I. Bde in BERTHONVAL Section as directed in O.O. No. 74 of 1st Sept.	
"	4/5		Quiet day. 9th Div. O.O. No. 75 issued directing relief of 27 Inf. Bd. by 1st S.A.I. Bd in the CARENCY Section on Sept. 6th. 9th Div. Instruction No. 29(?) as to Gas Measures issued.	O O 75 9th Div Inst. No 29(?)

Army Form C. 2118

WAR DIARY
or
INTELLIGENCE SUMMARY
(Erase heading not required.)

Instructions regarding War Diaries and Intelligence Summaries are contained in F.S. Regs., Part II. and the Staff Manual respectively. Title Pages will be prepared in manuscript.

Place	Date	Hour	Summary of Events and Information	Remarks and references to Appendices
CAMBLAIN L'ABBE	5/9		Quiet day.	
	6/9		Quiet day. 1.S.M. Bdr relieved 27 S.M. Bdr in CARENCY Section. 1 S.M.I. Bdr carried out by day and completed about 6 p.m. Relief carried out by day and completed about 6 p.m. On Sept. 5,6. 7th 50,51st F.A. Bdrs cut wire on the front Point 11 to TWIN CRATER.	
	7/9		Quiet day — Some shells were put over VILLERS-AU-BOIS about 10 p.m. no damage. 7th 50' & 51st Bdrs of Trench Mortars bombarded the hostile front line between TWINS CRATER and point 11. — The Heavy Artillery bombarded the trenches in the area 33,35, 16 to 15, also trenches 47 to 35, trench 3 to 5 to 7 and Point 112.14. B.G.C. 2 G.S.O.1 attended a Conference at Corps Headquarters at 10 A.M.	

WAR DIARY
or
INTELLIGENCE SUMMARY
(Erase heading not required.)

Army Form C. 2118

Place	Date	Hour	Summary of Events and Information	Remarks and references to Appendices
	5/9		Orders received verbally from 4 Corps for the Northumberland Fus. N. Stafford Regt (Pioneers) to rejoin the 34 Div	
	6/9		The Heavy Artillery (Corps) bombarded the enemy's trenches and CRATERS in the area S.15.a.4.6 - S.15.a.6.1 to S.15.c.4.9½ to S.15.c.4.5 and the CRATERS in S.15.c.d - The bombardment seemed to be satisfactory, except that a large percentage of the 6" How. were blind, and some of the 60 pr shells fell short into our own lines -	
	9/9		The Heavy Trench Mortars fired at 4 p.m. from its emplacement at S.20.b.55.1 at the enemy's trenches at S.15.c.1.9. The result was satisfactory -	

WAR DIARY
or
INTELLIGENCE SUMMARY
(Erase heading not required.)

Army Form C. 2118

Place	Date	Hour	Summary of Events and Information	Remarks and references to Appendices
CARNOY L'ABBÉ	9/9		4 Corps H.Q.S. 609 received at 10 p.m. directing the 9' Div. to extend its right as far south as LASSALLE AVENUE exclusive and relieve the 66 Div. in their trenches – The Southern Boundary of the 9' Div. on completion of relief to run from LASSALLE AVENUE (where LASSALLE AVENUE cuts the QUARRY (S.21.c.6.5.0.) along the diverting line between Squares S.21 & S.27 to Central BOYAU, and from there as at present – Relief to be completed by 6 p.m. on Sept. 11'. 9' Div. X 5/15 & 141 issued at 11 p.m. directing the 26'' Inf. Bde. to take over the new portion of front on Sept 11'' in accordance with the 4 Corps Instructions indicated above.	

WAR DIARY
or
INTELLIGENCE SUMMARY

(Erase heading not required.)

Army Form C. 2118

Place	Date	Hour	Summary of Events and Information	Remarks and references to Appendices
CAMBLAIN L'ABBÉ	10/9		G.O.C. & G.S.O. 1. attended a Conference at 4 Corps Headquarters at 10 A.M. when various questions in connection with future operations were discussed.	
"	11/9		Enemy put a heavy barrage on ZOUAVE VALLEY between 10 p.m. and 10.30 p.m in retaliation for a raid of 1st Division on our left. Our trench mortars active throughout the day — Enemy a little retaliated.	6
"	12/9		Our Artillery and Trench Mortars active against enemy's wire in CARENCY Section — Otherwise quiet otm.	
"	13/9		9ᵗʰ Dᴵⁿ O.O. No. 96 issued describing following reliefs and adjustment of fronts	

Army Form C. 2118

WAR DIARY
or
INTELLIGENCE SUMMARY
(Erase heading not required.)

Instructions regarding War Diaries and Intelligence Summaries are contained in F.S. Regs., Part II. and the Staff Manual respectively. Title Pages will be prepared in manuscript.

Place	Date	Hour	Summary of Events and Information	Remarks and references to Appendices
CAMBLAIN L'ABBÉ	13/9		63rd Inf. (a) 26th Inf. Bn to extend its left on 18 Inf. and relieve 1st S.A.Bn by 7 a.m. NORTH to UHLAN ALLEY inclusive (b) 63rd Inf Bn 37 Div to relieve 1st S.A. Bn in CAREMLY Section on Sept 17. (c) 27 Inf Bn to relieve 26 Inf Bn in the portion of its front from LASALLE AVENUE to VINCENT both exclusive — II Corps H.P.S. 677 B received dealing with future operations.	
"	14/9		1st S.A.I. Bn carried out a raid on the enemy trenches between ̶E̶A̶S̶T̶S̶ ̶E̶S̶T̶L̶I̶N̶ 120th Czalin — Raid took place & was quite successful — Five prisoners captured KENNEDY and 4.M.M. and at least twelve GERMANS killed — One Casualties one man wounded who returned and one man left badly wounded in enemy's lines — Report on the raid is attached —	Report on raid by 1st S.A.Bn attached

WAR DIARY
or
INTELLIGENCE SUMMARY

Army Form C. 2118

Place	Date	Hour	Summary of Events and Information	Remarks and references to Appendices
CAMBLAIN L'ABBE	14/9		A quiet day —	
	15/9		The 26' Inf. Bn. carried out a raid on the enemy trenches on night 14/15" at the same hour two veldts were blown at 10.7 p.m.n — At the same time Kennedy and Irish craters — between Kennedy and Irish craters one prisoner was made in the GERMAN trench — and about 38 GERMAN dead were left — A report on the raid is attached — The WORCESTERSHIRE Regt. (PIONEERS) 63rd Div. moved to BOIS DES DE LA HAIE for work under the 9' Div.	Report on raid by 26th Inf.
	16/9		The WORCESTERSHIRE Regt. (Pioneers) 63rd Div. moved to BOIS DES ALLEUX for work under 9' Div. A Corps route No. G/796 received concerning the relief of the 1st S.A.I. Bde by the 63' Inf. Bde 37 Div 9' Div X 5/1805 issued concerning Relies 1(0)-14) and 2.34 a.s. of 9' Div O.O No. 76	J [signature] X 5/1805

WAR DIARY
or
INTELLIGENCE SUMMARY

(Erase heading not required.)

Army Form C. 2118

Place	Date	Hour	Summary of Events and Information	Remarks and references to Appendices
CARNLAIN L'ABBÉ	16/9		9 Div G453 issued orders as to relief of Units of 37 Div attached to 9 Div. The 176 Tunnelling Company blew a small Camouflet under NEIDRGN CRATER at 2 A.M. on the night Sept 15/16 & ascertd the enemy blowing out gallery – Artillery and Trench Mortars were employed against enemy workers at the place where the blow bombarded the enemy; enemy answered the protest. – was struck to tell our enemy concerning the protest – The blow was successful. – No alterations in our dispositions were involved	G.45.3 / 10
	17/9		9 Div D.O. 47 issued ordering relief of 26 Inf. Bde by 27 Inf. Bde in the BERTHONVAL Sector on Sept 19. 7th 14 WORCESTERSHIRE Regt (Pioneer) returned to 63 Div	0047

Army Form C. 2118

WAR DIARY
or
INTELLIGENCE SUMMARY
(Erase heading not required.)

Instructions regarding War Diaries and Intelligence Summaries are contained in F. S. Regs., Part II. and the Staff Manual respectively. Title Pages will be prepared in manuscript.

Place	Date	Hour	Summary of Events and Information	Remarks and references to Appendices
CARNIN L'ABBÉ	18/9		Quiet day. Very wet - much damage done to trenches by rain.	
"	19/9		GERMANS blew a mine at 2.A.M. between KENNEDY and GUNNER CRATER. - Our casualties one officer and two men killed - otherwise the blow rather in our favour, as we occupied the near lip, and the lip on the enemy side so low, that we are in a posito of superiority. The 27 Inf Bde relieved the 26 Inf Bde in the BERTHONVAL Sector - Relief carried out by day - and completed about 6 p.m. IV Corps H.R.S. 609 received notifying that the 9 Div. would be relieved by the 24 Div [less Divl. Artillery] as soon as practical -	

WAR DIARY or INTELLIGENCE SUMMARY

Army Form C. 2118

Place	Date	Hour	Summary of Events and Information	Remarks and references to Appendices
CAMBLAIN L'ABBÉ	20/9		Quiet day. 9th Div. O.O. 78 issued ordering relief of the 9th Div. by the 24th Div. - Relief to commence on Sept 22nd. 43rd Bde to relieve 26th Bde in Reserve Area on Sept 22nd. 43rd Bde " 1st S.A. Bde " CARENCY Section on Sept 23rd. 1st S.A. Bde to relieve 1st S.A. Bde in Reserve Area on Sept 24th. 17th Inf Bde " 27th Inf Bde in BERTHONVAL Sec. on Sept 25th. Details as to further moves of 9th Div. to be issued later.	12 OO 78
	21/9		IV Corps O.O. 128 received as to relief of 9th Div. by 24th Div. A quiet day.	

Army Form C. 2118

WAR DIARY
or
INTELLIGENCE SUMMARY
(Erase heading not required.)

Place	Date	Hour	Summary of Events and Information	Remarks and references to Appendices
CAMBLAIN L'ABBÉ	22/9		9" Div O.D. 79 issued as to movements of the 9" Div. to 3rd Army Training Area. —	O.D. 79 /13
	23/9		26" Inf. Bde. relieved in Reserve Bde. area by the 73" S.J. Bde. 26" Inf. Bde. moved to the area VILLERS CHATEL – BETHONSART – CHELERS. —	
"	23/9		26th Inf. Bde. moved to Area LIENCOURT – ESTREE-WAMIN – DENIER. On completion of move the 26" Inf. Bde. disposed as under:- 26. Inf. Bde. HQ. BERLENCOURT 26. M.G.Co. 8. B. WATCH. DENIER L.T.M. Batty 5. CAMERONS. LIENCOURT 10. A&S Highlanders. BERLENCOURT 7. Seaforths. ETREE WAMIN	

Army Form C. 2118

WAR DIARY
or
INTELLIGENCE SUMMARY
(Erase heading not required.)

Instructions regarding War Diaries and Intelligence Summaries are contained in F. S. Regs., Part II. and the Staff Manual respectively. Title Pages will be prepared in manuscript.

Place	Date	Hour	Summary of Events and Information	Remarks and references to Appendices
CAMBLAIN L'ABBÉ	23/9		43rd Inf. Bde relieved 1st S.A. Bde in BERTHONVAL Section. 1st S.A. Bde moved back in relief to CHATEAU DE LA HAIE Area. 28th F. Amb. moved from GRAND SERVINS to HOUVIN-HOUVIGNEUL. 42nd Inf. Bde relieved four guns of S.A. Bde in BAJOLLE SWITCH.	
"	24/9		1st S.A. Bde relieved in Reserve Area by 17th Inf. Bde. 1st S.A. Bde moved to the VILLERS CHATTEL - MINGOVAL - CHELLERS area. 64th 4" Cy. R.E. moved from VILLERS-AU-BOIS to VILLERS BRULIN. S.A.F. Amb. moved from ESTRÉE CAUCHIE to GOUY-EN-TERNOIS. Quiet day on Divisional front.	

Army Form C. 2118

WAR DIARY
or
INTELLIGENCE SUMMARY
(Erase heading not required.)

Place	Date	Hour	Summary of Events and Information	Remarks and references to Appendices
CAMBLAIN L'ABBÉ	24/9		The 27 Inf. Bde carried out a raid on the enemy's front trench at S.15.c.1.2 at 4.15 A.m. - The raiding party was quite successful in entering the enemy's trench (EARL Trench Ref. M46 250v) but found it not occupied by the enemy - The party retired to our line without CASUALTIES - but three men were slightly wounded by a shell in the ZOUAVE VALLEY after their return - No identifications were procured. The 1st S.A. Bde moved to 3rd Army Training Area from the MINGOVAL Area. On completion of the move the Brigade was disposed as follows :-	

WAR DIARY
or
INTELLIGENCE SUMMARY

Army Form C. 2118

Place	Date	Hour	Summary of Events and Information	Remarks and references to Appendices
CAMBLAIN L'ABBE	25/9		2nd S.A. Bde HQ. AMBRINES	
			1 S.A. Regt MAIZIERES	
			2" LIGNEREUIL	
			3" MAGNICOURT	
			4" AMBRINES	
			26 M.G.Cy. MAIZIERES	
			S.A.L.T.M.Bath GOUYENTERNOIS	
			9th & 9th Seaforth (Pioneers) moved from VILLERS-AU-BOIS to VILLERS CHATEL	
			27 J. Amb. moved from QUATRE VENTS to BEAUFORT	
			20 Sm. Sec. moved from CAMBLIN L'ABBE to LE CAUROY	
			19 In Bde relieved 27th In Bde in BERTHONVAL Section.	
			On relief 27 In. Bde. moved to the BOIS DE LA HAIE Area.	

1875 Wt. W593/826 1,000,000 4/15 J.B.C. & A. A.D.S.S./Forms/C. 2118.

Army Form C. 2118

WAR DIARY
or
INTELLIGENCE SUMMARY
(Erase heading not required.)

Place	Date	Hour	Summary of Events and Information	Remarks and references to Appendices
CAMBLAIN L'ABBE	25/9		Gas attack on the CALONNE Section (Div on left of 9' Div) at 10 p.m., but this report proved to be unfounded.	
"	26/9		G.O.C. 9th Div. handed over command of right sector of 4 Corps Line to G.O.C. 24th Div. at 10. A.M., and which hour 9 Div. H.Q. closed at CAMBLAIN L'ABBÉ and opened at CAUROY (N.5.C. Street 51 C). The 27 Inf. Bde returned in the CHATEAU DE LA HAIE area & the 92 Inf. Bde and moved to the MINGOVAL Area - 90 Fd. Co. R.E. moved to the MINGOVAL Area from 6004 SERVINS. The 9' Sigbath (Pioneers) moved from VILLERS CHATTEL to AVERDINGT.	

WAR DIARY
or
INTELLIGENCE SUMMARY

Army Form C. 2118

Place	Date	Hour	Summary of Events and Information	Remarks and references to Appendices
CAVROY	27/9		27 Inf. Bde moved from MINGOVAL Area to the BEAUFORT Area, on completion of the move the Bde was disposed as under:- 27' Bde HQ. MANIN 6. K.O.S.B. BEAUFORT 9. S. Rifles GIVENCHY LE NOBLE 11. R. Scots VILLERS SUR SIMON 12. R. Scots MANIN 27. M.G. Co. BEAUFORT 27. L.T.M. Battery GIVENCHY LE NOBLE 90' T.M. moved to HOUVIN HOUVIGNEUL 63' F.Co. moved from BOIS DE LA HAIE to VILLERS KAOLIN	

Army Form C. 2118

WAR DIARY
or
INTELLIGENCE SUMMARY
(Erase heading not required.)

Instructions regarding War Diaries and Intelligence Summaries are contained in F.S. Regs., Part II. and the Staff Manual respectively. Title Pages will be prepared in manuscript.

Place	Date	Hour	Summary of Events and Information	Remarks and references to Appendices
CAUROY	28/9		63rd T.M.By. R.E. moved from VILLERS BRULIN to HOUVIN HOUVIGNEUL. On the morning of Sept 28th the Division was ordered to move in App. W	14
"	29/9		Nothing to record. All units at training.	
"	30/9		Nothing to record. All units at training.	

NOTE. 3 maps of the area occupied by this Division during this month are attached.

APPENDICES.

SECRET.

Copy No. 24

9th Division Operation Order No. 73.

1st Sept. 1916.

1. (a) The 26th Inf. Bde. will relieve the 63rd Inf. Bde. in the BOIS de la HAIE Area on September 2nd.

    (b) On relief the 63rd Inf. Bde. (less working parties of 500 men working under the C.R.A. and 350 men working under 9th Signals) will move back to the FRESNICOURT Area, and will come under the orders of the 37th Division.
    Details as to billets for the 63rd Inf. Bde. will be notified later.

    (c) The 63rd and 111th Light Trench Mortar Batteries will remain attached to the 26th Inf. Bde.

    (d) All details of relief will be arranged direct between Brigades concerned

2. (a) The working party of 100 men of the 8th Somerset L.I. working under the C.R.A. will remain at GOUY SERVINS, and will be attached to the Unit of the 9th Division billetted in that place.
    The remaining 400 men of the 63rd Inf. Bde. working under the C.R.A. will remain attached to Batteries as at present.

    (b) The working party of 350 men of the 63rd Inf. Bde. working under the 9th Signals will remain in their present billets at CARENCY.

                                          Lieutenant Colonel,
                                          General Staff,
Issued at 7 a.m.   9th (Scottish) Division.

Copies to:-
No. 1 to 26th Inf.Bde.
    2 to 27th Inf.Bde.
    3 to 1st S.African Bde.
    4 to C.R.A.
    5 to 50th Bde. R.F.A.
    6 to 51st Bde. R.F.A.
    7 to 52nd Bde. R.F.A.
    8 to 53rd Bde. R.F.A.
    9 to Trench Mortars.
    10 to Divisional Colm.
    11 to C.R.E.
    12 to 9th Seaforths.
    13 to 9th Div. Train.
    14 to 9th Signals.
    15 to A.A. & Q.M.G.
    16 to A.D.M.S.
    17 to A.D.V.S.
    18 to A.P.M.
    19 to 4th Corps.
    20 to 37th Division.
    21 to 60th Division.
    22 to 63rd Division.
    23 to 176th Tunnelling Coy.
    24 to 182nd Tunnelling Coy.
    25 to O.C. 'E' Coy. Special Battn.
    26/27 War Diary and File.
    28 to 63rd Bde.

SECRET.

Copy No 27

9th Division Operation Order No. 74.

1st Sept. 1916.

The 26th Inf. Bde. will relieve the 1st S.African Bde. in the BERTHONVAL Section on September 3rd.

All details of relief will be arranged direct between Brigades concerned.

Command will pass on completion of relief which will be reported by wire to Divisional Headquarters.

K Stewart
Lieutenant Colonel,
General Staff,
9th (Scottish) Division.

Issued at 7 a.m.

Copies to:-
No. 1 to 26th Inf. Bde.
2 to 27th Inf. Bde.
3 to 1st S.African Bde.
4 to C.R.A.
5 to 50th Bde. R.F.A.
6 to 51st Bde. R.F.A.
7 to 52nd Bde. R.F.A.
8 to 53rd Bde. R.F.A.
9 to Trench Mortars.
10 to Divisional Colm.
11 to C.R.E.
12 to 9th Seaforths.
13 to 9th Div. Train.
14 to 9th Signals.
15 to A.A. & Q.M.G.
16 to A.D.M.S.
17 to A.D.V.S.
18 to A.P.M.
19 to 4th Corps.
20 to 37th Division.
21 to 60th Division.
22 to 63rd Division.
23 to 176th Tunnelling Coy.
24 to 182nd Tunnelling Coy.
25 to O.C. 'E' Coy. Special Battn.
26/27 War Diary and File.

SECRET.

Copy No 24

9th Division Operation Order No. 75.

4/9/16.

1. The 1st South African Brigade will relieve the 27th Inf. Bde. in the CARENCY Section on September 6th.

2. All details of relief will be arranged direct between Brigades concerned.
Command will pass on completion of relief which will be reported by wire to Divisional Headquarters.

Lieutenant Colonel,
General Staff,
9th (Scottish) Division.

Issued at 7 a.m.

Copies to:-

No. 1 to 26th Inf. Bde.
2 to 27th Inf. Bde.
3 to 1st S.African Bde.
4 to C.R.A.
5 to 50th Bde. R.F.A.
6 to 51st Bde. R.F.A.
7 to 52nd Bde. R.F.A.
8 to 53rd Bde. R.F.A.
9 to Trench Mortars.
10 to Divisional Column.
11 to C.R.E.
12 to 9th Seaforths.
13 to 9th Div. Train.
14 to 9th Signals.
15 to A.A. & Q.M.G.
16 to A.D.M.S.
17 to A.D.V.S.
18 to A.P.M.
19 to 4th Corps.
20 to 37th Division.
21 to 60th Division.
22 to 63rd Division.
23 to 176th Tunnelling Coy.
24 to 182nd Tunnelling Coy.
25 to O.C. 'E' Coy. Special Battn.
26/27 War Diary and File.

9th Division Instructions No. 29 (G).

GAS MEASURES.

2/9/16.

1. Attention is called to the pamphlet "Defensive Measures against Gas Attacks" (S.S. 419) which was issued to all Units by the Stationery Depatment about the 11th June, 1916.

Every Officer and as many N.C.Os. as possible are to be in possession of the pamphlet, and Units are responsible that that newly joined Officers are furnished with a copy immediately on their arrival.

2. The instructions contained in S.S. 419 are to be carefully studied and strictly adhered to.

Attention is specially directed to the following paragraphs :-

"A" Part II (2) and amendment to para (2) (f).
Action when the wind is favourable for a gas attack, i.e. GAS ALERT PERIOD.
Note. In addition to the precautions laid down in S.S.419, working parties will not take off their coats, as without them it is impossible to adjust the helmet correctly.

"B". Part II (3). Arrangements for giving the gas alarm.

"C". Part II (4). Action to be taken on the gas alarm signal.

"D". Part III (1) (c). Method of carrying out tube helmet drill.

"E". Part III (3). Use of anti-gas fans.

3. Reference "A".

(a) When the wind is favourable to a hostile gas attack (i.e. an Easterly wind between North-East and South-South-East inclusive) a "GAS ALERT" period is declared.

(b) On the "GAS ALERT" being ordered, the measures indicated in "A" will be put into force at once.

(c) The "GAS ALERT" will usually be ordered by Divisional Headquarters but it will be ordered by Brigades or Battalions when it is noticed that the wind has changed. The next higher formation will in this later case be at once informed.

(d) The message to denote an actual gas attack is the word "GAS" followed by the name of the Section being attacked thus :-

```
       Gas BERTHONVAL
        "  CARENCY
        "  SOUCHEZ
        "  ANGRES.
```

(e) The message "CANCEL GAS ALERT" will be given by the Division when the wind changes to a direction favourable to us.

4. (a) Practice gas alarms will be carried out from time to time under orders issued by Divisional Headquarters and will also be carried out frequently under Battalion and Brigade Orders.

(b) It is not advisable to test the system of sound signals, but the test will include the passing of the alarm round all Units by the telephone.

In addition, the test should ensure that all ranks are efficient in the measures laid down in "C".

(c)

(c) When such practice alarms are ordered, the Units on both flanks should be warned.

(d) Part worn helmets are in the possession of Units for practice.

5. Brigadiers and C.R.E. will receive weekly certificates from Units that :-

    (a) Helmets have been inspected at least once during the week.

    (b) That all ranks including lately arrived drafts are trained in the rapid adjustment of the tube helmets under all possible conditions.

    (c) That all ranks including lately arrived drafts are ~~kxxixxx~~ properly instructed in defensive measures against gas attacks and that the Standing Orders on this subject are thoroughly understood.

    (d) That the arrangements for giving the alarm are efficient.

(Sgd.) A. E. McNamara.
Major,
for Lieutenant Colonel,
General Staff,
9th (Scottish) Division.

Copies to :-

26th Inf. Brigade	25.
27th Inf. Brigade.	25
1st S.African Bde.	25
C. R. A.	20
C. R. E.	10.
9th Seaforths.	5
9th Div. Train	5
Camp Commandant.	5
A. D. M. S.	4.
A. D. V. S.	3.
A. P. M.	1.
"Q"	1.
9th Div. Gas School.	1.

SECRET

26th Infantry Brigade   9th Seaforths.
27th Infantry Brigade   9th Divisional Train.
1st S.A. Infantry Brigade.   60th Division.
C.R.A.   "Q".
C.R.E.

No.X.5/1584/41   9th September, 1916.

---

1. The 26th Infantry Brigade will extend its right on the 11th September and will relieve the 180th Infantry Brigade, 60th Division, in the front line system of trenches as far south as LASSALLE AVENUE exclusive.

2. The 60th Division hold the front which is to be taken over by the 26th Inf. Bde. with one company.

3. All details of relief will be arranged direct between Brigadiers concerned. The relief is to be completed by 6 pm. on September 11th.
   The Headquarters of the 180th Inf. Bde. are at MONT St.ELOI.

4. The 26th Infantry Brigade will send an officer tomorrow to reconnoitre the trench to be taken over.

5. On completion of relief the southern boundary of the 9th Division will run from where LASSALLE AVENUE cuts the QUARRY (S.21.c.6½.0.) along the line dividing squares S.21 and S.27 to Central Boyau and from there as at present.

6. The G.O.C. 26th Inf. Bde. will assume command of the front taken over on completion of relief, which will be reported by wire to Divisional Headquarters.

Lieut. Colonel,
General Staff, 9th (Scottish) Division.

War Diary. 6

SECRET.

9th (Scottish) Division.
Operation Order No. 76.

Copy No 26

13th Sept. 1916.

1. The following reliefs and readjustment of fronts will take place:-

September 16th.
(a) The 63rd Machine Gun Company will relieve the 28th Machine Gun Company in the front system and one section of 27th Machine Gun Company in the BAJOLLE Switch.
(b) The 26th Infantry Brigade will extend its left and relieve the 1st S.African Bde. as far North as UHLAN Alley inclusive.

September 17th.
(c) The 63rd Infantry Brigade will relieve the 1st S.African Bde. in the CARENCY Section from UHLAN ALLEY (exclusive) Northwards. On completion of relief the 63rd Inf. Bde. will come under the orders of the 9th Division.

September 18th.
(d) The 27th Infantry Brigade will relieve the 26th Inf. Bde. in that portion of its front from LASSALLE AVENUE (exclusive) to VINCENT Avenue (exclusive).

2. All details of reliefs will be arranged direct between Brigadiers concerned.
Command in each case will pass on completion of relief which will be reported by wire to Divisional Headquarters.

3. The G.O.C. 26th Inf. Bde. will issue the necessary orders to the 63rd Light Trench Mortar Battery to relieve the S.African Light Trench Mortar Battery on the 17th instant.

4. Moves will take place as per Table "A" attached.
Accommodation available for formations in the front system is shown in Table "B".

5. Movements on roads East of a North and South line through VILLERS-AU-BOIS will be by parties not larger than a platoon.

Lieutenant Colonel,
General Staff,
Issued at 6 p.m.   9th (Scottish) Division.

Copies to:-

No. 1 to 26th Bde.   14 to A.A. & Q.M.G.
    2 to 27th Bde.   15 to A.D.M.S.
    3 to S.A.Bde.   16 to A.D.V.S.
    4 to C.R.A.   17 to A.P.M.
    5 to 50th R.A.Bde.   18 to 4th Corps
    6 to 51st R.A.Bde.   19 to 37th Division.
    7 to 52nd R.A.Bde.   20 to 60th Division.
    8 to Trench Mortars   21 to 63rd Division.
    9 to Div. Column.   22 to 176th Tunnelling Coy.
   10 to C.R.E.   23 to 182nd Tunnelling Coy.
   11 to 9/Seaforths   24 to 172nd Tunnelling Coy.
   12 to 9th Train.
   13 to 9th Signals.   26 to 63rd Inf. Bde.

TABLE A.

Date.	Divn.	Unit	From	To	Remarks.
Sep.15	37th	63rd Machine Gun Coy.	FREVILLERS & CALONNE	GRAND SERVINS.	
Sep.16	do	do	GRAND SERVINS	Line.	(a) 12 guns to relieve S.A.Bde. in front system. (b) 4 guns to relieve 27th Bde. in BAJOLLE SWITCH. (c) Wagon Lines of 63rd M.Gun Coy. to remain at GRAND SERVINS. (d) On relief the guns of the S.A.Bde. and 27th Bde. withdraw to GOUY SERVINS & VILLERS-AU-BOIS respectively.
Sep.16	do	A Bn. 63rd Inf. Bde.	FRESNICOURT	BOIS de la HAIE.	
		B Bn. " " "	HERMIN	CAMBLAIN l'ABBE.	
Sep.17	do	H.Q.	FRESNICOURT	VILLERS-AU-BOIS.	
		A Bn. " " "	BOIS de la HAIE.	} Front line	Relieve A & B Bns. 1st S.A.Bde.
		B Bn. " " "	CAMBLAIN l'ABBE.	} system.	
		C Bn. " " "	FRESNICOURT	HOSPITAL Corner, CARENCY & MAISTRE Line & BAJOLLE SWITCH N. of CARENCY.	
		D Bn. " " "	FREVILLERS	FRESNICOURT.	
	9th	1st S.A.Bde. H.Q.	VILLERS-AU-BOIS	FRESNICOURT.	
		A Bn. S.A.Bde.	} Front line	BOIS de la HAIE.	
		B Bn. S.A.Bde.	} system	CAMBLAIN l'ABBE.	
		C Bn. S.A.Bde.	CARENCY & BAJOLLE Line	VILLERS AU BOIS.	
		D Bn. S.A.Bde.	VILLERS AU BOIS	FREVILLERS.	

Date	Divn.	Unit	From	To	Remarks.
Sep.18	9th.	1 Bn. S.A.Bde.	VILLERS AU BOIS	HERMIN.	
		1 Bn. S.A.Bde.	BOIS de la HAIE.	GOUY SERVINS.	
	9th	27th Inf. Bde.	Reserve Area	Front system of trenches from LASSALLE Avenue exclusive to VINCENT exclusive.	In relief of portion of 26th Inf. Bde.

TABLE B.

Accommodation available for Brigades on completion of relief.

Unit	Accommodation available.	Remarks.
27th Bde. H.Q.	CHATEAU de la HAIE.	
26th Bde. H.Q.	VILLA D'AOQ.	
63rd Bde. H.Q.	VILLERS AU BOIS.	
S.African Bde. H.Q	FRESNICOURT.	
27th Brigade.	Front line system. COLISEUM. BAJOLLE Line. MAISTRE Line South of BOYAU 125. CAMBLAIN l'ABBE (1 Battn.)	
26th Brigade.	Front line system. ALHAMBRA. CABARET ROUGE. MAISTRE Line between BOYAU 125 & CARENCY both exclusive. VILLERS AU BOIS (1 Battn.)	
63rd Inf. Bde.	Front line system. CARENCY. MAISTRE Line (N. of CARENCY). BAJOLLE SWITCH. HOSPITAL CORNER (including Bn. H.Q. at DALYS).	Note (a) One Battn. 63rd Bde. in Reserve Area. (b) The transport of the 63rd Inf. Bde. will be at GRAND SERVINS.

1st South African Brigade.
14th September, 1916.

9th Division.

I forward herewith reports by the O.C., 2nd S.A.I. on raid carried out by members of his Unit on the night of 13th/14th.

The reports contain no information as to the enemy barrage, but this was furnished in my B.M.818 of to-day.

A few points I have referred to the O.C. 2nd S.A.I. for further report, the principal of which is the different opinions expressed as to the effect of our artillery fire on the enemy trenches. A report has also been asked for as to the approximate locality of the machine gun which opened fire. This information together with information on points which may not have been brought out in the report will be furnished early to-morrow.

I consider credit is due to Lt.Col. Christian and his staff in connection with the careful and thorough manner in which all preparations were made, and to the officers and men who took part in the raid.

(sd) H.T.Lukin, Brig.Genl.
Commanding 1st S.African Bde.

1st South African Infantry Brigade.
Headquarters.
15.9.16.

9th Division.

Adverting to my letter of the 14th instant forwarding report on raid 13th/14th instant I now have to report further.

1. **State of enemy trenches as reported by officers.**

   The two officers concerned entered the enemy trenches at diffeent points approximately 50 yards apart.

   The wire on the enemy trenches entered was well cut - On the left where 2nd Lieutenant Walsh entered, the trenches were not damaged, whereas, on the right, at the point entered by 2nd Lieut. Lilburn, considerable damage was done by our shell fire to enemy trenches.

2. **Enemy machine gun.**

   This gun fired from a point between KENNEDY CRATER and enemy trench.

3. **Enemy Trenches.**

   The officers state that they did not encounter any sentries on the fire steps. Enemy rifles with fixed bayonets were leaning up against the parapets.

4. **Raid equipment.**

   All concerned are agreed that a revolver is the most useful weapon in a small operation of this kind. They can be readily fired round traverses and into dug-outs without exposing oneself and were found of the greatest value.

   Bombs were also useful while rifles were cumbersome and could not be brought into action.

   (Sd) H.T.Lukin   Brig-General,
   Commanding 1st S.A. Infantry Brigade.

9th Division.

No. B.M.818.   14th September, 1916.

     During raid last night enemy barraged chiefly on ZOUAVE VALLEY, a few shells near SOUCHEZ. No barrage on "No Man's Land. Enemy opened their barrage at 4.8 a.m. One enemy machine gun in action but was not effective.

           1st S.African Brigade.   1 p.m.

2nd Regiment South African Infantry.

South African Brigade.

With reference to your B.M.214 and the raid which took place at 4 a.m. this morning, I beg to forward you:-

1. Copy of the Operation Orders issued.
2. Copy of the telephone messages sent you during the raid.
3. Copies of reports on the raid by 2nd Lieutenants Walsh and Lilburn.
4. Copies of the reports by two Company Commanders on their enquiries from the men as to the number of enemy casualties.

Having sent out 2nd Lts. Green, Walsh and Lilburn at 9 p.m. on the 13th inst. to report on the feasibility of getting through the enemy wire, and having receuved a favourable report from 2nd Lt. Green at 10.30 p.m. I wired you to this effect, and made all preparations for the raid to take place.

The night was a bright moonlight one with passing clouds, but this I considered would not interfere with the raid so long as the men could get into position on the enemy's side of our wire without being seen. The arrangements worked without a hitch and at 3.55 a.m. all the men were lying down in position on the enemy's side of our wire without having aroused the enemy's suspicions in getting there.

The barrage started at 3.59 a.m. on which the men jumped up and started doubling across "No Mans Land". They doubled across without any hesitation and jumped straight into the enemy trenches, the barrage having lifted just as they got there.

Prisoners were secured at once, some in the trench and some emerging from dug-outs. All the dug-outs were then bombed with both Mills and Phosphorous bombs, and the object having been obtained, the arranged signal was given and the whole party retired together. The whole party were back in our lines before the enemy barrage started.

I regret having to report that No. 8800 Pte. W.E. Sweetman was so severely wounded by a bullet through the chest that he could not be moved from the enemy trench. The officer in charge was of opinion that he would die in a few minutes. No. 950 Private J.B.Willis was wounded in the thigh but managed to get back to our own lines unassisted.

I consider that the success of the operation was due to two main causes:-

FIRST. The very effective and thorough scouting work performed by 2nd Lts. Walsh and Lilburn for several nights before the raid and their excellent leading and example during the raid.

SECOND. To the extremely accurate and well timed barrage of our guns. The men who took part in the raid have now such confidence in our guns that they would, I am certain, work right up to our own barrage in any future action. This is having a most excellent effect in the Battalion and I cannot express my gratitude to the 9th Division Artillery for the absolute perfect shooting they made last night.

I also wish to express my appreciation of the able and careful manner with which Captain Sullivan and Lieut.Davis the commanders of "B" and "D" Companies, did their part in organising and instructing their men for the raid. The signalling arrangements carried out by my signalling officer, Lieut.Knight, (who also acted as forward observing officer) were excellent and worked without a hitch.

I think the chief lessons to be learnt from this raid are:-

1. The necessity of a raiding party advancing right up to the barrage.

2. The necessity of careful patrolling of the area to be crossed by the officer leading party previous to the raid.

3. The advantage of raiding parties returning immediately their object is attained.

I may mention that on return both the officers concerned expressed their very decided opinion that it would have been better if the whole of the raiding party, with the exception of one or two men, had been armed with revolvers instead of with rifles and bayonets.

(sd) Irvan Christian,

Lieutenant Colonel,
Commanding 2nd Regiment S.A. Infantry.

IN THE FIELD.
14th September, 1916.

The Adjutant, 2nd S.A.I.

Lieut. Walshe killed two and Corporal Rees killed one of the enemy in last nights raid.
These are the only certain cases known.

14th Sept. 1916.
                            (sd) F.M.Davis, Lieut.
                                O.C. "D" Company.

The Adjutant, 2nd S.A. Infantry.

Re last nights raid. I have seen each N.C.O. and as far as possible am satisfied that the figures given below are correct. I have assured myself that the dead reported have not been duplicated, as each N.C.O. was in a different part of trench, and stated exactly where the enemy were.

Mr Lilburn only saw one dead himself, but the bombers on the right accounted for three, and on the left two at least were killed. If this return errs it is on the side of moderation.

    A. Killed - 9 at least.
    B. Wounded - NIL as far as known. All enemy seen were killed or captured.
    Dug-outs with enemy in were bombed - results unknown.

14th Sept. 1916.
                            (sd) A.A.Sullivan, Captain.

S.A. Brigade.

Copy of message sent you on night of 13th/14th Septr.

ROWING.
3.55   G.
3.59   Barrage started.
3.59½   Barrage good. 4 spray lights on the left and star-light on the left.
4.1   Barrage still good. From German lines.
4.2¼   Still more white lights.
4.2½   Nothing to report.
4.2¾   --- 4.9 5 prisoners coming down.
4.10   All reported with exception of one man.
4.12   All O.K.
4.17   We are searching the prisoners and will send them down as soon as possible.

Following in reply to query from Brigade Major.

4.45   They are all in with exception of one man who is badly wounded and could not be got out of the German trench.

4.55   All are in except the man who is so badly wounded that he could not be brought in. The prisoners are being sent under escort. OAR 4.57 a.m. message ends.

                              (sd) Ivan Christian, Lt.Col.
14th Sept. 1916.   Commanding 2nd Regt. S.A.I.

G. meant "All men over the parapet."

COPY.

The Adjutant,

   2nd S.A.I.

In accordance with pre-arranged plan, I proceeded with a party in conjunction with "D" Company to raid enemy's trench.

We left our lines by gap in our wire at 3.50 am between saps B.1 and B.2 and entered enemy's trench about 1½ minutes past 4, through gap in their wire, at the point we entered the trench was blown away.

I bombed one dug-out with Mills' bombs, also threw down one smoke bomb.

I captured three prisoners and to my knowledge one enemy was shot in trench.

The dug-out I bombed appeared to be occupied.

The trenches were about 8 to 9 feet deep and were "V" shaped, some Bays had fire-steps.

The greater part of enemy's trench was blown away.

We were altogether three minutes in trench.

I did all the damage I possibly could in the time we occupied enemy's trench.

In my opinion, our artillery was excellent and my party advanced right up to the barrage.

The wire was blown to pieces and enemy's trench could have been entered at many points.

I had one man mortally wounded and in my opinion he succumbed before we reached our own trench.

                          (Sd) Percy C. Lilburn,
                                     2nd/Lieut.
                                 2nd S.A.Infantry.

14th September, 1916.

O.C., 2nd S.A.I.

In accordance with the pre-arranged plan, in conjunction with an equal party from "B" Company, I took a party of 30 men on a raid into the enemy's trenches.

My party left by a gap in our wire at the head of sap B.3 at 3.50 a.m. and entered the enemy's trench almost before the artillery barrage lifted.

4 dug-out entrances were bombed with hand-grenades and groans were heard immediately afterwards.

The enemy were just emerging from their dug-outs, two were immediately shot and the rest surrendered very willingly and two prisoners were brought back.

The trenches were about eight feet deep and broad at the top, they were not revetted or duck-boarded except at the entrance of the dug-outs. The dug-outs were not entered.

The return was made after about three minutes and so there was no time to collect souvenirs, in fact nothing was seen to bring back, the trenches being quite clear.

The trenches did not appear to have been damaged by our artillery fire and trench mortars.

The barrage was excellent and we were able to advance right up to the trench as it lifted.

The enemy wire was badly cut and we had no trouble in crossing it.

A red and green light were put up as we went over and a green light was put up after our return apparently as a signal that the enemy artillery was firing short.

On my return I discovered a covered sap running out to "No Man's Land". A man was seen to run into this and he appeared up through a hole in "No Man's Land" and I shot him through the back with my revolver and I believe I killed him.

Our only casualty was one man wounded with a revolver shot in the right thigh. He was shot from a dug-out which was immediately bombed.

The whole party was back by 4.10 a.m.

(sd) F.Walshe, 2nd Lieut.
2nd Regiment S.A.Infantry.

14th September, 1916.

4th Corps.

No. X.5/1784/5.   17th September, 1916.

1.   A raid was carried out on the night September 14th/15th by the 8th Black Watch and 5th Camerons on the enemy trenches from S.15.c.1.7. to S.15.c.4½.4.

2.   The raid was carried out with the 8th Black Watch (4 officers and 77 other ranks) on the right and 5th Camerons (4 officers and 66 other ranks) on the left.

The point of entry into the enemy's trench allotted to the 8th Black Watch was Point 19 and to the 5th Camerons Point 29.

3.   Four Stokes Mortar Batteries in addition to the Medium Trench Mortar Batteries and Artillery covered this operation.

4.   The general plan was for the Stokes Mortars to open a hurricane bombardment of the German front line at Zero, the raiding parties advancing as close as possible to their objectives under cover of this fire.

At Zero plus 2 minutes the Stokes Mortars were to lift on to the German support line and the raiders to at once enter the German trench.

5.   The detailed plan of operations and table of barrages is given in the Operation Orders attached.

Zero was fixed for 10.7 p.m.

6.   In addition to the purpose of the raid set forth in the Operation Orders, it was intended to test the efficacy of an intense Stokes Mortar bombardment on the enemy's trenches and personnel.

7. The operation of the 8th Black Watch on the right was quite successful.

They advanced to within 40 yards of the German line under cover of the Stokes bombardment which was punctual and accurate.

The enemy put a barrage of whizz-bangs and 4.2s on his own front line at 10.8, and this made it difficult for the raiding party to pick up the lift of the Stokes and caused some slight delay, but at 10.12 the party entered the German trench exactly as arranged.

8. The German trench was found so damaged by our bombardment that in places it was difficult to follow.

Parties of dead Germans were found at the entrances to dug-outs, as if they had tried to rush to their dug-outs when the Stokes bombardment opened and had got caught in bunches at the entrances.

Groups of nine, eight, and six dead Germans were counted by the light of a torch at the entrances to their different dug-outs respectively. In addition to these there were several corpses lying about the trench.

The Black Watch found some eleven live enemy in the trench whom they killed.

Several dug-outs were bombed, and from the noises heard within during this operation, there is no doubt that some enemy were caught.

The whole Black Watch party returned to our lines at the appointed time.

At least 35 Germans were accounted for apart from enemy bombed in dug-outs.

9. The 5th Camerons were not so fortunate.

The Stokes Mortar barrage on their front opened two minutes too soon (i.e. 10.5 p.m. instead of at 10.7 p.m.) and some of the shells fell short of the German front line.

When the barrage lifted at 10.9 the guns that had been shooting short lifted on to the German front line, thus making matters difficult for the raiders.

The party however entered the enemy's trench. It was found to be very badly damaged, and almost flat in places.

No live Germans were met but one dead one was seen lying in the trench.

The raiding party returned at the pre-arranged hour. One prisoner was caught in "No Man's Land" and brought in.

10. The inaccurate shooting of the Stokes Mortar Battery covering the 5th Camerons has not yet been satisfactorily accounted for. The guns were carefully registered in advance, and I don't think this hitch should have occurred.

11. 30 Stokes guns were employed on a frontage of 300 yards.

The rates of fire employed were as follows:-

20 rounds per gun per minute for the first two minutes, and 8 rounds per gun per minute for the remaining 30 minutes.

Total rounds used, 5800.

12. This intense concentration of fire was intended to test the power of the Stokes against trenches and personnel.

The German trench was pretty well destroyed and the occupants killed, but the dug-outs were uninjured. I would not say that all this damage was due to the Stokes Bombs. It is possible that some of it had been caused by previous wire cutting by 18-pdrs. and 2" Trench Mortars.

The concussion of the bursting Stokes Bombs was so intense that our own troops felt the effects; and I believe

(we/

we should do better on another occasion to start with one minute of very rapid fire and then slacken the rate to 10, 5, and even 1 round per minute if we had concentrated mortars to the extent of 10 yards of front to a mortar.

13. The methods employed for recalling the parties were -

      (a) French Horns.
      (b) Bugles.
      (c) Green rockets fired in bunches from our trenches.

Of these the French Horns were found to be efficacious. The Bugles could not be heard nor were the rockets seen.

14. The enemy on this night put a barrage on to his own front trench within one minute of Zero. On the previous night during the raid of the 1st S.African Bde. he put his barrage on to the ZOUAVE Valley and did not open it till Zero plus 8.

15. Our casualties amounted to 14 wounded amongst the raiders, of whom 10 are still at duty.

In addition, one of our Stokes Mortars was knocked out by a shell which killed 2 and wounded 2 others of the detachment.

                                          Major-General,
                            Commanding 9th (Scottish) Division.

To :-

   Recipients of Operation Order 76.

No. X.5/1805.   16th September, 1916.

Paragraph 1 (c) and (d) and Paragraphs 2, 3, 4 and 5 of 9th Division Operation Order No. 76 are cancelled.

Please acknowledge.

[signature]
for Lieutenant Colonel,
General Staff,
9th (Scottish) Division.

"A" Form
MESSAGES AND SIGNALS.

Army Form C. 2121.

Prefix	Code	m.	Words	Charge	This message is on a/c of:	No. of Message
Office of Origin and Service Instructions.						Recd. at ___ m.
S.D.R.			Sent		10	Date ___
			At ___ m.		Service.	From ___
			To ___			
			By ___		(Signature of "Franking Officer.")	By ___

TO	26th Bde.	G.R.A.	Train	37th Divn.
	27th Bde.	G.R.E.	A.D.M.S.	
	S.A.Bde.	9/Seaforths	"Q"	

Sender's Number.	Day of Month	In reply to Number	
G 453	15/9		AAA

The 26th Machine Gun Coy. will relieve the 63rd M.G.
Coy. in the CARENCY Section to-morrow and the 27th
M.G.Coy. will relieve 4 guns of the 63rd M.G.Coy.
in the BAJOLLE SWITCH to-morrow AAA On completion
of relief the 63rd M.G.Coy. will concentrate at
GRAND SERVINS AAA The G.O.C. 1st S.African Bde. will
issue the necessary orders to the 63rd Machine Gun
Coy. AAA The 63rd Light Trench Mortar Battery will
move to GRAND SERVINS to-morrow under orders to be
issued by the 26th Inf. Bde. AAA The 153rd and
154th Field Coys. R.E. will concentrate at the Headquarters of their Companies to-morrow under orders
to be issued by C.R.E. and be ready to rejoin 37th
Division AAA The Medium Trench Mortar Batteries and
personnel of the Heavy Trench Mortar Battery of the
37th Division will be withdrawn from the line tomorrow
and will be ready to rejoin 37th Division AAA
ACKNOWLEDGE by wire

From	9th Division
Place	
Time	10.30 p.m.

The above may be forwarded as now corrected.

(Z)

Major,
G.S.

War Diary. 11

SECRET.
Copy No 25

9th Division Operation Order No. 77.

17.9.16.

1. The 1st S.African Brigade will extend its right on the 18th inst. and relieve the 26th Inf. Bde. as far South as GOBRON Trench inclusive.

2. The 27th Infantry Brigade will relieve the 26th Inf. Bde. in the BERTHONVAL Section on the 19th inst.

3. The 26th Inf. Bde. will relieve the section of the 27th Machine Gun Company in the BAJOLLE SWITCH on the 19th inst.

4. All details of reliefs will be arranged direct between Brigadiers concerned.
Command will pass on completion of relief which will be reported by wire to Divisional Headquarters.

K Stewart.
Lieutenant Colonel,
General Staff,
9th (Scottish) Division.

Issued at 7 a.m.

Copies to:—
No. 1 to 26th Bde.
2 to 27th Bde.
3 to 1st S.A.Bde.
4 to C.R.A.
5 to 50th R.A.Bde.
6 to 51st R.A.Bde.
7 to 52nd R.A.Bde.
8 to Trench Mortars
9 to Div. Colm.
10 to C.R.E.
11 to 9/Seaforths.
12 to 9th Train.
13 to 9th Signals.
14 to A.A. & Q.M.G.
15 to A.D.M.S.
16 to A.D.V.S.
17 to A.P.M.
18 to 4th Corps
19 to 37th Division.
20 to 60th Division.
21 to 63rd Division.
22 to 176th Tunnelling Coy.
23 to 182nd Tunnelling Coy.
24 to 172nd Tunnelling Coy.
25 " War Diary
26 " File.

War Diary

SECRET.

Copy No. 25

9th Division Operation Order No. 78.

20th Sept. 1916.

1. The 9th Division (less Divisional Artillery) will be relieved by the 24th Division in the Right Sector commencing on Septr. 22nd.

2. The Infantry reliefs will be carried out as per Table A. attached.
   All details of relief will be arranged direct between Brigade Commanders concerned.
   The Command of each Section will pass on completion of relief which will be reported by wire to Divisional Headquarters.

3. The Field Companies R.E. of the 9th Division will be relieved by the Field Companies of the 24th Division under arrangements to be made by C.R.Es. concerned.
   The arrangements made to be reported to Divisional Headquarters.

4. The 9th Seaforths (Pioneers) will be relieved on Sept. 25th by the Pioneer Battalion of the 24th Division.
   All details to be arranged between C.Os. concerned.

5. Details as to the relief of the Field Ambulances willbe arranged direct between A.Ds.M.S. concerned and of Mobile Veterinary Sections between A.Ds.V.S. concerned.
   The arrangements to be reported to Divisional Headquarters.

6. The command of the right Sector will pass to G.O.C. 24th Division at 10 a.m. on September 26th.

Lieutenant Colonel,
General Staff,
9th (Scottish) Division.

Issued at 7.30 p.m.

Copies to:-

No. 1 to 26th Bde.
    2 to 27th Bde.
    3 to 1st S.A.Bde.
    4 to C.R.A.
    5 to 50th R.A.Bde.
    6 to 51st R.A.Bde.
    7 to 52nd R.A.Bde.
    8 to Trench Mortars.
    9 to Div. Column.
    10 to C.R.E.
    11 to 9th Seaforths.
    12 to 9th Div.Train.
    13 to 9th Signals.
    14 to A.A. & Q.M.G.
    15 to A.D.M.S.
    16 to A.D.V.S.
    17 to A.P.M.
    18 to 4th Corps.
    19 to 37th Division.
    20 to 60th Division.
    21 to 24th Division.
    22 to 176th Tunnelling Coy.
    23 to 182nd Tunnelling Coy.
    24 to 172nd Tunnelling Coy.
    25   War Diary.
    26   File.

TABLE A.

Date.	Unit	From	To	To be relieved by	Remarks.
Sept. 22nd.	26th Inf. Bde.	CHATEAU de la HAIE Area.	*Training Area	73rd Inf. Bde.	
Sept. 23rd.	1st S.African Inf. Bde.	CARENCY Section	CHATEAU de la HAIE Area.	73rd Inf. Bde.	
Sept. 24th.	1st S.African Inf. Bde.	CHATEAU de la HAIE Area.	*Training Area	17th Inf. Bde.	
Sept. 25th.	27th Inf. Bde.	BERTHONVAL Section.	CHATEAU de la HAIE Area.	17th Inf. Bde.	
Sept. 26th.	27th Inf. Bde.	CHATEAU de la HAIE Area.	*Training Area	72nd Inf. Bde.	

*Further details will be issued as to the destination of Brigades.

SECRET.

Copy No. 29

9th Division Operation Order No. 79.

22.9.16.

Reference Sheets 36.b. and 51.c. 1/40,000.

1. The 9th Division will move to the Third Army Training Area in accordance with the attached table.

2. 9th Division Headquarters will close at CAMBLAIN l'ABBE at 10 a.m. on Septr. 26th and open at the CHATEAU, LE CAUROY at the same hour.

Lieutenant Colonel,
General Staff,
9th (Scottish) Division.

Issued at 7 a.m.

Copies to:-

No. 1 to 26th Inf. Bde.
2 to 27th Inf. Bde.
3 to 1st S.African Bde.
4 to C.R.A.
5 to 50th Bde. R.F.A.
6 to 51st Bde. R.F.A.
7 to 52nd Bde. R.F.A.
8 to Trench Mortars.
9 to 9th Div. Column.
10 to C.R.E.
11 to 9th Seaforths.
12 to 9th Div. Train.
13 to 9th Signals.
14 to A.A. & Q.M.G.
15 to A.D.M.S.
16 to A.D.V.S.
17 to A.P.M.
18 & 19 to 4th Corps
20 to XVII Corps
21 to XI Corps.
22 to 60th Division.
23 to 24th Division.
24 to 37th Division.
25 to 176th Tunnelling Coy.
26 to 182nd Tunnelling Coy.
27 to 172nd Tunnelling Coy.

MARCH TABLE.

Date	Unit	From	To	Remarks.
Sept.22nd.	26th Inf.Bde.	CHATEAU de la HAIE Area.	Area VILLERS CHATTEL MINGOVAL VILLERS BRULIN BETHONSART GUESTREVELLE. LE TIRLET HERLIN-LE-VERT. CHELERS.	To be clear of billets by 12 noon. Not to leave Reserve Brigade Area before 11.30 a.m.
Sept.23rd.	28th Inf. Bde.	MINGOVAL Area	Area LIENCOURT BERLENCOURT DENIER SARS LEZ BOIS. E.TREE WAMIN.	To use any roads W. of & including the VILLERS CHATTEL - AUBIGNY - MANIN - BEAUFORT Road. To be clear of VILLERS CHATTEL - TINQUES Road by 12 noon.
Sept.23rd.	28th Fld.Amb.	GRAND SERVINS.	HOUVIN - HOUVIGNEUL.	Via VILLERS BRULIN and TINQUES. Not to pass VILLERS CHATTEL before 12 noon.
Sept.24th	1st S.African Bde.	CHATEAU de la HAIE Area.	(Area VILLERS CHATTEL. (MINGOVAL. (VILLERS BRULIN. (BETHONSART. (GUESTREVILLE. (LE TIRLET. (HERZIN-LE-VERT. (CHELERS.	To be clear of billets by 12 noon. Not to leave Reserve Area till 11.30 a.m.
	64th Field Coy. RE	VILLERS AU BOIS.		64th Fd.Coy. to move and billet under orders to be issued by G.O.C. 1st S.African Bde.
	S.African F.Amb.	ESTREE CAUCHIE	GUOY-EN-TERNOIS.	To move at 10 a.m. via TINQUES.

2.

Date	Unit	From	To	Remarks.
Sept.25th	1st S.African Bde.	MINGOVAL Area	Area LIGNEREUIL. AMBRINES. MAIZIERES. MAGNICOURT. GOUY-EN-TERNOIS.	To use any roads W. of and including the VILLERS CHATTEL - AUBIGNY - MANIN - BEAUFORT Road. To be clear of VILLERS CHATTEL by 12 noon.
	64th Field Co. RE	MINGOVAL Area.	HOUVIN HOUVINEUL.	To move under orders to be issued by G.O.C. 1st S.A.Inf.Bde. C.R.E. to arrange billeting.
	9. Seaforths (Pnrs)	VILLERS-AU-BOIS	VILLERS CHATTEL	Not to reach VILLERS CHATTEL till 12 noon. To be clear of CAMBLIGNEUL by 12.40 p.m.
	27th Fld.Amblce.	LES QUATRE VENTS.	BEAUFORT.	To move via CAMBLIGNEUL. Not to enter CAMBLIGNEUL till 12.45 p.m.
	20th Scn.Section.	CAMBLAIN l'ABBE.	LE CAUROI.	
Sept.28th.	27th Inf. Bde.	CHATEAU de la HAIE Area.	Area VILLERS CHATTEL MINGOVAL. VILLERS BRULIN. BETHONSART. GUESTREVILLE. LE TIRLET HERMIN-LE-VERT. CHELERS.	To be clear of billets by 12 noon. Bde. Area till 11.30 to leave Reserve 90th Fd.Coy. R.E. to move and billet under the orders of G.O.C. 27th Inf.Bde.
	90th Fd.Coy. R.E.	GOUY SERVINS.		
	9/Seaforths (Pnrs)	VILLERS CHATTEL.	AVERDOING.	To be clear of VILLERS CHATTEL by 11 a.m.

3.

Date	Unit	From	To	Remarks.
Sept.27th.	27th Inf.Bde.	MINGOVAL Area	Area BEAUFORT MANIN GIVENCHY-LE-NOBLE VILLERS-SIR-SIMON.	To be clear of VIL- LERS BRULIN by 12 noon. To use any roads West of and including the VILLERS CHATTEL - AUBIGNY - MANIN - BEAUFORT Rds.
	90th Fd.Coy. R.E.	MINGOVAL Area.	HOUVIN HOUVINEUL.	To move under orders of G.O.C 27th Inf. Bde. C.R.E. to arrange billeting.
	63rd Fd.Coy. R.E.	BOIS de la HAIE.	VILLERS BRULIN.	Not to enter VILLERS BRULIN till 12 noon.
Sept.28th.	63rd Fd.Coy. R.E.	VILLERS BRULIN.	HOUVIN HOUVINEUL.	

War Diary

9th (Scottish) Division.
Dispositions of Units.

9th Div. Hd.Qrs.	LE CAUROY.
26th Bde. H.Q.	LIENCOURT.
5th Cameron Hlrs.	LIENCOURT.
7th Seaforth Hlrs.	ESTREE WAMIN.
8th Black Watch.	DENIER.
10th Arg. & Suth. Hlrs.	BERLINCOURT.
26th Trench Mortar Bty.	SARS-LE-BOIS.
26th Machine Gun Coy.	SARS-LE-BOIS.
27th Bde. H.Q.	MANIN.
6th K.O.S.Bs.	BEAUFORT.
9th Scottish Rifles	GIVENCHY LE NOBLE.
11th Royal Scots.	VILLERS SIR SIMON, DOFFINE, FERME.
12th Royal Scots.	MANIN.
27th Machine Gun Coy.	BEAUFORT.
27th Trench Mortar Bty.	GIVENCHY LE NOBLE.
1st S.African Bde.	AMBRINES.
1st Bn. S.A.Infy.	MAIZIERES.
2nd Bn. S.A.Infy.	LIGNEREUIL.
3rd " "	MAGNICOURT sur CANCHE.
4th " "	AMBRINES.
28th Machine Gun Coy.	MAIZIERES.
S.African Trench Mortar Bty.	GOUY en TERNOIS.
9th Seaforth Hlrs. (Pioneers)	AVEROINGT.
A.D.M.S.	LE CAUROY.
27th Field Ambulance.	PENIN.
28th Field Ambulance.	HOUVIN HOUVIGNEUL.
S.African Fld. Ambulance.	GOUY en TERNOIS.
20th Sanitary Section.	LE CAUROY.
C.R.E.	LE CAUROY.
63rd Field Coy. R.E.	VILLERS CHATEL.
64th " " "	HOUVIN HOUVIGNEUL.
90th " " "	HOUVIN HOUVIGNEUL.
A.D.V.S.	LE CAUROY.
21st Mobile Vet. Sec.	PENIN.
9th Divisional Train.	HOUVIN HOUVIGNEUL.
104th Coy. A.S.C. (attd. 9th D.A.)	GAUCHIN LEGAL.
105th Coy. A.S.C.	ESTREE WAMIN.
106th Coy. A.S.C.	BLAVINCOURT.
107th Coy. A.S.C.	GOUY en TERNOIS.
D.A.D.O.S.	LE CAUROY.
Salvage Coy.	LE CAUROY.
9th Div. Supply Colm.	TENQUES.
Divisional School.	MAISNIL BOUCHE.

27/9/16.

B.M. 2/290.
27th. Infantry Brigade.
8th. September 1916.

To, 9th.(Scottish) Division.

****

Owing to other and more pressing work required in the line - it was not possible to assist the T.M. Battery with R.E. or infantry labour.

The following work were undertaken & completed by the battery -

(1). No. 3 emplacement.

(2). A new central bomb store at Battery Headquarters.

(3). Camouflage work on emplacements 2, 3, 4 & 7.

(4). The provision of cupola bomb stores in emplacements where required.

As regards (3), the emplacements were covered with sods & wire secured over the top. This was unnecessary & resulted from a misunderstanding as to what was actually required.

There is no excuse for the dirty condition of some of the guns and ammunition. They were not generally in this state, & on occasions when emplacements have been visited, the guns & ammunition were always found to be clean.

The existing bomb emplacements would appear to afford insufficient protection to the ammunition in wet weather.

The attention of the O.C. 27th T.M.Battery has been drawn to the points dealt with in the report of the Divisional T.M.B Officer.

Brigadier General,
Commanding 27th Inf.Brigade.

27th Infantry Brigade.

No. X.5/1760.   7th September, 1916.

With reference to attached report on the condition of the emplacements of the Trench Mortar Battery under your command, the G.O.C. wishes to be informed whether there is any adequate reason for the Trench Mortar Battery to have failed in improving the emplacements during the time the Brigade was in the line.

He also wishes for an explanation as to the condition of the guns and of the ammunition referred to.

The inspection of the emplacements was carried out by the Divisional Trench Mortar Officer under the instructions of the G.O.C.

Lieut. Colonel,
General Staff,
9th (Scottish) Division.

9th Division.

Herewith report on Stokes Mortar Emplacements handed over on Sept 6th 1916 by 27th Inf. Bde. to S.A. Inf. Bde.

No 1 Emplacement. S.14.b.8.6.

Head cover comprises 2 layers sand-bags only. Bed plate is badly laid, and is not at right angles to line of fire. This would involve a great deal of work to switch the gun on to its full zone. The bomb store is a small cupola, with one layer of sand-bags as protection, which is inadequate.
The Ammunition is rusty and damp. No dug-out for men.

No 2 Emplacement. S.14.b.7½.8.

No revetting to emplacement. Embrasure not on a gradient sufficient to allow extreme range. Bomb store has no head cover, and Ammunition is rusty and damp. Gun also has been neglected. Mens dug-out measures 3' x 3' and has no protection, beyond one sheet of corrugated iron.

No 3 Emplacement. S.14.b.5½.9.

This was constructed by 27th Inf. Bde. The pit has been dug too far forward, and thereby prevents gun from firing at extreme range. Head cover is 2 layers of sand-bags. Gun rusty. Bomb store is small and could be improved.

No 4 Emplacement. S.8.d.7½.3.

Head cover inadequate. Revetting of emplacement is poor. 2 rifles G.S. being used as supports. The Ammunition is stored in the gun pit, and this I consider dangerous, and also invites dampness, through water running down slope of embrasure. Mens dug-outs foul and should be improved.

No 5 Emplacement. S.8.d.7½.5.

Was full of water, and in no way fit for use. Will entail much work to put same in working order.

No 6 Emplacement. S.8.b.4.3.

Has been demolished by hostile fire. Ammunition however was not removed, and 140 rounds are damp and rusty, having no protection against the weather.

No 7 Emplacement. S.8.b.5.2.

[margin: Iron rails / 2 layers sandbags]

Has no overhead cover, and no revetting. The bomb store is simply an excavation, and has no protection of any kind. Ammunition in same was rusty and damp. The dug-out for men is 300 yards away, but there are several dug-outs near emplacement which could be improved and made good.

The Head-quarters dug-out requires a great deal of improvement, the entrance being particularly bad.

Generally.

Not one emplacement could in my opinion be passed as satisfactory for several reasons :-

(1) Each gun pit should have 3 excavations for bed plate so as to increase zone of fire. This is taught at all schools, and is an essential point.

(2) Protection for detachment is entirely inadequate. In many cases the roofs of emplacements were simply resting on one sheet of corrugated iron, which was supported by

sand-bag walls, and would easily fall in.

(3) Bomb stores have had little or no trouble taken in their construction. 3 placed in the gun pit itself, and at that just below the muzzle of the gun. This proved at the Somme to be a very dangerous habit, one detachment being wiped out through a premature burst detonating Ammunition. The Ammunition on the whole was rusty and damp.

(4) Dug-outs for men were very poorly constructed, and afforded no protection against hostile shelling.

(5) No use has been made of "camouflage" for protection against aerial photography of emplacements.

I might mention that to the best of my knowledge the emplacements, with the exception of No 3 were constructed by the 2nd Division.

J D Jaidman
Capt. R.A.
Comdg.
9th Trench Mortar Brigade.

4/9/16.

First Army

9th (Scottish) Division.

INTELLIGENCE SUMMARY.
4 p.m. 16/9/16 to 4 p.m. 17/9/16.

BERTHONVAL.
Enemy movement. Enemy transport was heard behind the enemy lines between 8.30 p.m. and 9.15 p.m. from OLD BOOT Sap.
Enemy work. Enemy were heard working on DUKE and GARTER. Our Lewis guns fired on them and work ceased.
New sandbags are visible on the parapet at S.15.c.5½.7. and S.15.c.5.4.
New wire has been erected in front of TOM and HARRY, at S.21.a.9½.9½ and S.21.b.4.2.

CARENCY II.
Enemy work. Enemy appeared to be busy repairing his trenches.
General. A pigeon was observed at 5.40 p.m. flying from the enemy's line towards VILLERS AU BOIS.
The enemy's attitude has been very quiet on this front for the last few days.
Aircraft. At 7.30 a.m. about 22 of our planes crossed the enemy lines going in an Easterly direction.

Reported by Divisional Observers.
Enemy movements. At 4.8 p.m. at T.12.c. cart going North to MERICOURT
4.25 p.m. at U.7.d. cart going to ROUVROY from ACHEVILLE.
4.15 p.m. Motor lorry left ROUVROY going S.W. for about 1000 yards,
    Returned without turning round. It appeared to be on rails
7.10 p.m. 9 motor lorries left MERICOURT on the VIMY Road.
    8 motor lorries left ROUVROY on VIMY Road.
4.30 - 5 p.m. 40 infantry marching from MERICOURT cross roads
    T.18.a. in batches of 10 at 100 yards interval, along
    VIMY Road for 1500 yards. They halted here and appeared
    to be engaged in some sort of signalling, using bright
    metal discs.
Enemy work. At T.10.c. 8 or 9 men observed working in fold of ground.
At U.15.b. about 40 people working on harvest.
At S.15.a. enemy support trenches appear to have been strongly wired.
At S.9.c. fresh wire put out behind IRISH Crater. A lot of fresh wire appears to have been thrown in front of enemy's trenches between IRISH and KENNEDY Craters.
At M.27.a.6.6. more chalk has been thrown up - suspected dug-outs.
At S.9.c.3.3. snipers post suspected.
At T.16.c.4.5. flash of a gun observed in front of shed.

Captain,
General Staff,
9th (Scottish) Division.

First Army

9th (Scottish) Division.

INTELLIGENCE SUMMARY.
4 p.m. 17/9/16 to 4 p.m. 18/9/16.

BERTHONVAL.
Enemy signals. About 6.45 p.m. several lines of continuous white lights were observed coming from the enemy's left. Each line had from 10 to 12 lights. On reaching a certain height the lights went out.
Enemy work. A man was observed working on the enemy parapet. He was fired on and seen to fall.
At S.15.a.2.1½. new sandbags are visible built into the parapet.

CARENCY.II.
Enemy work. A working party was observed at S.8.d.9.8½. Our Lewis guns fired on them and the party was dispersed.

Reported by Divisional Observers.
Enemy work. At S.22.b.1.7. enemy working in trench; a considerable amount of chalk has been thrown up and is clearly visible.
At S.22.c.4.8. a sandbag redoubt has been observed. Fairly large loop-hole is visible.
General.
Owing to the bad weather conditions observation was very difficult.

G. Pearson
Captain,
General Staff,
9th (Scottish) Division.

First Army.

9th (Scottish) Division.

INTELLIGENCE SUMMARY.
4 p.m. 19/9/16 to 4 p.m. 20/9/16.

BERTHONVAL.
Enemy signals. At 6.30 p.m. a hostile aeroplane was seen to drop two white lights. No action followed.
At 7.15 p.m. enemy sent up a white light which burst into seven white lights - no result observed.
Enemy movement. At 1 p.m. enemy transport heard opposite right sub-section front, apparently a good distance away.
At 5 p.m. an enemy aeroplane attempted to cross our lines but was driven off by our machine guns and artillery.
Enemy work. Two or three stakes and fresh wire observed opposite MANDORA Central.
Work has been carried out during the night in repairing enemy parapet where blown in by our trench mortars.
Fresh earth has been observed at several places.

CARENCY I.
Enemy movement. A hostile plane endeavoured to cross our lines at 5.30 p.m. but was driven Eastwards by our guns.
Enemy work. An enemy working party attempted to repair his wire but was frustrated by our Lewis guns.
General.
The enemy appears to have changed his tactics and is more agressive than formerly.

CARENCY II.
Enemy work. Two working parties seen at S.9.c.2.9. and S.9.a.1.4. were dispersed by our Lewis guns.

Reported by Divisional Observers.
Enemy movement. Two 4-horse G.S. wagons loaded entered ROUVROY from ACHEVILLE with 10 men walking behind.
About 300 men moved off from T.4.a. and b. in broken order and proceeded towards SALLAUMINES and MERICOURT.
At 1.35 p.m. a party of about 250 men moving towards ACHEVILLE along VIMY - ACHEVILLE Road were observed at T.22.b. and T.17.c. and d. This was reported to IVth Corps Heavy Artillery.
At M.36.b.5.5. 8 men walking along road to AVION.
At T.24.b. about 50 infantry going South from ACHEVILLE disappeared from sight in sunken road.
At T.24.b. about 50 infantry going North into ACHEVILLE.
At T.18.a. about 50 men going to-wards ROUVROY.
Enemy work. At S.9.a.2.0. a suspected O.P. has been constructed.
At S.9.a.1.6. what appears to be an O.P. was observed.
At S.8.b.8.0. a fairly large loop-hole is visible.

GENERAL. A man in civilian clothes was found in garden of ruined house at X.10.a.2.1. having no pass. He was arrested and handed over to the Military Police whose report has not yet been received.

Captain.
General Staff
9th (Scottish) Division.

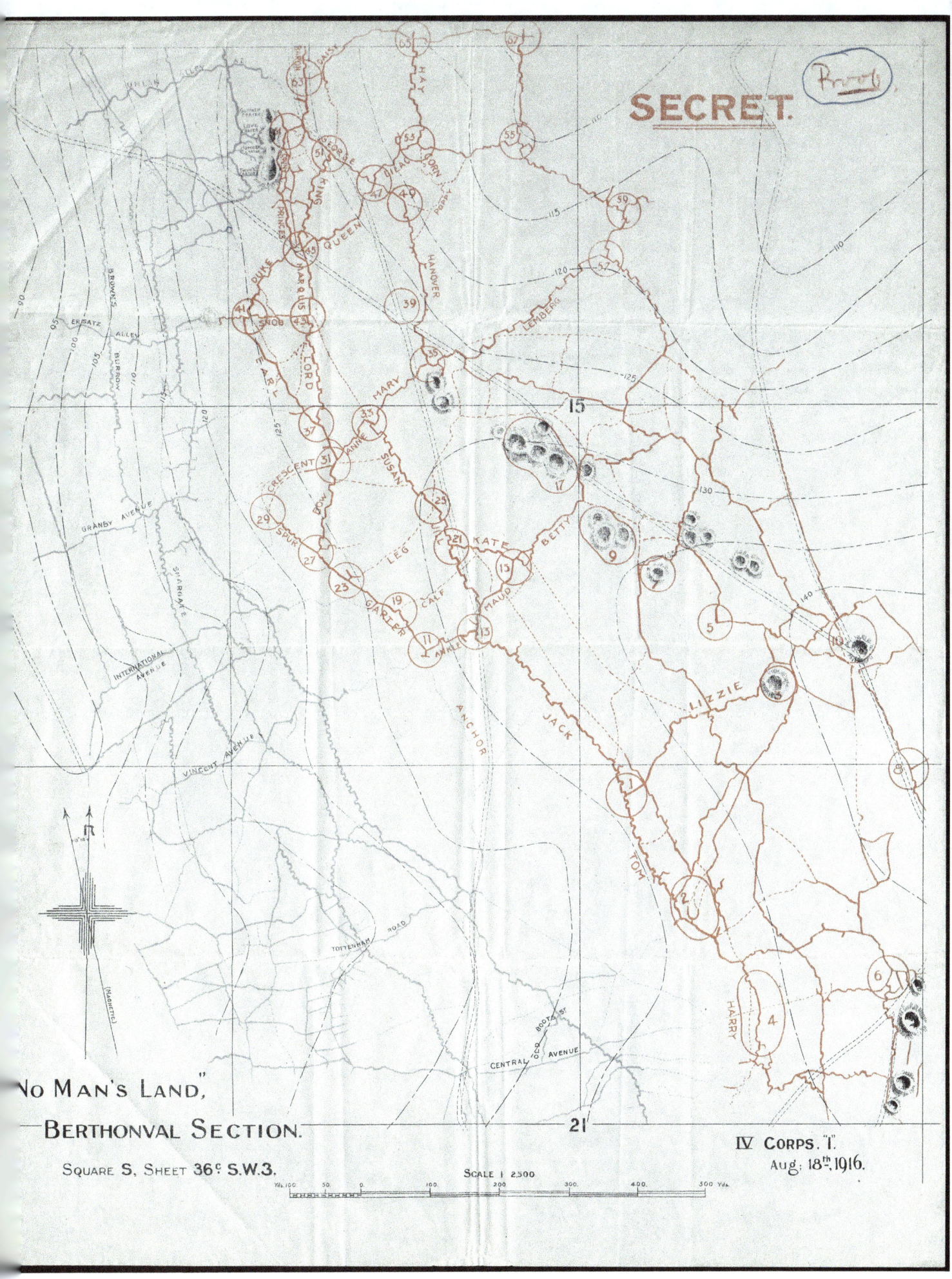

For Wier Drury

For War Diary

War Diary

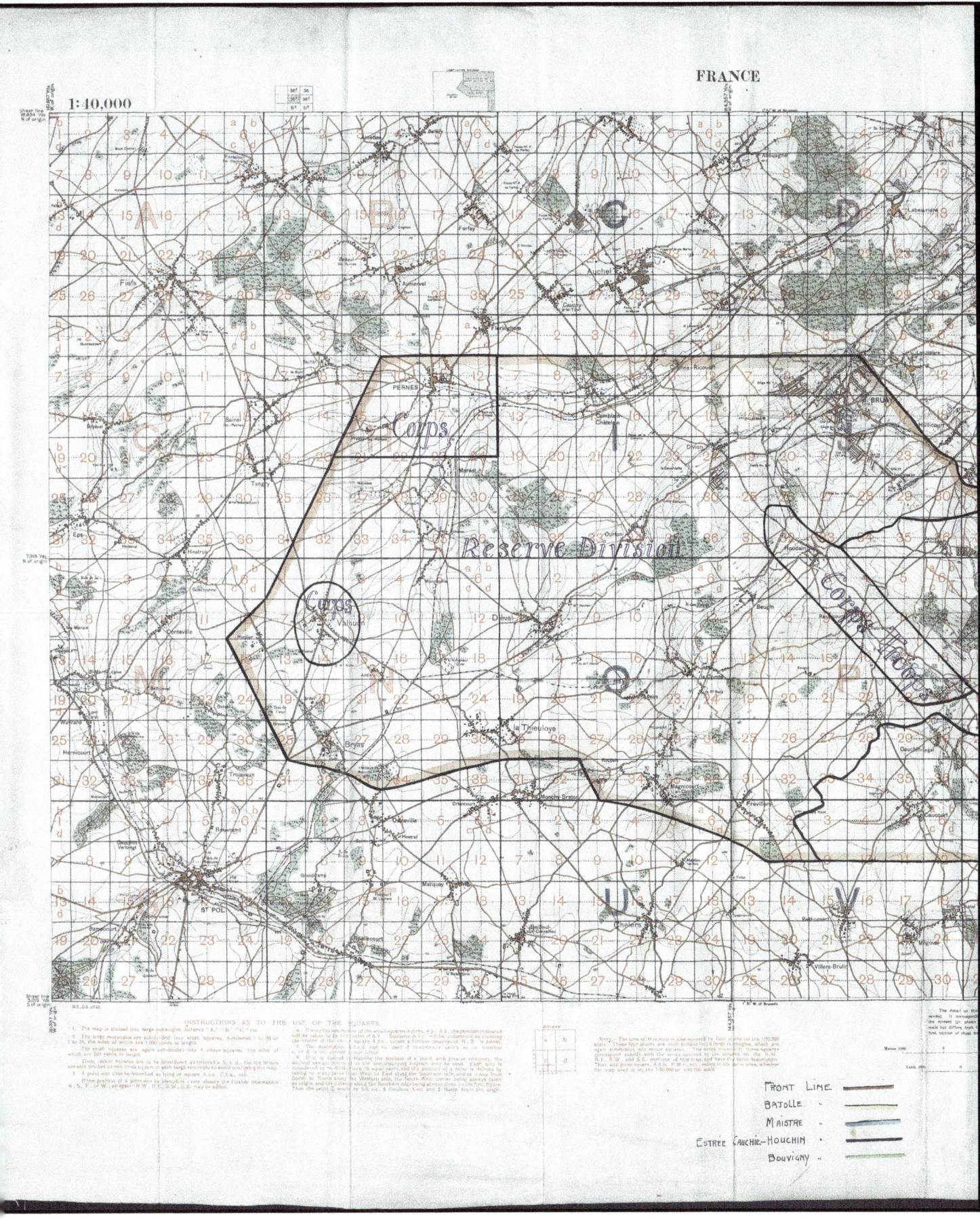

Four à coke	Coke oven.
Ganterie	Glove Factory.
Gare	Station.
Garenne	Warren.
Garnison	Garrison.
Gommerie	Gum-works.
Fab.^e de glaces	Mirror Factory.
Glacière	Ice factory.
Gué	Ford.
Guérite	Sentry-box, Turret.
" à signaux	Signal-box (Ry.)
Halte	Halt.
Hangar	Shed, Hangar.
Hôpital	Hospital.
Hôtel-de-Ville	Town hall.
Houillère	Colliery.
Huilerie	Oil factory.
Imprimerie, Impr.^{ie}	Printing works.
Jetée	Pier.
Laminerie	Rolling mills.
Ligne de butte	
Laisse de marée	High water mark.
" de basse marée	Low " "
Maison Forestière M.^{on} F.^{re}	Forester's house.
Malterie	Malt-house.
Marbrerie	Marble works.
Marais	Marsh.
Marais salant	Salters.
"	Salt marsh.
Marché	Market.
Mare	Pool.
Meule	Rick.
Mine	Mine.
Monastère	Monastery.
Moulin, M.ⁿ	Mill.
" à vapeur	Steam-mill.
Mer	Well.
" artésien	Deep-holed well.

Nacelle	Ferry.
Orme	Elm.
Orphelinat	Orphanage.
Oseraie	Osier-beds.
Ouvrage	Fort.
Ouvrages hydrauliques	Water works.
Papeterie	Paper-mill.
Parc	Park, yard.
" aérostatique	Aviation ground.
" à charbon	Coal yard.
" à pétrole	Petrol store.
Passage à niveau, P.N.	Level-crossing.
Passerelle, Pass.^{lle}	Foot-bridge.
Pépinière	Nursery-garden.
Peuplier	Poplar tree.
Phare	Light-house.
Pilier, Pil.^r	Post.
Plaine d'exercice	Drill ground.
Pompe	Pump.
Ponceau	Culvert.
Pont	Bridge.
" levis	Drawbridge.
Poste de garde	
Station côte	Coast-guard station.
Poteau P.^{au}	Post.
Poterie	Pottery.
Poudrière, Poud.^{re}	Powder magazine.
Magasin à poudre	
Prise d'eau	Water supply.
Puits	Pit-head, Shaft, Well.
" artésien	Artesian well.
" d'avage	
" ventilateur	Ventilating shaft.
" de sondage	Boring.
Quai	Quay, Platform.
" aux bestiaux	Cattle platform.
" aux marchandises	Goods platform.
Raccordement	Junction.
Raffinerie	Refinery.
" de sucre	Sugar refinery.
Râperie	Beet-root factory.

Remblai	Embankment.
Remise des Machines	Engine-shed.
Réservoir, Rés.^r	Reservoir.
Route cavalière	Bridle road.
Rubanerie	Ribbon Factory.
Ruine	
Ruines	Ruin.
En ruine	
Ruiné - e	
Salière	Sand-pit.
Sablonnière, Sablon.^{re}	
Sapin	Fir tree.
Saule	Willow tree.
Saunerie	Salt-works.
Scierie, Sc.^{ie}	Saw-mill.
Sondage	Boring.
Source	Spring.
Sucrerie, Suc.^{ie}	Sugar factory.
Tannerie	Tannery.
Tir à la cible	Rifle range.
Tissage	Weaving mill.
Tôlerie	Rolling mill.
Tombeau	Tomb.
Tour	Tower.
Tourbière	Peat-bog, Peat-bed.
Tourelle	Small tower.
Tuilerie	Tile works.
Usine à gaz	Gas works.
" d'électricité	Electricity works.
" métallurgique	Metal works.
" d'agglomérés	Briquette factory.
Verrerie, Verr.^{ie}	Glass works.
Viaduc	Viaduct.
Vivier	Fish Pond.
Voie de chargement	
" déchargement	
" d'évitement	Siding.
" formation	
" manœuvre	
Zingerie	Zinc works.

FRANCE.

SHEET 36 B.

THIRD EDITION.

INDEX TO ADJOINING SHEETS.

Scale $\frac{1}{40,000}$.

Army Form A 2007.

CENTRAL REGISTRY.

Central Registry No. and Date.

502/88(G)

Attached Files.

SUBJECT, AND OFFICE OF ORIGIN.

Minor Operation - Raid.
Raid carried out by 8th Black Watch and 5th Camerons against enemy trenches from S.15.c.1.7. to S.15.c.4½.4.

9th Div

Referred to	Date	Referred to	Date	Referred to	Date
G.	18.9.16.				
I	24/9/16				
F.M. ~~A.R.A~~	24.9.16				
~~C.E.~~	~~24.9.16~~				
G.	25.9.16				

P.A.	Date
F.M.	25/9/16

Schedule of Correspondence

1736

Inter-office Minutes.

Note.—Inside sheets to be attached to this page.

SECRET

1st ARMY GENERAL STAFF
No. 502/88
Date 19.9.16

IV Corps No. H.R.S. 641.

First Army.

Forwarded in continuation of my H.R.S. 641 dated 18th September, 1916.

Henry Wilson

H.Q., IV Corps,
19th September, 1916.

Lieutenant-General,
Commanding IV Corps.

IVth Corps.
27th Infantry Brigade,
1st S.African Brigade,

No. X.1811,   19th September, 1916.

The attached copy of 26th Infantry Brigade letter No. 26/2129 of 17th September is forwarded for information.

Lieutenant Colonel,
for Major General,
Commanding, 9th (Scottish) Division.

26/2129.

9th Division.

The following points seem to have been brought out with regard to the employment of a Stokes barrage.

1. Although the infantry are able to get within 40 yards of the barrage, the concussion is so terrific that they should not be asked to remain close to such a barrage for more than one minute.

2. A Stokes barrage at the later stages should not be closer than 100 yards to the infantry.

3. Probably one gun to 20 yards, firing at the rate of 10 rounds per minute is sufficient for an intensive barrage.

4. With systematic registering and well trained batteries the accuracy of a Stokes barrage may be relied on.

(Sgd.) A. B. Ritchie.
Brigadier General,
17.9.16. Commanding 26th Infantry Brigade.

1st Army.

I forward a clear report of an excellent little raid carried out by the 2 parties of the 8th Black Watch & of the 5th Cameron. On the whole it worked well & there is no doubt of the severe punishment it inflicted on the enemy.

It is interesting to me as being the first raid we have tried which was, chiefly, dependent on the fire of the Stokes mortar; and it is very satisfactory to read that Gen. Furse considers that the Stokes were almost too powerful at the rate of fire employed.

The whole enterprise was creditable and successful.

Henry Wilson.
H Gen'l
Comm'd IV Corps.

18.9.16.

HRS 641

SECRET

4th Corps.

No. X.5/1784/5.   17th September, 1916.
---

1.   A raid was carried out on the night September 14th/15th by the 8th Black Watch and 5th Camerons on the enemy trenches from S.15.c.1.7. to S.15.c.4½.4.

2.   The raid was carried out with the 8th Black Watch (4 officers and 77 other ranks) on the right and 5th Camerons (4 officers and 66 other ranks) on the left.

The point of entry into the enemy's trench allotted to the 8th Black Watch was Point 19 and to the 5th Camerons Point 29.

3.   Four Stokes Mortar Batteries in addition to the Medium Trench Mortar Batteries and Artillery covered this operation.

4.   The general plan was for the Stokes Mortars to open a hurricane bombardment of the German front line at Zero, the raiding parties advancing as close as possible to their objectives under cover of this fire.

At Zero plus 2 minutes the Stokes Mortars were to lift on to the German support line and the raiders to at once enter the German trench.

5.   The detailed plan of operations and table of barrages is given in the Operation Orders attached.

Zero was fixed for 10.7 p.m.

6.   In addition to the purpose of the raid set forth in the Operation Orders, it was intended to test the efficacy of an intense Stokes Mortar bombardment on the enemy's trenches and personnel.

7.   The operation of the 8th Black Watch on the right was quite successful.

They advanced to within 40 yards of the German line under cover of the Stokes bombardment which was punctual and accurate.

The enemy put a barrage of whizz-bangs and 4.2s on his own front line at 10.8, and this made it difficult for the raiding party to pick up the lift of the Stokes and caused some slight delay, but at 10.12 the party entered the German trench exactly as arranged.

8.   The German trench was found so damaged by our bombardment that in places it was difficult to follow.

Parties of dead Germans were found at the entrances to dug-outs, as if they had tried to rush to their dug-outs when the Stokes bombardment opened and had got caught in bunches at the entrances.

Groups of nine, eight, and six dead Germans were counted by the light of a torch at the entrances to three different dug-outs respectively. In addition to these there were several corpses lying about the trench.

The Black Watch found some eleven live enemy in the trench whom they killed.

Several dug-outs were bombed, and from the noises heard within during this operation, there is no doubt that some enemy were caught.

The whole Black Watch party returned to our lines at the appointed time.

At least 35 Germans were accounted for apart from enemy bombed in dug-outs.

9. The 5th Camerons were not so fortunate.

The Stokes Mortar barrage on their front opened two minutes too soon (i.e. 10.5 p.m. instead of at 10.7 p.m.) and some of the shells fell short of the German front line.

When the barrage lifted at 10.9 the guns that had been shooting short lifted on to the German front line, thus making matters difficult for the raiders.

The party however entered the enemy's trench. It was found to be very badly damaged, and almost flat in places.

No live Germans were met but one dead one was seen lying in the trench.

The raiding party returned at the pre-arranged hour. One prisoner was caught in "No Man's Land" and brought in.

10. The inaccurate shooting of the Stokes Mortar Battery covering the 5th Camerons has not yet been satisfactorily accounted for. The guns were carefully registered in advance, and I don't think this hitch should have occurred.

11. 30 Stokes guns were employed on a frontage of 300 yards.

The rates of fire employed were as follows:-

20 rounds per gun per minute for the first two minutes, and 8 rounds per gun per minute for the remaining 30 minutes.

Total rounds used, 5800.

12. This intense concentration of fire was intended to test the power of the Stokes against trenches and personnel.

The German trench was pretty well destroyed and the occupants killed, but the dug-outs were uninjured. I would not say that all this damage was due to the Stokes Bombs. It is possible that some of it had been caused by previous wire cutting by 18-pdrs. and 2" Trench Mortars.

The concussion of the bursting Stokes Bombs was so intense that our own troops felt the effects, and I believe

(we/

we should do better on another occasion to start with one minute of very rapid fire and then slacken the rate to 10, 5, and even 1 round per minute if we had concentrated mortars to the extent of 10 yards of front to a mortar.

13. The methods employed for recalling the parties were -

    (a) French Horns.
    (b) Bugles.
    (c) Green rockets fired in bunches from our trenches.

Of these the French Horns were found to be efficacious. The Bugles could not be heard nor were the rockets seen.

14. The enemy on this night put a barrage on to his own front trench within one minute of Zero. On the previous night during the raid of the 1st S.African Bde. he put his barrage on to the ZOUAVE Valley and did not open it till Zero plus 8.

15. Our casualties amounted to 14 wounded amongst the raiders, of whom 10 are still at duty.

In addition, one of our Stokes Mortars was knocked out by a shell which killed 2 and wounded 2 others of the detachment.

Major-General,
Commanding 9th (Scottish) Division.

SECRET.   COPY NO......7

26th INFANTRY BRIGADE, OPERATION ORDER No. 39.
....

Ref. Map 1/5000, Enemy Trenches Southern Sector
                  (BERTHONVAL).
    ----

1. The 8th Black Watch and 5th Cameron Highlanders will carry
   out a combined raid on Z day at zero hour on the frontage
   S.15.c.5.4 — S.15.c.05.75.

2. OBJECTIVES.   (a). To capture prisoners (essential).
                 (b). To obtain identifications and information.
                 (c). To kill the enemy.
                 (d). To capture or destroy material.

3. PLACES OF ENTRY.

       8th Black Watch. at Point 19 on a front of 50 yards.
       5th Camerons at point 27 on a front of 50 yards.

4. ACTION.   The 8th Black Watch. To clear Garter up to

             (a). Its junction with ANKLE, establishing a block
                  at this point.
             (b). To clear CALF for 25 yards.
             (c). To clear GARTER up to its junction with LEG.
             (d). To clear LEG for 25 yards, in co-operation
                  with 5th Cameron Highlanders.

       5th Cameron Highlanders.

             (a). To clear SPUR up to its junction with CRESCENT
                  establishing a block at this point.
             (b). To clear BOW for 25 Yards.
             (c). To clear SPUR up to its junction with LEG.
             (d). To clear LEG for 25 yards in co-operation
                  with 8th Black Watch.

5. STRENGTH OF RAIDING PARTIES.
                                              61
       8th Black Watch.   4 Officers and 70 O.R's.
       5th Camerons.   do.   do.

6. POSITION OF READINESS. In NO MANS LAND in front of our
       wire, opposite the place of entry.

7. TIME. At zero the Raiders will advance from position of
       readiness under the STOKES MORTAR BARRAGE.
           At zero + 23 the signal to withdraw will be given,
       by means of (a) High G note on bugles.
                   (b) French Horns.

8. BARRAGES.   (a). STOKES and TWO INCH T.M's.   Appendix 1.
               (b). ARTILLERY.   Appendix 11.

9. M.G.   The 26th Machine Gun Coy., will co-operate by bringing
          bursts of fire to bear on the following targets to zero +
          35. from zero.

                       DUKE - CRATERS, 35, 17, 9, 7, 3.

No. 2.
-----

10. <u>PRISONERS & BOOTY.</u>   To be sent to Advanced Brigade Headquarters, by the unit concerned.

11. <u>COUNTERSIGN.</u>   Will be given on Z Day to the troops concerned.

12. <u>DRESS.</u> Nothing that will enable the enemy to obtain information or identification is to be worn or carried by the Raiders.
    Kilts will not be worn.

13. <u>REPORTS.</u> To be sent as frequently as possible to Advanced Brigade Headquarters at CABARET ROUGE.

14. PLEASE ACKNOWLEDGE.

JSDrew.
Major,
Brigade Major,
26th Infantry Brigade.

11:9:16.

Copy No. 1. 8th Black Watch.
         2. 7th Seaforths.
         3. 5th Camerons.
         4. 10th A. & S. H.
         5. 26th M. G. Coy.,
         6. 26th T. M. Batty.
         7. 9th Division.
         8. C. R. A.
         9. 50th R. F. A.
        10. 51st R. F. A.
        11. 52nd R. F. A.
        12. 9th Division T. M.

Appendix I.

BARRAGES.

      0 to 0+2   STOKES. ―――――――――   2 inch T.M. ||||||

      0+2 to 0+30 STOKES. ~~~~~~~~~   "   "   "   ⦿

(Special 0+2 to 0+7 STOKES). • • • •

      0+30 to 0+32 STOKES. ―――――――   "   "   " |||||

      0+2 to 0+30 XXXX ARTILLERY. ―――――――――

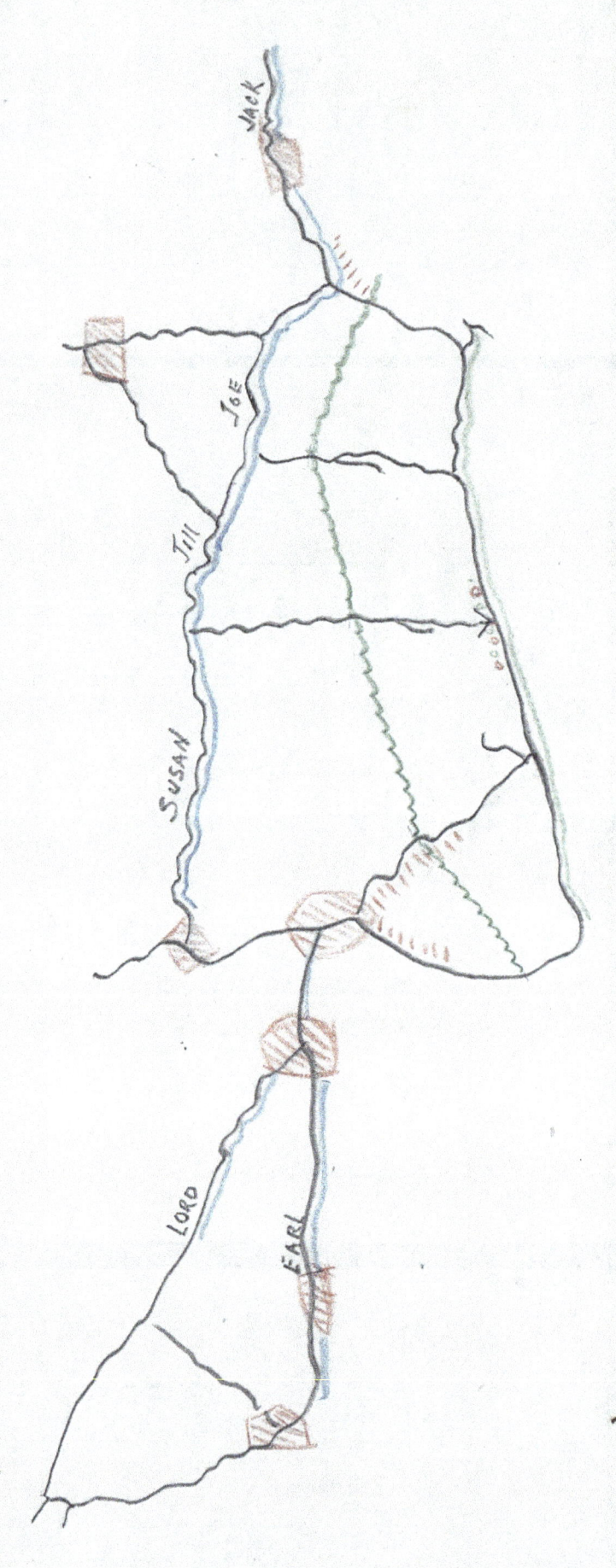

9th Bn.   13-9-16

Please acknowledge
J.E.A.wrong to
HQ 26.18 ✓ Done

OPERATION ORDER.
9th Bn. The Black Watch.

1. **INFORMATION.** The 9th Black Watch and 5th Camerons will carry out a raid on Hun Front Line between Points 11 and 29, to include C.T's CALF, LEG and BOW.

2. **OBJECT.** To Kill.
   To capture Prisoners, M.G's and get information.

3. **ZERO.** Date and hour will be notified later.

4. **FORMATION OF RAID.** As per attached "A".

5. **COMMANDS.** Lieut. Hamilton will command the Black Watch portion of raid, and will move at head of covering party which will line out at point 19 on the west side of the Hun parapet, or in the trench as seems best on arrival.
   He will establish his telephone in the best place at this point with all speed. The Stretcher Bearers will join this party and act as situation demands.

   "A" Party will be commanded by
   "B"   "   "   "   "
   "C"   "   "   "   "

6. **BARRAGES.** As per attached order.

7. **POSITION OF ASSEMBLY.** In MANDORA STREET, 2 hours before Zero where raiding party will organise in exact order of leading out as detailed.

8. **ADVANCE TO POSITION OF READINESS.** At   the parties will lead out and take up positions as practised.
   Absolute silence will be maintained, and the lines will crawl and lie down when they have reached their points.

9. **ASSAULT.** At zero the raiding party will commence crawling forward under the barrage, and will only halt when they can get no further. On the barrage lifting zero ± 2, the raid will rise up and walk speedily forward, not losing a moment in getting to their objective.

10. **ARRIVAL AT HUN FIRING LINE.** Black Watch to enter at point 19.
    Camerons to enter at point 27.
    "B" party taking CALF C.T. up to barrage and form block.
    "A" party entering beside "B" and bombing to right up to Barrage where they form a block.
    "C" party entering beside "B" and bombing to left to point 23 where they meet Camerons - first party at 23 drop two men at junction and carry down LEG with four men up to barrage and form block. Should either Black Watch or Camerons not arrive at point 23, the party who do arrive must do the best possible with the situation.

11. **COMMUNICATIONS.** A tape will be paid out by leading file of covering party which will start at our firing line and finish at Hun firing line at Point 19.
    Along this line Signallers will also pay out D.5 wire. Connecting files will drop out on this line as practised.

No. 2.

12. ACTION IN TRENCHES.

Any enemy discovered in hostile trench will be made prisoners - any who resist will be killed at once. Prisoners will be dealt with by cleaning party, who will hand them over to "collecting" party, who will conduct them to covering party, who will pass them out down the tape, 1 man conducting 2 prisoners.
BOMBING GROUPS will proceed as indicated. When the bombing party halt to make their block, the riflemen of each group will lie on the top of the ground to deal with any men who crawl over the top of the ground between the trenches. CLEANING PARTIES, working in pairs, will follow immediately on the heels of their bombing party and deal with dugouts and all else left behind by the bombing parties, who will on no account halt till they have reached their objective.
Dugouts will be bombed with one tear shell, one smoke bomb, and one MILLS No. 5 if nothing appears.
Any dugout so left will be guarded by two men.
Collecting parties will follow hard on the heels of cleaning parties and act as detailed, bearing in mind that a live hun is best value, wounded huns should be encouraged to get up and walk to the covering party - caps - badges - papers and shoulder straps must not be forgotten.

[margin note: if so, they sh'd be tied up.]

13. RETURN.

Minutes after zero, the signal will be given for the raiding parties to withdraw.
The signal will consist of :-
1. French horn blown in "Boche" lines.
2. Bugles (Regimental call) sounded in our lines.
No other Signal will be regarded on no account must the whistle be used, or the word "Retire" used - if heard it will be regarded as an enemy signal.
BOMBING GROUPS in C.T's will be warned by their clearing party in addition to the sounding of horn and bugle. The first to pass out will be the collecting parties, followed by the cleaning parties, followed by the bombing parties - all parties passing out by the way they entered - leaders reporting their parties present or otherwise to Lieut. Hamilton at Point 19, who must withdraw by zero x 29.
The absence of any man must be fully explained - i.e., Dead, etc., The dead must, if possible, be brought in. The covering parties will cover the retirement and picking up the tape, and telephone wire as they go. Stretcher bearers will accompany the last bombing party who leave the trench. The line of the tape will be used for the retirement as much as possible, but congestion must be avoided.
All parties will exit by point 19, the leader of his group being the last man to leave the trench.

14. ARRIVAL IN OLD TRENCHES.

On arrival back in our Fire Trench the raiding party will re-assemble in ZOUAVE VALLEY at Battn. Headquarters, there a roll call will be called. Booty collected, and the party will occupy Reserve Line dugouts.
Major Abercromby will undertake the above and will be responsible for placing of Police at points in VINCENT STREET and NORTHUMBERLAND AVENUE to keep men on the right road.
In addition to this roll call, the raiding party will be counted in at point X on map and controls will be placed at Y and Z to count in any men who leave the tape line - these controls will report to Lieut. Murray who will organise this.

No. 3.

The names of any men returning by other routes must be reported at once.
If short of the number, Lieut. Murray will telephone down to Major Abercromby for his count and should the number still be short, the search party of "A" Company (standing by) will be at once despatched under orders of Lieut. Murray.

15. DRESS & ARMS IN GENERAL.
As per order, but all ranks will wear trousers and blacken hands and face. Officers will carry revolver and torch - French Horn - luminous watch- 1 smoke bomb, N.C.O's in charge of parties carry torch - luminous watch - One tear bomb.
Officers and senior N.C.O. of "C" party will in addition to above each carry a Roman Candle, one of which they will light before approaching point 23 to enable the Camerons to see the whereabouts of the bombing party as they approach - Camerons will do likewise when approaching point 23 from their side. Each party will carry one pairwire cutters. Discs and all marks of identification will be removed from every man going over the parapet, should a man be captured all he is bound to give is his rank and name - anything else it should be a point of Honour not to divulge. counter- *Countersign* sign.

GARRISON OF MANDORA STREET will move into "A" assembly trench when raiding party move into firing line at   o'clock. When raiding party have moved out, they will return to their original positions.

16. CASUALTIES.
M.O. will establish 4 S.B's at point R, from there they will evacuate or if necessary carry men down VINCENT STREET C.T. to Battalion Aid Post where M.O. will remain.

17. Signal station will be located at point S to communicate with Lieut. Hamilton at Point 19 and Battn. Headquarters, Lieut. Glen will arrange.

18. Stores will be arranged by Lieut. Gouldie.

19. Advanced Battn. Headquarters will be at Battle H.Q.

20. Prisoners will be taken over at Point X by the Provost Sergeant who will have Police collected at that point.
On being taken over they will be at once despatched to Battn. Headquarters at ZOUAVE VALLEY via VINCENT STREET under adequate escort, where they will be handed over to Major Abercromby at Battn. H.Q. who will send them to Adv. Brigade Headquarters.

C.W.
(Sd). Hmt. H. Gordon, Lt.Col.
Commanding, 8th Black Watch.

9:9:15.

Formation and Constitution.

```
        A.                  C.          ■ Officeʳ    A.
                            □                         ·
                            · 6          · 6          · 6    Bombing parties.
                            ·            ·            ·
                            6 paces      6 paces

                            ■ Officeʳ
                            ·
                            · 6          · 6                 Cleaning parties
                            ·            ·

                            6 paces.
                            · 3          · 3               · 3 Collecting
                                                             parties.

                                        6 paces
                                        ■ Officeʳ
                                        ·
                                        · 6                 Covering Party.
                                        ·

                                        4 paces
                                          2                 Signallers.

                                        4 Paces.
                                          2                 S.B's.

                                        4 Paces.
                                        ·· 6                Connecting Files.
```

To Carry:

BOMBING PARTY.   2 Riflemen each.   1 Rifle, 20 S.A.A. in right trouser pocket. 2 bombs in haversack. 2 sandbags slung.

2 Bombers. each.   1 Knobkerrie 10 S.A.A. in right trouser pocket, 6 bombs, in haversack, 2 sandbags slung.

1 Spare Rifleman.   1 Rifle. 15 S.A.A. in pocket, 6 bombs in haversack, 1 small pick slung on back, 2 sandbags tied round pick.

1 Spare Bomber.   1 Kerry, 6 bombs in haversack 1 spade with 2 sandbags wrapped round it – slung.

CLEANING PARTY.   3 Riflemen. each.   1 Rifle, 20 rounds in pockets, 1 smoke bomb.

3 bombers. each.   1 Knobkerrie, 10 rounds in R.T.P. 6 bombs in haversack, 2 Tear bombs in haversack.

No. 2.

3rd Party.

Collecting   o)
)
duty to   o) 3 Bombers each with.
)
1. Take over o)
   prisoners from
   2nd party and
   conduct them
   to covering party.

1 Knobkerry, 10 S.A.A. in R.T.P. 2 Bombs in right coat pocket, 2 sandbags tied together into which goes useful booty.

2. Collect booty.

4th Party.

Covering party.

   duty to

1. Take over prisoners.

2. Conduct them back to connecting files and then return.

3. To cover the retirement.

Each man with 1 Rifle, 20 S.A.A. in T.P's, 4 bombs in R.C.P.

5th Party.

2 Signallers with telephone and Reel and torch for signalling, unarmed.

6th Party.

2 Stretcher bearers, unarmed with One long stretcher.

7th Party.

Duty to take over prisoners
As 1st pair get a job, next
pair move up to take over next
job leading pair becoming 3rd
pair when they have conducted
huns to our parapet.

6 connecting files in 3 pairs

armed with knobkerries.

Para. 3. OBJECT.

    (A). To capture prisoners (essential).
    (B). To obtain identifications and information.
    (C). To kill the enemy.
    (D). To capture or destroy material.

OPERATION ORDER.

6th Cameron Highlanders.

GENERAL IDEA.

1. The Battalion will carry out a raid on the enemys trenches in conjunction with 8th Black Watch on Z day at an hour which will be notified later.

2. **FRONTAGE.** From Junction of BOW and SPUR to a point 40 yards from Junction of SPUR and CRESCENT. Ref. Map Sheet, Enemy Trenches Southern Sector, Scale 1/5000.

3. **OBJECT.** See para. 2 of Brigade Orders.

4. **STRENGTH.**
A. Bombing party	1 Officer, 1 N.C.O. and 5 Men.
B. " "	" " "
C. " "	" " "
A. Dugout party	1 N.C.O. and 5 Men.
B. " "	" "
C. " "	" "
A. Salvage party	1 N.C.O. and 2 Men.
B. " "	" "
C. " "	" "

   Support Party   1 Officer, 3 N.C.O.s. and 12 Men.
                    4 Stretcher bearers, 2 Signallers.

   Total   4 Officers.
            60 Other Ranks.
            6 Stretcher bearers & Signallers.
            ——
            70

SPECIAL IDEA.

5. (1). **Bombing party A.**, under Lt. MacAulay will enter the enemy trench at junction of BOW and SPUR and will at once clear BOW for a distance of approximately 30 yards and block the trench. The N.C.O. will unreel a tape from starting point to enemy line.

   BOMBING party B., under Lt. RIACH will enter the enemy trench on the left or N of Bombing party A and will at once clear SPUR and block as near to junction of SPUR and CRESCENT as STOKES barrage will allow (see below).

   Bombing party C., under Lt. Doak will enter the enemy trench on the right or S of bombing party A and will at once clear GARTER and affect a junction with BLACK WATCH at junction of GARTER and LEG. If this party arrives at this junction before the BLACK WATCH it will proceed to block LEG.

   (11). Bombing parties will carry the following equipment.
   Officers. Revolver and 10 spare rounds in pocket, Electric torch, luminous watch, horn, knobkerry.
   The Officer in charge of C party will also carry special musical instrument and 2 Roman Candles.

   N.C.O's and Men. Two with Rifles and Bayonets and 20 extra rounds each in pocket of coat and wirecutters.
   Two with knobkerries, 10 rounds S.A.A. in pocket and 6 bombs in haversack.
   One with Rifle, 10 extra rounds in pocket, 6 bombs and 1 pick (slung).
   One with knobkerry, 10 Rounds S.A.A. in pocket, 6 bombs and one shovel (slung).

No. 2.

Every N.C.O. and man will in addition carry two
sandbags.
Total for bombing parties :-
9 Rifles, 240 Rounds S.A.A., 30 Bombs, 3 Picks,
3 Shovels, 36 Sandbags, 6 pairs wirecutters,
3 electric torches, 9 knobkerries.

6. Bombing parties will move across NO MANS LAND as per diagram
below :-

```
              B.           A.           C.

Officer.    o         Off. o       Off. o
Rifle.      .              .             .
Rifle.      .              .             .
Bomber.     . 10 paces.    . 10 paces.   .
Carrier.    .              .             .
Blocker.    .              .             .
N.C.O.      .              .             .
```

7. (1). DUGOUT PARTIES. A. Will follow bombing party A as close in
rear as possible and enter the enemy trench at the same point.
It will then proceed to clear dugouts if any in BOW. If there
are no dugouts or the existing ones have been cleared before the
time of withdrawal it will assist the other dugout parties, as
required.
DUGOUT PARTY B., will follow bombing party B and enter the enemy
trench at the same point. It will then proceed to clear DUGOUTS
in SPUR.
DUGOUT PARTY C., will follow bombing party C and enter the enemy
trench at the same point. It will then proceed to clear DUGOUTS
in GARTER.

(11). On no account are DUGOUTS to be entered if they have been
treated with Tear Bombs.
Dugout parties will carry the following equipment :-
Three with Rifles and 20 rounds S.A.A. carried in the pocket.
Three with Knobkerries, 10 rounds S.A.A. in pocket, 5 grenades
and 2 tear grenades.

          Total.   9 Rifles.
                   9 Knobkerries.
                 270 Rounds S.A.A.
                  45 Grenades.
                  18 Tear Grenades.
                   6 Electric Torches - 2 per party.

(111). Dugout parties will proceed across NO MANS LAND in the
following order as per diagram :-

```
Bombing parties.         |          |          |
                         | Rifle.   | Rifle.   | Rifle.
                         . N.C.O.   . N.C.O.   . N.C.O.
                         . Bomber.  .          .
Dugout parties.          . Rifle.   .          .
                         . Bomber.  .          .
                         . Rifle.   .          .
                         . Bomber.  .          .
```

No. 5.

(IV). **Method of clearing dugouts.** Parties will work in pairs of one rifle and one bomber. Each pair will call down and order the inmates to come up and surrender. If there is no response to this the bomber will throw down one grenade and one tear grenade and pass on to another entrance leaving the rifleman to deal with Huns when they emerge. If there are a number willing to surrender not more than one at a time will be allowed up.

8. (1). **SALVAGE PARTY.** Each Salvage party will consist of One N.C.O and two Men and will follow their respective dugout parties as in diagram.
Their duties will be to collect all articles of military value found in their respective trenches, search any dead Huns for papers, etc., remove all identifications, place them in sandbags for the purpose and hand them over to SUPPORT party. They will also escort any Live Huns and hand them over to SUPPORT party, previously having removed all arms. Each prisoner will have a cord round his neck.

(11). **EQUIPMENT.** Each man knobkerry, 10 Rounds S.A.A. in pocket, 2 Bombs, 2 sandbags for loot, 3 cord nooses for prisoners.

Total.   Knobkerries.   9.
         S.A.A.   90 Rounds.
         Bombs.   18.
         Sandbags.   18.
         Nooses.   27.

(111). Position of SALVAGE PARTIES crossing NO MANS LAND :-

Bombing parties.

Dugout parties.

                     N.C.O.   N.C.O.   N.C.O.
                       .   .   .
Salvage parties.   .   .   .
                       .   .   .

9. (1). **SUPPORT PARTY.** Lt. RUNTER in command of raiding party.
This party will advance in rear of Salvage party A, Officer leading, Stretcher Bearers and Signallers in rear. The Signallers will lay a wire from starting point to enemy trench.
This party will drop connecting files and stretcher as per diagram on way across.
This party will line along the enemy trench on each side of point of entry and act as covering party. It will collect all loot and prisoners from SALVAGE parties and pass them back through connecting files along the laid tape.

11. **FORMATION.**

Bombing parties.

Dugout parties.

Salvage parties.

                                           O.C. raiders.

No. 4.

```
.  Stretcher.
.  bearers.
.  Signallers dropping wire.
.    "        "     "    "


.
.  Connecting file.


..  Connecting file.
..  Stretcher.

..  Connecting file.
```

(111). **Equipment of SUPPORT PARTY.** Nine N.C.O's and men with rifles and 20 rounds S.A.A. in pockets. In addition each will carry 4 bombs as a reserve. Stretcher bearers and Signallers will have no arms - Connecting files, knobkerry only - Three trench ladders will be brought up by this party.

Total. 9 Rifles.
180 S.A.A.
36 Bombs.
3 Trench ladders.
2 Electric torches.

10. <u>THE ADVANCE.</u> The entire raiding party will be drawn up in a position of readiness [*In NoMans Land*] by zero hour, when the STOKES barrage will commence on the objective. During the barrage which will last till + 2 the party will creep forward as near the barrage as is consistent with safety.
At + 2 the barrage will lift as per enclosed map and the raiders will push forward to their objectives.

11. <u>METHOD OF WITHDRAWAL.</u> At + 23 Officers will sound their horns and a bugler will sound high notes from our trenches signifying withdrawal. Each party will then proceed to the place of entry and withdraw along the tape, seniors in rear of each party The last to leave will be the SUPPORT party who however, must withdraw by + 29 as the STOKES barrage will return at + 30 to its original line.
Should parties find it impossible to withdraw along the tape, they will leave the Hun trenches at the most suitable place.
In the event of hostile barrage on our own front line the raiding party will remain in NO MANS LAND until the barrage has lifted before re-entering.
On re-entering our own lines every individual Officer, N.C.O. and man will report to Lt. ELLICE at junction of INTERNATIONAL AVENUE AND MANDORA STREET who will check names from his nominal roll. After reporting to Lt. ELLICE every one will move at once to his dugout where numbers will be again checked by Lt. FOULIS. The SUPPORT party will bring in the tape and wire if possible.

12. <u>RESERVE.</u> Two platoons A Coy., under Lt. ELLICE.
Lt. ELLICE will arrange to send out search parties in the event of wounded or dead being left out in NO MANS LAND. He will also collect all loot and prisoners and send them to CAPT. CRICHTON at Battalion Headquarters.

No. 8.

Capt. CRICHTON will arrange to send all prisoners and Loot after the party has returned, to BRIGADE HEADQUARTERS, CABARET ROUGE.

13. The M.O. will arrange evacuation of all wounded brought in to our front line.

14. MISCELLANEOUS.

(1). On no account will any halt be made in the advance – Any wounded will be collected by search parties of the Reserve.
(2). The countersign will be given out later. *at what hour?*
(5). All watches will be synchronised before zero hour. *at Bn H*Q*
(6). The O.C. raiding party will keep the O.C. battalion thoroughly informed as to progress.
(7). Advanced Battn. Headquarters will be at 9th Black Watch Advanced Headquarters.
(8). All marks of identification will be removed before the advance – Khaki trousers will be worn instead of Kilts and all faces and hands will be blackened. All ranks are forbidden to carry anything in their pockets that might lead to their identification.
(9). No Whistles will be blown and the word "Retire" is forbidden. Any Whistles blown will be presumed to come from an enemy source. The word "Retire" will be treated in the same way.
(10). All ranks are reminded that if taken prisoners they must only give their name and rank. It must be a point of honour that no other information is given.
(11). In the event of the enemy trench being found empty or only very lightly held it will be left to the discretion of the O.C. to withdraw before 23 if he considers that no useful object can be obtained by remaining the full time, but the 9th Black Watch raiders must be informed.
(12). O.C. parties are responsible that no promiscuous bomb throwing takes place. Every bomb thrown must have a definite object in view.

12.9.16.

(Sd) H. R. Brown, Lt. Col.
Commanding 5th Cameron Highlanders.

AMENDMENT

to

9th Divisional Artillery

Operation order No. 59.

****

13th September 1916.

PARA 2.

<u>DELETE</u>

'The 2" Trench Mortars will bombard Point 41, machine gun'
'emplacement just North of 1 of Earl, Points 37, 31, 33, 15,'
'50" from 13 along JACK, 1, 2, 4.'

After 'The Guns, Howitzers"

<u>DELETE</u>   "and Mortars"

<u>DELETE</u> PARA 3

and SUBSTITUTE

3. <u>MORTARS.</u>

<u>The 2" Trench Mortars</u> will keep up a steady fire from 0 + 2 mins. to 0 + 30 mins. on Point 41, Machine Gun North of 1 in Earl Points 37, 31, 33, 15, and 50 yards from Point 13 along JACK and 1, 2, 4.

Also from zero to 0 + 2 mins. and from zero + 30 mins. to zero + 32 mins. one 2" Trench Mortar will fire at each of the following:- Point 13, Point 31 to S.15.o.2½.8. and Point 31 to S.13.o.1½.8½.

<u>The Stokes Mortars</u> will bombard the front line from Point 11 to 29 from 0 to 0 + 2 mins. then lift to the line S.15.o.5½.4½. -- S.15.o.4½.6½. -- S.15.o.2½.8. -- S.15.o.1½.8½., where they will fire from 0 + 2 mins. till 0 + 30 mins. At 0 + 30 mins. the Stokes Mortars will return to their first barrage till 0 + 32 mins.

<u>Special Stokes Mortars</u> will bombard Point 23 from 0 + 2 to 0 + 7 mins.

F Rose
Major R.F.A.
Brigade Major.
R.A., 9th Division.

9th Divisional Artillery.

Operation Order

No. 59

Copy No.

Reference Map 1/5,000.

10th September 1916.

1. The 26th Inf. Brigade will carry out a raid on the enemy's line from about S.15.c.1.7. to S.15.c.4½.4 on X day at Zero hour.

2. Previous to Zero the enemys front line trenches will be bombarded by Stokes Mortars.

3. In support of this operation an intermittant artillery barrage will be formed as under:-

    52nd Brigade. Point 41 to Point 31.
    50th Brigade   Point 31 to 33 to 25.
    51st Brigade   Point 25 to 21 to half way between 13 and 15
                         to 50^X S.E. of Point 13 along Jack

Howitzers will cover along the same front as these brigades.

The 2" trench mortars will bombard Point 41, machine gun emplacement just N of 1 of Earl Point 37, 31, 33, 13, 50^X from 13 along Jack 1, 2, 4.

The guns, howitzers and mortars will fire from zero to + 5

                                                           "   " + 8 to + 14

                                                           "   " +18 to + 22

                                                           "   " + 25 to + 30

rate of fire for guns and howitzers 2 rounds per minute.

4. <u>Liason.</u> The 51st Bde will detail an officer as liason officer at the H.Q. of the battalion that carries out the raid.

5. <u>Watches.</u> Will be synchronised with H.Q. 26th Bde

Major R.F.A.
Brigade Major.
R.A., 9th Division.

NOT TO BE WRITTEN ON.

Army Form A 2007.

CENTRAL REGISTRY.

Central Registry No. and Date.

502/87(9).

Attached Files.

SUBJECT, AND OFFICE OF ORIGIN.

Minor Operation – Raid.
Carried out by South African Bde on night
13/14 September, 1916.

9th Divⁿ

Referred to	Date	Referred to	Date	Referred to	Date
G.	19-9-16				
I	19-9-16				
For ~~A.G.R.A.~~	19-9-16				
CE	19-9-16				
G	20-9-16				

P.A.	Date
1731	

Schedule of Correspondence

4

Inter-office Minutes.

Note.—Inside sheets to be attached to this page.

IVth Corps No. 1701/10 (G)

First Army.

      I forward herewith a report on a raid carried out on the enemy's trenches between Kennedy and Irish Craters by the 1st South African Brigade on the night of 13th/14th instant.

I have nothing to add to Gen¹ Furse's minute

16th September, 1916.

Henry Wilson
Lieutenant General,
Commanding IVth Corps.

H.R.S. 641.

4th Corps.

No. X.5/1776/3.   15th September, 1916.

1. I forward herewith the report of the 1st S.African Inf. Brigade on the raid carried out on the night of September 13th/14th. on the enemy's trenches between KENNEDY and IRISH Craters.

The report referred to in para 2 of the letter of the G.O.C. 1st S.African Bde. is attached.

2. It was in accordance with my orders that the party returned to our trenches immediately prisoners had been secured, my instructions being that the party should return as soon as two prisoners had been secured, and under any circumstances at the end of 20 minutes.

3. In my opinion the O.C. raiding party made an error of judgement in not bringing in the wounded man.

Major-General,
Commanding 9th (Scottish) Division.

1st South African Brigade.

14th September, 1916.

9th Division.

I forward herewith reports by the O.C., 2nd S.A.I. on raid carried out by members of his Unit on the night of 13th/14th.

The reports contain no information as to the enemy barrage, but this was furnished in my B.M.818 of to-day.

A few points I have referred to the O.C. 2nd S.A.I. for further report, the principal of which is the different opinions expressed as to the effect of our artillery fire on the enemy trenches. A report has also been asked for as to the approximate locality of the machine gun which opened fire. This information together with information on points which may not have been brought out in the report will be furnished early to-morrow.

I consider credit is due to Lt.Col. Christian and his staff in connection with the careful and thorough manner in which all preparations were made, and to the officers and men who took part in the raid.

(sd) H.T.Lukin, Brig.Genl.
Commanding 1st S.African Bde.

1st South African Infantry Brigade.

Headquarters.

15.9.16.

9th Division.

Adverting to my letter of the 14th instant forwarding report on raid 13th/14th instant I now have to report further.

1. State of enemy trenches as reported by officers.

The two officers concerned entered the enemy trenches at diffeent points approximately 50 yards apart.

The wire on the enemy trenches entered was well cut - On the left where 2nd Lieutenant Walsh entered, the trenches were not damaged, whereas, on the right, at the point entered by 2nd Lieut. Lilburn, considerable damage was done by our shell fire to enemy trenches.

2. Enemy machine gun.

This gun fired from a point between KENNEDY CRATER and enemy trench.

3. Enemy Trenches.

The officers state that they did not encounter any sentries on the fire steps. Enemy rifles with fixed bayonets were leaning up against the parapets.

4. Raid equipment.

All concerned are agreed that a revolver is the most useful weapon in asmall operation of this kind. They can be readily fired round traverses and into dug-outs without exposing oneself and were found of the greatest value.

Bombs were also useful while rifles were cumbersome and could not be brought into action.

(Sd) H.T.Lukin   Brig-General,
Commanding 1st S.A. Infantry Brigade.

9th Division.

No. B.M.818.   14th September, 1916.

      During raid last night enemy barraged chiefly on ZOUAVE VALLEY, a few shells near SOUCHEZ. No barrage on "No Man's Land. Enemy opened their barrage at 4.8 a.m. One enemy machine gun in action but was not effective.

      1st S.African Brigade.   1 p.m.

2nd Regiment South African Infantry.

South African Brigade.

With reference to your B.M.214 and the raid which took place at 4 a.m. this morning, I beg to forward you:-

1. Copy of the Operation Orders issued.
2. Copy of the telephone messages sent you during the raid.
3. Copies of reports on the raid by 2nd Lieutenants Walsh and Lilburn.
4. Copies of the reports by two Company Commanders on their enquiries from the men as to the number of enemy casualties.

Having sent out 2nd Lts. Green, Walsh and Lilburn at 9 p.m. on the 13th inst. to report on the feasibility of getting through the enemy wire, and having receuved a favourable report from 2nd Lt. Green at 10.30 p.m. I wired you to this effect, and made all preparations for the raid to take place.

The night was a bright moonlight one with passing clouds, but this I considered would not interfere with the raid so long as the men could get into position on the enemy's side of our wire without being seen. The arrangements worked without a hitch and at 3.55 a.m. all the men were lying down in position on the enemy's side of our wire without having aroused the enemy's suspicions in getting there.

The barrage started at 3.59 a.m. on which the men jumped up and started doubling across "No Mans Land". They doubled across without any hesitation and jumped straight into the enemy trenches, the barrage having lifted just as they got there.

Prisoners were secured at once, some in the trench and some emerging from dug-outs. All the dug-outs were then bombed with both Mills and Phosphorous bombs, and the object having been obtained, the arranged signal was given and the whole party retired together. The whole party were back in our lines before the enemy barrage started.

I regret having to report that No. 8800 Pte. W.E. Sweetman was so severely wounded by a bullet through the chest that he could not be moved from the enemy trench. The officer in charge was of opinion that he would die in a few minutes. No. 950 Private J.B.Willis was wounded in the thigh but managed to get back to our own lines unassisted.

I consider that the success of the operation was due to two main causes:-

FIRST. The very effective and thorough scouting work performed by 2nd Lts. Walsh and Lilburn for several nights before the raid and their excellent leading and example during the raid.

SECOND. To the extremely accurate and well timed barrage of our guns. The men who took part in the raid have now such confidence in our guns that they would, I am certain, work right up to our own barrage in any future action. This is having a most excellent effect in the Battalion and I cannot express my gratitude to the 9th Division Artillery for the absolute perfect shooting they made last night.

I also wish to express my appreciation of the able and careful manner with which Captain Sullivan and Lieut.Davis the commanders of "B" and "D" Companies, did their part in organising and instructing their men for the raid. The signalling arrangements carried out by my signalling officer, Lieut.Knight, (who also acted as forward observing officer) were excellent and worked without a hitch.

I think the chief lessons to be learnt from this raid are:-

1. The necessity of a raiding party advancing right up to the barrage.

2. The necessity of careful patrolling of the area to be crossed by the officer leading party previous to the raid.

3. The advantage of raiding parties returning immediately their object is attained.

I may mention that on return both the officers concerned expressed their very decided opinion that it would have been better if the whole of the raiding party, with the exception of one or two men, had been armed with revolvers instead of with rifles and bayonets.

(sd) Irvan Christian,

Lieutenant Colonel,
Commanding 2nd Regiment S.A. Infantry.

IN THE FIELD.
14th September, 1916.

The Adjutant, 2nd S.A.I.

     Lieut. Walshe killed two and Corporal Rees killed one of the enemy in last nights raid.
     These are the only certain cases known.

14th Sept. 1916.
                                    (sd) F.M.Davis, Lieut.
                                        O.C. "D" Company.

The Adjutant, 2nd S.A. Infantry.

     Re last nights raid. I have seen each N.C.O. and as far as possible am satisfied that the figures given below are correct. I have assured myself that the dead reported have not been duplicated, as each N.C.O. was in a different part of trench, and stated exactly where the enemy were.
     Mr Lilburn only saw one dead himself, but the bombers on the right accounted for three, and on the left two at least were killed. If this return errs it is on the side of moderation.

     A. Killed - 9 at least.
     B. Wounded - NIL as far as known. All enemy seen were killed or captured.
     Dug-outs with enemy in were bombed - results unknown.

14th Sept. 1916.
                                    (sd) A.A.Sullivan, Captain.

S.A.Brigade.

     Copy of message sent you on night of 13th/14th Septr.

ROWING.
- 3.55   G.
- 3.59   Barrage started.
- 3.59½   Barrage good. 4 spray lights on the left and star-light on the left.
- 4.1   Barrage still good. From German lines.
- 4.2¼   Still more white lights.
- 4.2½   Nothing to report.
- 4.2¾   --- 4.9 5 prisoners coming down.
- 4.10   All reported with exception of one man.
- 4.12   All O.K.
- 4.17   We are searching the prisoners and will send them down as soon as possible.

Following in reply to query from Brigade Major.

- 4.45   They are all in with exception of one man who is badly wounded and could not be got out of the German trench.

- 4.55   All are in except the man who is so badly wounded that he could not be brought in. The prisoners are being sent under escort. OAR 4.57 a.m. message ends.

                                    (sd) Ivan Christian, Lt.Col.
14th Sept. 1916.
                                    Commanding 2nd Regt. S.A.I.

G. meant "All men over the parapet.

COPY.

The Adjutant,

    2nd S.A.I.

        In accordance with pre-arranged plan, I proceeded with a party in conjunction with "D" Company to raid enemy's trench.

        We left our lines by gap in our wire at 3.50 am between saps B.1 and B.2 and entered enemy's trench about 1½ minutes past 4, through gap in their wire, at the point we entered the trench was blown away.

        I bombed one dug-out with Mills' bombs, also threw down one smoke bomb.

        I captured three prisoners and to my knowledge one enemy was shot in trench.

        The dug-out I bombed appeared to be occupied.

        The trenches were about 8 to 9 feet deep and were "V" shaped, some Bays had fire-steps.

        The greater part of enemy's trench was blown away.

        We were altogether three minutes in trench.

        I did all the damage I possibly could in the time we occupied enemy's trench.

        In my opinion, our artillery was excellent and my party advanced right up to the barrage.

       x The wire was blown to pieces and enemy's trench could have been entered at many points.

        I had one man mortally wounded and in my opinion he succumbed before we reached our own trench.

                              (Sd) Percy C. Lilburn,
                                            2nd/Lieut.
                                        2nd S.A. Infantry.

14th September, 1916.

O.C., 2nd S.A.I.

In accordance with the pre-arranged plan, in conjunction with an equal party from "B" Company, I took a party of 30 men on a raid into the enemy's trenches.

My party left by a gap in our wire at the head of sap B.3 at 3.50 a.m. and entered the enemy's trench almost before the artillery barrage lifted.

4 dug-out entrances were bombed with hand-grenades and groans were heard immediately afterwards.

The enemy were just emerging from their dug-outs, two were immediately shot and the rest surrendered very willingly and two prisoners were brought back.

The trenches were about eight feet deep and broad at the top, they were not revetted or duck-boarded except at the entrance of the dug-outs. The dug-outs were not entered.

The return was made after about three minutes and so there was no time to collect souvenirs, in fact nothing was seen to bring back, the trenches being quite clear.

The trenches did not appear to have been damaged by our artillery fire and trench mortars.

The barrage was excellent and we were able to advance right up to the trench as it lifted.

The enemy wire was badly cut and we had no trouble in crossing it.

A red and green light were put up as we went over and a green light was put up after our return apparently as a signal that the enemy artillery was firing short.

On my return I discovered a covered sap running out to "No Man's Land". A man was seen to run into this and he appeared up through a hole in "No Man's Land" and I shot him through the back with my revolver and I believe I killed him.

Our only casualty was one man wounded with a revolver shot in the right thigh. He was shot from a dug-out which was immediately bombed.

The whole party was back by 4.10 a.m.

(sd) F.Walshe, 2nd Lieut.
2nd Regiment S.A.Infantry.

14th September, 1916.

NOT TO BE WRITTEN ON.

Scheme J.

S.A. Bde. Operation Orders.

Scheme J.   Copy No. 13

1ST SOUTH AFRICAN INFANTRY BRIGADE.

Sketch map attached.   11th October 1916.   achd

OPERATION ORDER NO. 66.

The 9th Division will attack the enemy's position on the high ground between M.17.d.9.9. and the LE SARS – BAPAUME road on the 12th October at ZERO.

ZERO will be notified later.

The 1st S.A.I. Brigade will be on the left of the Divisional front, with the 26th Brigade on the right. The 44th Infantry Brigade is holding in the line on the left of the 9th Division.

BRIGADE BOUNDARY. The boundary between the 26th Brigade and this brigade runs between M.23.A.6.8. and M.17.B.2.7.

OBJECTIVES. The Brigade will have two objectives.
(1) Enemy trench in M.17.C. and
(2) Enemy trench from M.17.B.2.7. to the LE SARS – BAPAUME road, including the BUTTE de WARLENCOURT.

ASSAULTING TROOPS. The assault will be carried out by the 2nd and 4th S.A.I. (2nd leading) with the 3rd and 1st in reserve. The assault will be carried out on a one battalion front in column of companies (each company less one platoon – carriers).

ASSEMBLY. The battalions to carry out the assault will be assembled in the front trenches 20 minutes before ZERO.

The 3rd S.A.I. will move forward into the trenches at present occupied by the 4th S.A.I. 10 minutes after ZERO, provided the enemy barrage permits of their doing so.

The 1st S.A.I. will be ready to move into the trenches in HIGH WOOD at present occupied by the 3rd S.A.I. immediately that regiment moves forward.

BASE. Provided the creeping barrage permits the base from which the Brigade will "jump off" will be a line between the Post at present occupied by the 2nd S.A.I. at M.16.D.9.3. to the right of our present front line at M.23.A.8.8.

CARRIERS. There will be one platoon carriers to each company of the assaulting battalions. Carrying platoons will follow in rear of the 4th Regiment in column of half-companies. There will thus be, eight waves of fighting troops followed by four waves of carriers.

BARRAGES There will be two barrages – one a standing barrage, the other a creeping barrage.

The standing barrage will open on the first objective and thereafter lift to the second objective.

The creeping barrage will commence 200 yards in advance of our front line and after three minutes will lift 50 a minute until it is about 200 yards beyond the first objective. From there it will again creep forward at O plus 23 minutes at the same rate until it reaches about 200 yards beyond our first objective.

THE ATTACK. The 2nd S.A.I. will go over the parapet at ZERO and form up in four waves on the BASE provided the barrage permits. It will be followed by the 4th S.A.I.

The first wave will creep up as close as possible to the barrage and succeeding waves will follow at 50 yards distance between waves.

The leading wave will move forward with the creeping barrage the other waves conforming – care being taken that the distance of 50 yards between waves is maintained.

It is essential that the assaulting infantry shall keep as close up as possible to our own barrage.

The first three waves will advance over the first objective, the fourth wave remaining in that objective, until O plus 23 when the creeping barrage again proceeds by lifts of 50 yards.

The fifth and following waves will lie down (provided they have not to re-inforce) until the leading waves again move forward, when all excepting the eight wave will advance over the first objective which will be cleared and held by the eighth wave.

STRONG POINTS AND CONSOLIDATION. On attaining the second objective strong points will be established on the forward slopes at approximately M.17.A.3.8. and M.17.B.2.6. to be made and held by the 2nd S.A.I. Each strong point will be under the command of an officer.

Lewis guns will be placed immediately in both of these strong points being replaced by Vickers guns as soon as the positions are consolidated.

Machine guns in the strong point on the right will be placed so as to cover the west face of the spur running N.W. from M.17.B.5.7.

Stops will be placed to prevent the enemy counter-attacking up his trench on the N.W. face of the BUTTE spur.

Advanced posts of not more than sixmen in each will be thrown forward by the second S.A.I. in front of the final objective.

The position of these advanced posts will be sited by an officer who will remain in command of them until they are withdrawn.

The officers in command of the strong points will inform the Officer in charge of advanced posts when they consider the strong points sufficiently consolidated to justify the withdrawal of the posts. These posts will then be withdrawn.

The final objective will be held by means of machine guns and Lewis guns and as thinly as possible as regards garrison.

The main consolidation will be just south of the crest of the BUTTE spur so as to avoid direct land observation on the enemy's part from the LOUPART WOOD high ground.

The line to be consolidated runs approximately from M.17.central to M.17.C.3.7.

A strong point will be made at the latter point.

The 4th S.A.I. will dig this main consolidated trench.

Emplacements for Stokes' guns will be prepared in the line to be consolidated, if it is possible to "Stokes mortar" the BUTTE de WARLENCOURT from there. If it is not possible to do so from the line of consolidation as sited, Trench mortar emplacements will be made in front of that line to enable this being done

ROYAL ENGINEERS. The 64th Field Co, R.E. (less two sections) is attached to the Brigade for the operations. It will construct the T.M. emplacements with such assistance from infantry working parties as may be necessary.

Two N.C.O.s and six sappers will report to the O.C. 2nd S.AI at his H.Q. at M.22.D.5.8. two hours before ZERO. These N.C.Os and sappers will advise infantry working parties regarding construction and consolidation of the strong points on the right and left of our final objective and at M.17.C.3.7.

O.C. 64th Field Co. R.E. will report at the H.Q. 2nd S.A.I. half an hour before ZERO. He will proceed forward with a section of his company to the line to be consolidated immediately the final objective is gained.

The second section of the Field Co will remain in reserve under the orders of the O.C. 64th Field Co, R.E.

MACHINE GUNS. The O.C. Machine Gun Company will detail the following guns to move forward immediately the final objective has been gained, viz., (A) a section of guns to proceed to the final objective - two to be placed in the strong points forward of the BUTTE de WARLENCOURT and two in the strong point at M. 17.B.2.6.

(B) two guns to proceed to strong point M.17. C.3.7. the officers in charge of these guns will report to the O.C., 2nd S.A.I. at his H.Q. half an hour before ZERO.

The four guns at present in the FLERS Switch will from ZERO onwards during the attack water the valley in M.11.C.D.

The remaining guns will be held in Brigade reserve.

The O.C., 28th M.G.Coy will report at Brigade H.Q. one hour before ZERO.

Unless under exceptional circumstances once a machine gun has been placed by an officer of the machine gun company it will not be moved except under the orders of a battalion Commander or the Brigade.

TRENCH MORTARS. The O.C., L.T.M.Battery will hold four stokes mortars in readiness to proceed from their present position in the trenches to the line to be consolidated in M.17.C immediately the final objective is gained. The Officer in charge of these guns will report at the H.Q. of the 2nd S.A.I. half an hour before ZERO.

The O.C., L.T.M.Battery will report at Brigade Headquarters one hour before ZERO.

The O.C., L.T.M.Battery will detail 10 men to report to the O.C., 2nd S.A.I. two hours before ZERO, each of these men will have two stokes' bombs prepared for use to assist in destroying dug-outs or other works in the BUTTE de WARLENCOURT.

PIONEERS "B" Company, 9th Seaforth Pioneers is attached to the Brigade for the operations. It will assemble at the S.W. side of High Wood half an hour before ZERO and will proceed in advance of the 3rd S.A.I. to the trenches at present occupied by the 4th S.A.I., and from thence to the front line trenches which it will be ready to leave immediately the final objective is gained.

It will dig communication trenches up to the Brigade's final objectiv

The O.C. "B" Company (9th Seaforth Highrs, will report at the H.Q. of the 2nd SMAMI. half an hour before ZERO, and will proceed with the O.C. 64th Field Co, R.E. The latter officer will site the communicat trenches to be dug by the pioneers

SIGNAL COMMUNICATIONS. Visual signal stations will be established.
Ample service of runners to be arranged by _ _ _ Battalions.
Os. C.Units will keep Brigade H.Q. fully posted regarding the progress of the battle.

The importance of prompt and accurate reports cannot be over estimated.

The Brigade has to report the situation to the Division every hour and battalion commanders will send in reports at least as frequently

MEDICAL ARRANGEMENTS. The line of evacuation for wounded is from collect.. at EAUCOURT L' ABBAYE by railway to west of High Wood, thence by ambulance to advanced dressing station at BAZENTIN LE PETIT.

Walking wounded will be directed along this route

FIGHTING OUTFIT. The normal fighting outfit for each man will be as per appendix "B" of Instructions for training issued by 9 th Division, excepting that the pack may be substituted for the haversack, the S.A.A. carried on the man is reduced to 120 rounds and every man will carry two bombs.

Every thing in excess of the normal outfit will be dumped by battalio at a spot near their H.Q. and left in charge of a guard,

All men will ~~~~ the infantry entrenching tool andall men except-

speciallists, i,o, snipers, Lewis gunners Machine Gunners etc, will carry a pick or a shovel in the proportion of six shovels to one pick.

MATERIAL TO BE CARRIED Carrying platoons will cary the material etc., set forth in the attached shhedule.

CONTACT AEROPLANE A contact aeroplane will fly over the trenches at 1 hour after ZERO and the advanced infantry will light yellow flares in reply to aeroplane signal.

CONNECTING POST. The 4th S.A.I. will gain touch with the 44th Brigade on their left by establishing a post in the neighbourhood of road junction M.16.B.9.0.

ZERO HOUR. A representative from each unit will report at Brigade H.Q tomorrow, 12th instant, at 10 am when ZERO hour will be notified and watches set.

BRIGADE H.Q. Brigade H.Q. will be at S.15.B.3.5.

Page 4.

Simultaneously with our attack the 44th Brigade on our left will attack enemy's strong point in the valley at approximately M.16.B.6.3.

The 15th Division is arranging for a smoke screen to be maintained on the enemy's position between LE SARS and WARLENCOURT from ZERO to O plus 45.

The BUTTE will be kept under smoke by them until our leading infantry are approaching it about O plus 28.

All ranks are reminded that in addition to gaining their own objective it is their duty to assist their neighbours to gain theirs.

[signature]
Major.
Brigade Major.

12.10.16
Issued by orderly at 6.30 am/as per S.A.Bde distribution list.

ARTICLES TO BE CARRIED BY THE REAR (CARRYING) PLATOONS.

	Each Section.	Total per platoon	Total per battalion.
Sandbags	100	400	1600
Rolls French wire	2	8	32
Rifle grenade No.23	50	200	800
Very pistols	1	4	16
Very lights, pkts.	1	4	16

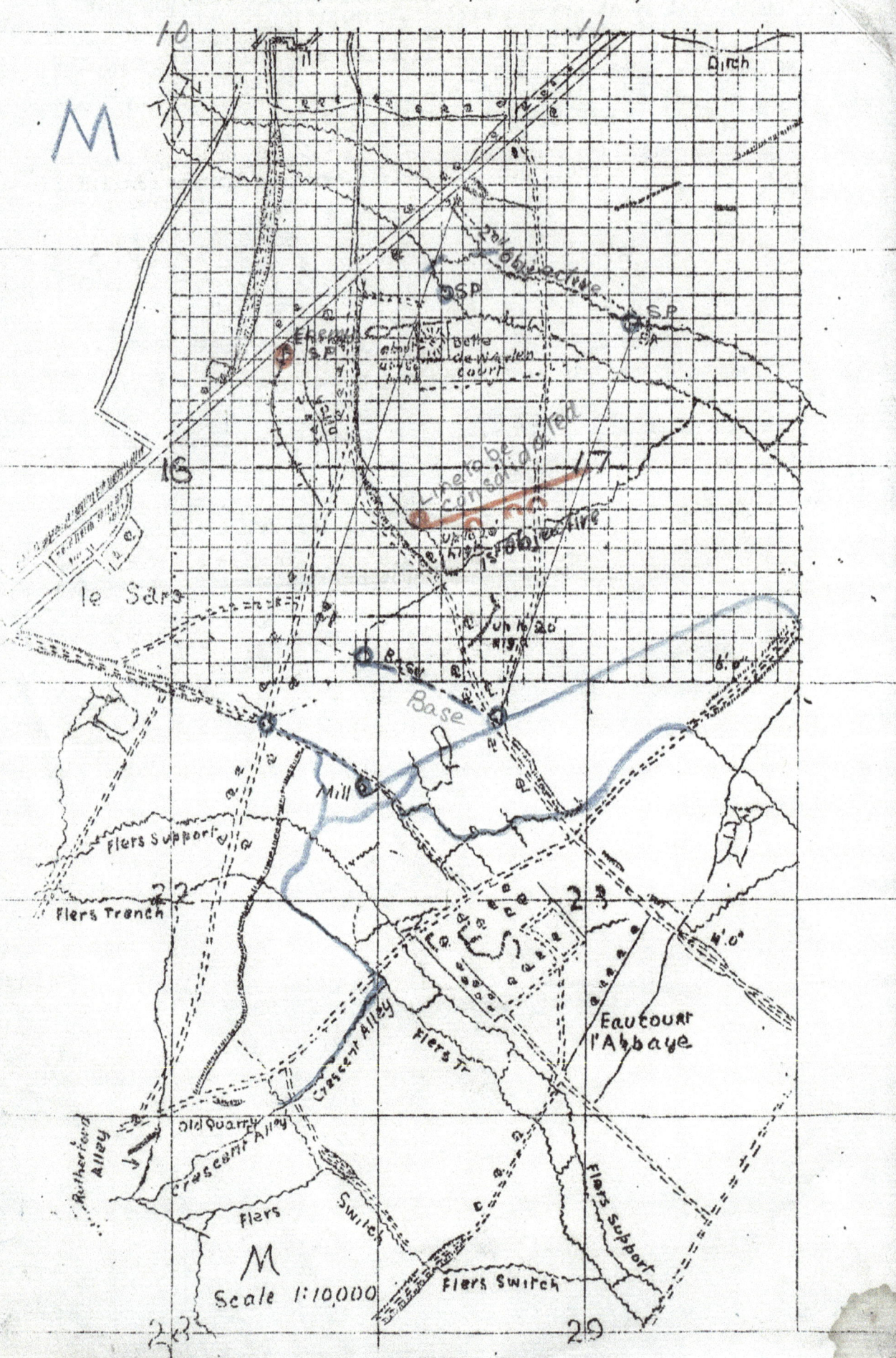

Copy No. 13

1st S.A. Infantry Brigade.
15th October 1916.

OPERATION ORDER NO. 67.

The 1st S.A.I. will relieve the 3rd S.A.I. in the line tomorrow night (16th) after the moon rises. Time of the relief to be arranged between Commanding Officers.

Troops will move by platoons at 200 yards distance.

Completion of relief to be reported to Brigade Headquarters by message "ALBERT".

On relief the 3rd S.A.I. will occupy the line now held by the 1st S.A.I.

Please acknowledge.

Major.

Issued by orderly as per
S.A. Brigade distribution list, at 6.30 am.
16/10/16.

Brigade Major.

H.Q., 1st South African Infantry Brigade.
17th October 1916.

SECRET. URGENT.
Map Reference.
Sketch Map attached.

Copy No. 13

OPERATION ORDER NO 68.

The 9th Division will attack the enemy's position in M.17.C and D on 18th October 1916.
The hour of ZERO will be notified later.
The 1st S.A.I.Brigade will be on the left of the Divisional front with the 26th Brigade on the right.
The 46th Infantry Brigade is holding the line on the left of the 9th Division.

BRIGADE BOUNDARY. The boundary between the 26th Infantry Brigade and the 1st S.A.I.Brigade is a North and South line through M.17.C.9.9. at which point there is a single tree which forms a directing mark as shown on sketch map attached.

OBJECTIVE. The Brigade's objective will be the enemy's trenches in M.17.C.

ASSAULTING TROOPS AND FORMATION OF ATTACK. The assault will be carried out by the 1st S.A.I. with three companies in line, each on a platoon frontage with the fourth company in support and one company of the 3rd S.A.I. in reserve

ASSEMBLY. The 1st S.A.I. will be assembled in the front trenches 20 minutes before ZERO. The company of the 3rd S.A.I. in reserve will be assembled in the support trench 20 minutes before ZERO.

CARRIERS. There will be one platoon of carriers to each company.
Carrying platoons will be assembled 20 minutes before ZERO in the communication trench running up to point M.16.D.9.3. They will advance and join their companies as soon as the objective has been gained.

BARRAGE. The attack will be preceded by an artillery barrage on the enemy's line from ZERO to ZERO plus one minute.
The barrage will be intensified by a Stokes mortar barrage which will be maintained on the enemy's trench till ZERO plus 2 minutes.
A smoke barrage will be arranged so as to blind the BUTTE de WARLENCOURT and the valley between the BUTTE and Le SARS north of the line joining M.17.central and M.16.central.

THE ATTACK. The assaulting troops will be formed up in NO MAN'S LAND in three waves by ZERO. When the barrage opens the leading wave will creep up as close as possible under it, assaulting the enemy's line as soon as the barrage lifts.
A special party will be detailed to fight up the SWITCH TRENCH on the left of the Brigade's objective, and to clear it of the enemy as far as approximately M.17.C.1.8., where it will be blocked and held.

STRONG POINTS AND CONSOLIDATION.
On gaining the objective a strong point will be established at trench junction M.17.C.4.4. The enemy's line will be consolidated immediately it is captured, covering patrols being pushed forward at once.

MACHINE GUNS. The guns at present in the support trench and those in M.22.D. and 28.A and B., will from ZERO onwards during the attack fire on enemy's trenches and roads north of a line drawn East and West through M.17.central but will not shoot on any ground West of M.11 and 17. The BAPAUME main road should be traversed.

Immediately the objective is gained, the O.C., Machine Gun Coy will move four machine guns into the captured trench. One of these guns will be placed in the strong point at trench junction M.17.d.4.4. and another at approximately M.17.C.1.8.

Positions for the other two will be selected by the Machine Gun officer in charge in consultation with the Infantry officer in Command on the spot.

Once the Machine Gun officer has decided on a position for a Machine gun, it is NOT to be changed except under the orders of the Brigade or the Battalion Commander.

STOKES MORTARS. The O.C., S.A.L.T.M.Battery will make all arrangements for the 2 minutes barrage from ZERO being carried out by his battery and for an adequate supply of ammunition being forward with the mortars.

He will, immediately the barrage ceases, have his mortars ready to fire at extreme range over the objective to deal with any counter attack from the north.

ENGINEERS AND PIONEERS. One section of 64th Field Co. R.E. and half a company of 9th Seaforths (Pioneers) are attached to the Brigade for the operations.

The Engineers will assist the Infantry in making the strong point at M. .C.4.4. and the block at M.16.C.1.8.

The Pioneers will cut a communication trench from approximately M.17.C.7.1. to M.17.C.7.6.

The Officers in command of the Engineers and Pioneers will report to the O.C., 1st S.A.I. at his headquarters at M.22.D.3.2. at least two hours before ZERO.

COMMUNICATIONS. A main Divisional receiving station has been established M.29.D.4.4. which is visible from the whole front to be attacked.

Arrangements as ordered by the O.C., Signal Section will be made for visual communication to be established with this station from the captured line.

Where staples supporting telephone lines in trenches are found detached they should be replaced. All ranks are required to assist in this way in the maintenance of communications.

LIGHTS. Red flares will be shown by the advanced Infantry to show their positions to the contact aeroplanes which will fly over the front as soon as light permits.

If progress up the SWITCH TRENCH is held up by our own barrage a single red light should be sent up as a signal to the artillery to lift gradually. If the signal has to be repeated, there should be at least half-a-minute interval between signals.

FIGHTING OUTFIT. The normal fighting outfit for each man will be as per appendix "D" of Instructions for training issued by 9th Division, excepting that the pack may be substituted for the haversac the S.A.A. carried on the man is reduced to 120 rounds and every man will carry two bombs. Every thing in excess of the normal outfit will be dumped by battalions at a spot near their H.Q. and left in charge of a gu. All men will carry the Infantry entrenching tool and all men excepting specialists, i.e., snipers, Lewis gunners, Machine Gunners, etc., will carry a pick or a shovel in the proportion of six shovels to one pick.

Page 3.

MATERIAL TO BE CARRIED.-
Carrying platoons will carry the material etc., setforth in the Annexed Schedule.

REPORTS. Situation reports will be sent in as frequently as possible.

DUMP. The Brigade advanced Dump is at M.28.d.5.4. Ammunition, Bombs and Stores will be sent forward by the Brigade carriers on receipt of a request for same - The bearer of the request acting as guide.

MEDICAL ARRANGEMENTS.
The line of evacuation for wounded is from collecting posts at EAUCOURT L'ABBAYE by railway to WEST of HIGH WOOD thence by Ambulance to advanced Dressing Station at BAZENTIN LE PETIT.
Walking wounded will be directed along this route.

PRISONERS.
The Collecting station is at BAZENTIN LE PETIT S.8.d.4.5. Escorts which should be in proportion of 15% to 20% will proceed as far as this collecting station only and then return to their Battalions - Prisoners will not be searched by Units except for arms.

ASSISTANCE BY BRIGADE ON LEFT.
The 45th Brigade are assisting with Machine gun fire on Enemy trenches ; The BUTTE de WARLENCOURT , and on known and suspected enemy Machine gun positions but will not fire on any ground SOUTH of a line EAST and WEST through M.17 CENTRAL.
Their STOKES MORTARS will also be in action ready to deal with any hostile Machine guns about M.10.d.

BATTALION HEADQUARTERS.
The Headquarters of the 1st S.A.I. will be at M.22.d.2.3

BRIGADE HEADQUARTERS.
Brigade H.Qrs will be at S.15.b.3.5.

ALL RANKS ARE REMINDED THAT IN ADDITION TO GAINING THEIR OWN OBJECTIVE IT IS THEIR DUTY TO ASSIST THEIR NEIGHBOURS TO GAIN THEIRS.

Major,
Brigade Major.

Issued by Orderly at 2.30 p.m. as per S.A.Brigade distribution list.

ARTICLES TO BE CARRIED BY THE REAR (CARRYING) PLATOONS.

	Each Section.	Total per Platoon.	Total per Battalion.
Sandbags	100.	400.	1600.
Rolls French Wire.	2.	8.	32.
Rifle Grenade No.23	50.	200.	800.
Very Pistols.	I.	4.	16.
Very Lights, Pkts.	I.	4.	16.

ZERO WILL BE 3.40 a.m. on 18th inst. - Divisional time will be given over phone to Officer Commanding 1st Regt. S.A.I. at 9.30 p.m. tonight.

Os/C. Machine Gun Coy and Trench Mortar Battery will send a representative either to Brigade Headquarters or to those of 1st S.A. Infantry to set watches.

Major,
Brigade Major.
1sr S.A.I.Brigade,....

SA I Bde SECRET

Sketch Map

Accompanying OO No 66. 17th Oct 1916

Reference
- Enemy Trs (new) ⌇⌇⌇
- " old ⊡⊡
- Our " ⌇⌇⌇
- Light Rlys ┼┼┼
- Main " ━━━
- Roads ═══
- Form Lines —100—

SCALE 1:10000

H.Q. 1st S.A.I. Brigade.
18th October 1916.

SECRET & URGENT.
Map reference.
ALBERT 1/40,000.

Copy No. 13

OPERATION ORDER NO. 69.

The 1st S.A.I. Brigade will be relieved in the line on the 19th and the night of the 19th/20th October, by the 27th Infantry Brigade in accordance with the attached schedule.

Advanced parties to take over the camping areas from the 6th K.O.S.Bs and the 11th Royal Scots will be sent by the 4th and 2nd S.A.I., respectively to report to the H.Q. of the 27th Infantry Brigade at S.30.a.6.6. at 8 am on the 19th. Similarly advanced parties of the 6th K.O.S.Bs and 11th Royal Scots will report at 8 am on the 19th at the H.Q. of the 4th S.A.I. and 1st S.A.I. Brigade to take over camping sites from the 4th and 2nd S.A.I. respectively. The O.C. 2nd S.A.I. will send a guide to Brigade H.Q. (S.A.) to meet the advance party of the 11th Royal Scots.

On relief the 3rd S.A.I. will proceed to BAZENTIN LE GRAND and take over camping area vacated by the 11th Royal Scots and the 1st S.A.I. on relief will proceed to the camping area in HIGH WOOD vacated by the 6th K.O.S.Bs. The Os.C. 1st and 3rd S.A.I. will send advance parties to take over these camping sites at 4 pm on the 19th.

The 2nd and 4th S.A.I. will take with them all picks and shovels in their possession.
The 1st and 3rd will hand over to their relieving battalions all picks, shovels, bombs and ammunition.

Completion of relief to be reported to Brigade Headquarters by the message "NATAL".

Brigade Headquarters will remain at BAZENTIN LE GRAND.

ACKNOWLEDGE.

Major.
Brigade Major.

Issued by orderly at 9.15 pm
as per S.A.Brigade distribution
list.

SCHEDULE ACCOMPANYING OPERATION ORDER NO. 69.

UNIT BEING RELIEVED.	UNIT RELIEVING	Hour of relief	Hour and place at which guides will meet relieving units.	REMARKS.
2nd S.A.I.	11th Royal Scots.	11 a.m, 19/10/16.	---	---
4th S.A.I.	6th K.O.S.Bs	11.15 a.m., 19/10/16.	---	
1st S.A.I.	6th K.O.S.Bs	About 6 pm., 19/10/16.	5 pm 19/10/16 at Headquarters 6th K.O.S.Bs, HIGH WOOD.	17 guides will be sent. One for each platoon, one for Headquarters.
3rd S.A.I.	11th Royal Scots	About 6-30pm	5-30 pm 19/10/16 at H.Q. of 11th Royal Scots BAZENTIN LE GRAND. (Near Bde H.Q.)	-do-
28th M.G.Coy	27th M.G.Coy	About noon 19/10/16	11.30 am H.Q. 4th S.A.I.	
S.A. L.T.M.Battery	27th Bde L.T.M.Battery	11 am. 19/10/16.	10 am S.A.Bde H.Q.	The S.A.Brigade Trench Mortars will be left in the line.

Scheme J.

27th Bde. Operation Orders

SECRET.

B.M.2/971.
Headquarters,
27th.Inf.Brigade.
17th.Oct.1916.

To, Recipients of O.O. 101.

1. Zero hour will be at 3.40 a.m. 18th.Oct.

2. A contact aeroplane will fly over the front as soon as light permits.

Red flares will be shown by the advanced Infantry in reply to aeroplane signals.

3. Acknowledge.

Major,
Brigade Major.
27th.Infahtry Brigade.

SECRET.

Copy No. 1

27th. Infantry Brigade Operation Order No. 101.

acknowledged

17th. October 1916.

1. The 9th.Division will attack the enemy's trenches from M.18.c.2.5. to M.17.c.0.3. on the 18th.inst. in conjunction with the 30th. Division which will attack the enemy's firing & support lines running S.E. from M.18.c.4.6. and M.18.c.6.8.

The 15th.Division on the left will co-operate by bringing machine gun fire to bear on the BUTTE de WARLENCOURT and on the enemy's trenches E. of the BUTTE, both during the attack and during the consolidation of the position.

Their Stokes Mortars will also be in action ready to deal with any hostile machine guns about M.10.d.

2. The dividing line between the 9th. & 30th.Divisions will be the sunken road in M.18.c. and M.17.d. exclusive to the 9th.Division.

3. The hour of Zero will be notified later.
It will be two or three hours prior to dawn.

4. The attack will be carried out by the 26th.Inf.Bde on the right and the S.African Bde on the left.

The dividing line between the Brigades will be a line between the bending tree in the Quarry just North of the cross roads at M.23.a.9.4. and a lone tree about M.17.a.9.0. i.e. a North and South line 50 yards West of the dividing line between M.17.c. and M.17.d.

5. The attack will be preceded by an artillery barrage on the enemy's line from Zero to Zero plus 1 minute. The barrage will be intensified by a Stokes Mortar barrage which will be maintained on the enemy's trench till Zero plus two minutes.

Where our trench is closest to the enemy at about M.17.d.4.2. the barrage on the enemy's trench will be entirely Stokes.

6. A Smoke barrage will be arranged so as to blind the BUTTE de WARLENCOURT and the Valley between the BUTTE and LE SARS North of the Line joining M.17. central and M.16 central.

7. The leading wave of the attacking infantry will form up outside their front trench under cover of darkness and will advance as close under the barrage as possible, assaulting the enemy's line as soon as the barrage lifts.

8. As soon as the line is captured the S.African Bde will send a party up the trench running N.W. from M.17.c.4.4., and the 26th.Inf.Bde. will similarly send a party up the trench running N.W. from M.17.d.2½.6½. The 26th.Inf.Bde will also co-operate with the 30th.Division by enfilading with rifle and Lewis Gun fire the trench running N.E. across the sunken road from the right of their objective at M.18.c.3.5. This will however only be done provided the 26th.Inf.Bde is not delayed in attaining its objective. Should the advance of the 26th.Inf.Bde be delayed fire in this direction will not be opened unless it is clear to our infantry that the trenches East of them are still in the hands of the enemy.

The right of the 26th.Bde will not enter the sunken road which will be kept under fire by Stokes Mortars of the 30th.Division.

9. The enemy's line when captured will be consolidated. Strong points being made :-
  (a) Immediately W. of the sunken road) by 26th.Inf.Bde.
  (b) At trench junction M.17.d.2½.6½.)
  (c) At trench junction M.17.c.4.4.   by S.A.Bde.

contd

The trenches running N.W. from M.17.d.2½.6½. and M.17.c.4.4. will be blocked at about M.17.c.8.10.and M.17.c.1.8.respectively. with a view to their being joined up on the following night to form a new front line.

10. Each Brigade will open up a communication trench from the present front line to the captured line, 26th.Inf.Bde about M.17.d.5.3. to 5.5. and the S.African Bde about M.17.c.4.0. to M.17.c.4.4.

11. Red flares will be used by the Infantry to show their positions to contact aeroplane.

12. A main divisional receiving station has been established at M.29.d.4.4. which is visible from the whole front to be attacked.
Brigades will arrange for visual communication to be established with this station from the captured line.

13. Arrangements for evacuation of wounded will be similar to those detailed in 27th.Bde O.O.No.100.

14. 26th. and S.African Bde Headquarters will be at BAZENTIN LE GRAND, S.15.b.3.5.
9th.Divisional Headquarters will remain at FRICOURT FARM.

15. The 27th.Inf.Brigade is in Divisional reserve, and will be ready to move at one hours notice.
Arrangements will be made by O.C's 12th.R.Scots & 6th.K.O.S.B. to recall working parties quickly if required.

27th.Inf.Brigade Headquarters will remain in present position.

Issued at 11.a.m.

Cop.No.1 to 9th.Division.
 2 11th.R.S.
 3 12th.R.S.
 4 6th.K.O.S.B.
 5 9th.S.R.
 6 27th.M.G.Coy.
 7 27th.T.M.Bty.
 8 90th.F.Coy.R.E.
 9. 27th.F.Ambce.
 10. 106th.Coy.A.S.C.
 11. 214th.A.T.Coy.R.E.
 12. 26th.Inf.Bde.
 13. 1st.S.A.Brigade.

14 / 20 Office.

Major,
Brigade Major,
27th.Infantry Brigade.

Scheme J.

Special Co. R.E.
Operation Orders

Copy No. 3

Operation Order No. 18
No. 4 Special Company R.E.

1. On the 18th inst. "N" Section — O.C. Lieut WISDOM — will establish a smoke barrage, combined with lachrymatory shells, at zero, to screen the attack of the 9th Division, on enemy trenches in M.17.c. and M.17.d.

2. Emplacements will be made on the night of the 17th inst.

3. (A) Four guns including one gun firing lachrymatory shells, will fire from emplacements in and about our front line trench in M.16.b. and d.
These guns will drop bombs at varying heights on the slopes in M.17.a. and in the bottom in M.16.b, with the following objects:—
   (1.) Blinding the BUTTE de WARLENCOURT.
   (2.) Preventing observed enemy machine-gun fire from M.16.b. being brought to bear on the attacking troops.

Lachrymatory bombs will be dropped in and about the BUTTE de WARLENCOURT.

The barrage should be continuous, starting from the bottom in M.16.b. and continuing to the highest slope possible to reach in M.17.a.

(B) Three guns, including one gun firing lachrymatory shells will fire from emplacements in and about S.W. of M.16.a.
These guns will drop bombs on the slopes in M.15.b. and M.16.a. and will form a barrage, to be continuous with that described in (A), with the following objects:—
   (1.) To prevent aimed machine-gun fire from M.10.c. and d. being brought to bear on the attacking troops.
   (2.) To induce enemy to expect an attack by the 15th Division.

P.T.O.

Continued
Sheet 2.

4. Firing must not take place with any wind which will cause smoke or lachrymatory to come South of a line through M.18 — 17 central — M.16.b.7.0 — M.16.b.1.8 — CHALK PIT.
The decision as to whether wind is favourable will rest with O.C. "N" Section.

5. Duration of barrage:- 45 minutes.
Number of rounds per gun:- 40 smoke, 20 lachrymatory.

6. Firing will commence at Zero.

7. O.C. (A) Firing Party   2nd Lt. BENTLEY.
   O.C. (B) Firing Party   2nd Lt. JONES.

8. Watches will be synchronised, and zero time obtained at 46th Inf. Bde. H.Q. under arrangements to be made by O.C. "N" Section, at 11.p.m on the 17th inst.

9. Firing Parties will leave Coy. H.Q. at 3 p.m on the 17th inst, pick up guns at MARTINPUICH, and proceed to battle positions.

10. Ammunition carrying party under 2nd Lt. NASH will leave Coy H.Q. at 4 p.m on the 17th inst, pick up ammunition at MARTINPUICH, and proceed to the cutting E. of LE SARS, where it will be met by guides from (A) & (B) firing parties. After depositing ammunition at required positions, the carrying party will return to billets.

11. O.C. "N" Section will be present at Batt. H.Q. 26th Avenue, and will be in communication with 46th Bde by telephone and orderlies, and with O.C. Firing Parties by orderlies. He will report to

P.T.O.

Continued.
Sheet 3.

46th Bde H.Q. before proceeding to the Battn H.Q.

12. After the conclusion of the barrage, guns and personnel will be withdrawn at the discretion of O.C. Firing Parties.

Date: 17th Oct 1916.
Copy No 1.   III. Corps.
 "   " 2.   15th Division
 "   " 3.   9th Division
 "   " 4.   46th Inf Bde
 "   " 5.   O.C. 'N' Section.
 "   " 6.   2nd Lt Bentley
 "   " 7.   2nd Lt Cates.
 "   " 8.   O.C. Special Companies R.E
 "   " 9.   File

A. E. Kent Capt
O.C. No 4 Special Coy
R.E

"C" Form (Duplicate).
MESSAGES AND SIGNALS.

Army Form C. 2123.

Sender's Number	Day of Month	In reply to Number	AAA
G 587	11th		

TO: 9th Div

Reference a.a. no 14 by special company to end of para 3 (A) add the words "and will continue to zero plus 45" aaa Please arrange to carry this out addressed Special to 44th inf Bde rep'td 9th Div

FROM PLACE & TIME: 15° Div

Copy No. 3.

Operation Order No. 17.
No. 4. Special Company. R.E.

1. On the 12th inst "P" Section – O.C. Lieut THOMPSON will establish a smoke barrage at zero, to screen the attack of the 9th Division.

2. Emplacements will be made on the night 11th/12th.

3. (a) Two guns will fire from emplacements about M.16.d.2.9 with the object of screening attack of the 9th Division, from enemy observation in and about BUTTE de WARLENCOURT.
Duration of barrage :- 28 minutes.
Directly 9th Division's troops have reached the BUTTE de WARLENCOURT, fire will lift behind the BUTTE to screen consolidation of this position & will continue to zero + 45

(b) Two guns will fire from emplacements about M.16.b.2.4. with two objects :-
1. To screen local attack of 15th Division from machine-gun emplacements in M.16.c.r.d. the exact position of which will be obtained from O.C. Battalion in the line.
2. To screen attack of 9th Division, from enemy observation N. & W. of BUTTE de WARLENCOURT.
Number of rounds per gun :- 30.
Duration of barrage :- 28 minutes.

(c) Two guns will fire from emplacements about M.15.b.9.2. with the object of smoke barraging from proximity of M.9.d.1.4 to M.10.c.5.2.
Number of rounds per gun :- 20.
Duration of barrage :- 20 minutes.

4. O.C. of (a) & (b) Firing Parties :- 2nd Lieut JONES.
O.C. of (c) Firing Party :- 2nd Lieut NASH.

5. Firing and Carrying Parties will leave Coy. H.Q.

Continued:- Sheet ij

at 6 p.m. on the 11th inst. They will proceed to previously arranged rendez-vous at MARTINPUICH, where they will be met at 8 p.m. by the O's C Firing Parties, who will take charge of their Firing and Carrying Parties, and lead them to previously reconnoitred positions.

6. O.C. "P" Section will be present at Batt. H.Q. near M.16 central, and will be in communication with O'sC Firing Parties by orderlies, and with 44th Bde H.Q by orderlies & Telephone.

7. O.C. "P" Section will arrange that watches will be synchronised and zero time obtained at 44th Bde H.Q. at 10 hours before zero.

8. Firing will take place with any of the following winds:- S. SW. W. SE. E.

9. The decision as to whether wind is favourable, will rest with O.C. "P" Section.

10. After the conclusion of the barrage, guns & personnel will be withdrawn at the discretion of O.C. "P" Section.

Date:- 11th Oct. 1916.

A.E. Kent Capt
O.C. No 4 Special Coy. R.E.

Copy No 1. III Corps.
" " 2. 15th Division
" " 3. 9th Division
" " 4. 44th Inf. Bde
" " 5. 45th Inf. Bde
" " 6. O.C. "P" Section.
" " 7. 2nd Lt Jones
" " 8. 2nd Lt Nash
" " 9. O.C. Special Companies R.E.
" " 10. File

Scheme J

2nd 9th
47th / Div. Artillery

Operation Order

ADDENDUM NO. 2   Copy No........

TO

9TH DIVISIONAL ARTILLERY

OPERATION ORDER

NO. 68

****

October 17th 1916.

From zero + 3 onwards the 25th, 39th, 50th and 52nd Brigades will each detail one battery to search all ground back from their Brigade barrage to the GIRD LINE.

Please acknowledge by wire.

                                      Major R.F.A.
                                    Brigade Major.
                                  R.A., 9th Division.

Copy No. 1 to 50th Brigade, R.F.A.
Copy No. 2 to 51st Brigade, R.F.A.
Copy No. 3 to 52nd Brigade, R.F.A.
Copy No. 4 to 25th Brigade, R.F.A.
Copy No. 5 to 39th Brigade, R.F.A.
Copy No. 6 to III Corps R.A.
Copy No. 7 to 9th Division.

Acknowledged

ADDENDUM NO. 1

to

9th Divisional Artillery

Operation Order

No. 86

October 17th 1916.

1. Zero hour will be 3.40 a.m. on 18th October 1916.

2. A red light, which is not to be repeated at a less interval than half a minute, will be the signal referred to in Para. 4.

3. Brigades will send an officer to meet a member of III Corps Staff at 26th Infantry Brigade Headquarters at BAZENTIN LE GRAND at 9 p.m. 17th October, who will give them Corps time.

   Time will be checked again from this office by telephone one hour before zero.

   [signed]

   Major R.F.A.
   Brigade Major.
   R.A., 9th Division.

Copy No. 1 to 9th Division.
Copy No. 2 to 50th Bde. R.F.A.
Copy No. 3 to 51st Bde. R.F.A.
Copy No. 4 to 52nd Bde. R.F.A.
Copy No. 5 to 39th Bde. R.F.A.
Copy No. 6 to 25th Bde. R.F.A.
Copy No. 7 to 9th Trench Mortar Brigade.
Copy No. 8 to Left (15th) Divl. Artillery Group.
Copy No. 9 to 12th Divisional Artillery.
Copy No. 10 to III Corps Heavy Artillery.
Copy No. 11 to R.A., III Corps.
Copy No. 12 to 26th Infantry Brigade.
Copy No. 13 to 27th Infantry Brigade.
Copy No. 14 to 1st S.African Inf. Bde.

Copy No. 1

9th Divisional Artillery

Operation Order No. 68.

17th October 1916.

1. The 9th Division are attacking Trench line from H.17.c.0.3. to H.18.c.1.4. at Zero hour on X Day.

2. Tasks for the Artillery.

At Zero hour the Right Divisional Artillery Group and 4 Brigades of Left Divisional Artillery Group will open an intense bombardment as follows :—

Right Divisional Artillery Group.

Zero to Zero + 1 minute.

Rate of fire 4 rounds per gun per minute. H.E. only.

9th [18 LR] Brigade R.F.A. from H.18.c.1.4. to H.17.d.7.4.
52nd Brigade R.F.A. from M.18.c.1.4. to M.17.d.7.4.
50th Brigade R.F.A. from H.17.d.3.5. to M.17.c.9.5.
25th Brigade R.F.A. from H.17.c.9.5. to H.17.c.4.4.

Left Divisional Artillery Group.

Zero to Zero + 1 minute

Rate of fire 4 rounds per gun per minute. H.E. only.

One Brigade from H.17.d.3.5. to H.17.c.4.4.

At Zero + 1 minute

Rate of fire 2 rounds per gun per minute. H.E. only.

The above batteries will move their fire due North 50 yards per round, for four rounds, where they will remain till further orders.

3. Two Brigades Left Divisional Artillery Group.

Zero to Zero + 1 minute

Rate of fire 4 rounds per gun per minute.

H.E. only will be used by guns firing within 300 LR yards of first objective; the remainder will fire half H.E., half Shrapnel.

Triangle H.17.c.4.4. along Trench running North West by side of sunken road towards BUTTE de WARLENCOURT to H.16.b.1.6. to BUTTE de WARLENCOURT LR

At Zero + 1 minute

Rate of fire 2 rounds per gun per minute.

All Guns.....

All guns within 200 yards of objective will move their fire due North 50 yards after each round for four rounds and remain on this barrage till further orders.

One Brigade of Left Divisional Artillery Group.

From Zero

Will search and sweep ridge in H.10.c. and H.16.a. at a safe distance beyond our line to keep down Machine Gun fire.

Rate of fire 3 rounds per gun per minute for 5 minutes, then 2 rounds per gun per minute for 5 minutes, then drop to one round per gun per minute till further orders.

4. Coloured lights will be sent up by the Infantry when they require Artillery to lift to establish blocks in the two trenches running North West from the first objective: colour will be notified later.
Brigades covering these two trenches will arrange lookouts to watch for these lights, so as to lift barrage at once 200 yards beyond block (See 9th Division Operation Order No. 86, para. 9.)

5. A high rate of fire is called for but it must be distinctly understood that this must not be attained by a sacrifice of accuracy. A slower rate is preferable to a loss of accuracy.

6. The 50th and 52nd Brigades will each LR establish a visual Signal Station in our present front line, for communication back LR to a forward telephone station.
Positions of these stations will be fixed by Brigade Commanders and reported to this office for communication to all concerned.

7. **Action of Heavy Artillery**

Zero to Zero + 3 LR minutes.

60 Pounders will barrage at an intense rate of fire along Ridge from H.17.a.0.4. through H.17.b.0.3. to ~~H.18.a.4.7.~~ M.18.c.5-8 LR to keep down Machine Gun fire.

Heavy and Medium Howitzers

Zero ~~onwards~~ to Zero + 15 minutes LR

Bombard the GIRD LINE from the BUTTE de WARLENCOURT to H.18.c.4.7. concentrating particularly on that portion in H.18.c.

8. **Trench Mortars**

Zero to Zero + 2 LR minutes.

The Stokes will bombard the front trenches and particularly that portion between M.17.d.7.4. and M.17.d.3.5.

Medium Mortars

Will fire one salvo at Zero and then cease fire.

9. Lieut. Colonel G.A.S. Cane, 51st Brigade R.F.A. will act as Liaison Officer with the 26th and 1st South African Infantry Brigades.

10. The 50th Brigade R.F.A. will detail a F.O.O. and party to follow the attack of the South African Brigade and the 52nd Brigade will detail a F.O.O. and party to follow the attack of the 26th Brigade.

11. Watches will be synchronised from this office, one hour before Zero.

Major, R.F.A.,
Brigade Major,
R.A. 9th. Division.

Copy No. 1 to 9th Division.
Copy No. 2 to 50th Bde. R.F.A.
Copy No. 3 to 51st Bde. R.F.A.
Copy No. 4 to 52nd Bde. R.F.A.
Copy No. 5 to 39th Bde. R.F.A.
Copy No. 6 to 25th Bde. R.F.A.
Copy No. 7 to 9th Trench Mortars.
Copy No. 8 to Left(15th) Div. Arty. Group.
Copy No. 9 to 12th Divl. Artillery.
Copy No. 10 to III Corps Heavy Artillery.
Copy No. 11 to R.A. III Corps.
" " 12 - 26th Infantry Brigade
" " 13 - 27th Infantry Brigade
" " 14 - 1st S. African Brigade

Distribution:-

Copy No. 13   G" office
" " 14   76th Bde
" " 15   27th "
" " 16   S.H. "
" " 17   2nd Corps
" " 18   30th Div.
" " 19   15th "
" " 20   CRE
" " 21   9th Seaforths
" " 22 & 23   Spare

SECRET.   COPY NO. 23

ADDENDUM NO. 1 TO RIGHT DIVISIONAL ARTILLERY GROUP OPERATION
ORDER NO. 65.

1.   With reference to Table "B" STATIONARY BARRAGE, nothing but H.E. will be fired one minute before each lift.

2.   With reference to Table "A" CREEPING BARRAGE, nothing but H.E. is to be fired one minute before and during creeps.

3.   Lieut. Col. E.C. MASSY, 235th. Brigade R.F.A., will act as Liaison Officer at 26th. Infantry Brigade Headquarters during the operation.

4.   With reference to para 2 (c) of Right D.A. Group Operation Order No. 65, the Zones for S.O.S. barrages will be the final barrage lines allotted in the schedules of fire.

5.   With reference to Tables "A", "B" and "C", where "Zero plus 20" occurs read "Zero plus 23". All times subsequent to Zero plus 20 will therefore now be 3 minutes later: thus 25th. Brigade R.F.A. will reach final barrage at plus 32 instead of at plus 29.

H.Q. 47th. D.A.   Major R.A.,
                                             Brigade Major,
11th. October 1916.   Right D.A. Group.

Issued to all recipients of Right D.A. Group Operation Order No. 65.

Distribution

Copy no. 13. G. Office.
" " 15. 26th Bde.
" " 16 27th "
" " 17 1st S.A. "
" " 18 3rd Corps
" " 19 30th Division
" " 20 15th "
" 21 CRE
" " 22 9th Seaforths
" 14•23 Spare.

SECRET.   COPY NO. 23

ADDENDUM NO. 2 TO RIGHT DIVISIONAL ARTILLERY GROUP OPERATION

ORDER NO. 65.
✽✽

1.   At Zero plus 36, 4.5" Howitzer Batteries will fire on following objectives :-

   D/25 Battery   - Houses about M.10.d.5.9½.
   40th. Battery
   (section)   - House about M.10.b.9.1½.
   D/236 Battery   - Cross Roads in M.5.c.
   30th. Battery   - (BAPAUME Road at M.11.b.8.5.
                      (Banks in M.11.d., southern portion.
   D/235 Battery   - Road between M.11.a.0.3 and M.11.b.6.4

2.   Rates of fire :-

   Final lift off GIRD LINE to plus 1 hour 30 minutes - one round per gun per 6 minutes.

   Plus 1 hour 30 minutes onwards - occasional bursts.

                                            [signature]
H.Q. 47th. D.A.   Major R.A.,
                                            Brigade Major,
12th. October 1916.   Right D.A. Group.

Issued to all recipients of Right D.A. Group Op. O. No. 65.

SECRET.   COPY NO. 23

RIGHT DIVISIONAL ARTILLERY GROUP OPERATION ORDER NO. 65.
✻✻

Reference Map :- 1/10,000
Fourth Army Trench Map No. 694.   11th. October 1916.

1. INFORMATION.

(a) The Right Division of the lllrd. Corps in conjunction with the XVth. Corps is attacking on the 12th. instant the GIRD TRENCH both front and support from the Corps boundary to M.17.a.4.7½. and the BUTTE DE WARLENCOURT.

(b) The objective of the 9th. Division is the GIRD line from M.17.d.0.9. to the BUTTE DE WARLENCOURT as shown on map attached to Right D.A. Group Operation Order No. 64 dated 6/10/16.

(c) Zero hour will be communicated later.

2. ARTILLERY ACTION.

(a) Right D.A. Group and four F.A. Brigades of Left D.A. Group will fire as per attached schedule.

(b) On the 12tH. instant during the day, previous to Zero hour each Brigade will detail one battery to search the ground methodically from our trenches up to the GIRD LINE.

(c) If the S.O.S. Signal is seen fire will be quickened to, or at once opened at, 3 rounds per gun per minute for 5 minutes and then dropped to 1 round per gun per minute till situation clears.

3.   Watches will be again synchronized from 47th. D.A. H.Q. one hour before Zero.

H.Q. 47th. D.A.   Major R.A.,
                                   Brigade Major,
11th. October 1916.   Right D.A. Group.

Copies to :-

       No. 1. War Diary.
           2. File.
           3. 25th. Brigade R.F.A.
           4. 39th. Brigade R.F.A.
           5. 235th. Brigade R.F.A.
           6. 236th. Brigade R.F.A.
           7. 237th. Brigade R.F.A.
           8. 238th. Brigade R.F.A.
           9. 47th. D.A.C.
          10. D.T.M.O. 47th. Division.
          11. lllrd. Corps R.A.
          12. lllrd. Corps H.A.
    13 to 23. 9th. Division.
    24 to 28. Left D.A. Group.
          29. 21st. D.A. Group.

S E C R E T.

SCHEDULE OF FIRE -- TABLE "A" -- (To accompany Right D.A. Group Op. Order No. 65).

C R E E P I N G   B A R R A G E.

UNIT.	TIME.	OBJECTIVE.	PROCEDURE.	REMARKS.
235th. Brigade R.F.A.	Zero to plus 3.	M.17.c.5.3½. to M.16.d.6.2.	Barrage.	At Zero plus 3 starts creeping back by 50 yards per minute till it reaches a line 300 yards beyond the 1st. objective where it remains till zero plus 20.
"	Zero plus 20.	Creeps back by 50 yards per minute till it arrives 200 yards beyond final objective on line M.11.c.3.3½ - M.18.a.0.7½. where it remains till further orders.		
237th. Brigade R.F.A.	Zero to plus 3.	M.17.c.5.3½. to M.17.c.5.3½.	Barrage.	As for 235th. Brigade R.F.A.
"	Zero plus 20.	As for 235th. Brigade R.F.A.		
238th. Brigade R.F.A.	Zero to plus 3	M.18.c.0.4. to M.17.d.2.4.	Barrage.	As for 235th. Brigade R.F.A.
	Zero plus 20.	As for 235th. Brigade R.F.A.		

(1) Howitzer Batteries of the Brigades mentioned above will be included in the Creeping barrage but will fire 100 yards beyond the 18-pounders.

(2) On reaching the final line of the Creeping barrage 1 Battery of 237th. Brigade and 1 Battery of 235th. Brigade will sweep the road from WARLENCOURT to the BAPAUME - ALBERT road.

SECRET.

SCHEDULE OF FIRE -- TABLE "B" -- (To accompany Right D.A. Group Op. Order No. 5).

STATIONARY BARRAGE.

UNIT.	TIME.	OBJECTIVE.	PROCEDURE.	REMARKS.
25th. Bde. R.F.A.	Zero to plus 3.	Trench M.18.c.0.4. to M.17.d.5.4.	Barrage.	At plus 3 lifts.
"	Plus 3 to plus 20.	Line M.18.c.0.8. to M.17.b.5.2.	"	At plus 20 lengthens range 100 yards on to GIRD Front line.
"	Plus 20 to plus 26.	GIRD Front line	"	At plus 26 lifts on to GIRD Support line.
"	Plus 26 to plus 29.	GIRD Support line.	"	At plus 29 lengthens 200 yards and remains on that line till further orders.
39th. Bde. R.F.A.	Zero to plus 3.	M.17.d.5.4. to M.17.d.0.5.	"	At plus 3 lifts.
"	Plus 3 to plus 20.	M.17.b.5.2. to M.17.b.0.4.	"	At plus 20 lengthens range 100 yards on to GIRD Front line.
"	Plus 20 to plus 27.	GIRD Front line.	"	At plus 27 lifts on to GIRD Support line.
"	Plus 27 to plus 29.	GIRD Support line.	"	At plus 29 lengthens range 200 yards and remains on that line till further orders.
1 Brigade R.F.A. Left D.A. Group.	Zero to plus 5.	M.17.d.0.5. to M.17.c.5.4½.	"	At plus 5 lifts.
"	Plus 5 to plus 20.	M.17.b.0.4. to M.17.a.5.6.	"	At plus 20 lengthens range 100 yards on to GIRD Front line.
"	Plus 20 to plus 28.	GIRD front line.	"	At plus 28 lifts on to GIRD Support line.
"	Plus 28 to plus 29.	GIRD Support line.	"	At plus 29 lengthens range 200 yards and remains on that line till further orders.

SECRET.

TABLE "B" CONTINUED.
****

UNIT.	TIME.	OBJECTIVE.	PROCEDURE.	REMARKS.
1 Brigade R.F.A. Left D.A. Group.	Zero to plus 5.	M.17.c.5.4½. to M.16.d.7.4.	Barrage.	At plus 5 lifts.
	Plus 5 to plus 20.	M.17.a.5.6. to M.17.a.0.6.	"	At plus 20 lengthens range 100 yards on to GIRD Front line.
	Plus 20 to plus 29.	GIRD Front line.	"	At plus 29 lifts on to Support line.
	Plus 29 to plus 30.	GIRD Support line.	"	At plus 30 lengthens range 200 yards and remains on that line till further orders.

SECRET.

SCHEDULE OF FIRE -- TABLE "C" -- (To accompany Right D.A. Group Op. Order No. 65).

UNIT.	TIME.	OBJECTIVE.	PROCEDURE.	REMARKS.
1 Brigade R.F.A. Left D.A. Group.	Zero to plus 20.	Rectangle - M.17.c.0.4. - M.17.c.3.4. M.16.b.9.7. - M.17.a.3.7.	Bursts of fire.	At plus 20 lengthens 50 yards per minute until it reaches the line M.17.a.0.6. - M.11.c.4.½. where it will form a barrage and remain till further orders.
1 Brigade R.F.A. Left D.A. Group.	Zero to plus 5.	Enemy machine gun emplacements at - M.17.c.4.5. - M.17.c.3½.7. M.17.c.1½.8.		At plus 5 lengthens 50 yards per minute for 200 yards. At plus 20 lengthens 50 yards per minute until it reaches the line M.17.a.0.6. - M.11.c.4.½. where it will form a barrage and remain till further orders.

RATES OF FIRE.

TABLES "A", "B" and "C".   18-Pounders and Howitzers.

ZERO to plus 6	--	3 rounds per gun and How. per minute.
Plus 6 to plus 20	--	1 round " " " " "
Plus 20 to plus 26	--	3 rounds " " " " "
Plus 26 to plus 30	--	2 rounds " " " " "
Plus 30 onwards	--	1 round " " " " "

SECRET.   COPY NO. 22

ADDENDUM NO. 1 TO RIGHT DIVISIONAL ARTILLERY GROUP OPERATION
                        ORDER NO. 65.

****

1.   With reference to Table "B" STATIONARY BARRAGE, nothing but H.E. will be fired one minute before each lift.

2.   With reference to Table "A" CREEPING BARRAGE, nothing but H.E. is to be fired one minute before and during creeps.

3.   Lieut. Col. E.C. MASSY, 235th. Brigade R.F.A., will act as Liaison Officer at 26th. Infantry Brigade Headquarters during the operation.

4.   With reference to para 2 (c) of Right D.A. Group Operation Order No. 65, the Zones for S.O.S. barrages will be the final barrage lines allotted in the schedules of fire.

5.   With reference to Tables "A", "B" and "C", where "Zero plus 20" occurs read "Zero plus 23". All times subsequent to Zero plus 20 will therefore now be 3 minutes later: thus 25th. Brigade R.F.A. will reach final barrage at plus 32 instead of at plus 29.

H.Q. 47th. D.A.   Major R.A.,
                                          Brigade Major,
11th. October 1916.   Right D.A. Group.

Issued to all recipients of Right D.A. Group Operation Order No. 65.

SECRET.   COPY NO. 22

RIGHT DIVISIONAL ARTILLERY GROUP OPERATION ORDER NO. 65.
****

Reference Map :- 1/10,000
Fourth Army Trench Map No. 694.   11th. October 1916.

1. INFORMATION.

   (a) The Right Division of the IIIrd. Corps in conjunction with the XVth. Corps is attacking on the 12th. instant the GIRD TRENCH both front and support from the Corps boundary to M.17.a.4.7½. and the BUTTE DE WARLENCOURT.

   (b) The objective of the 9th. Division is the GIRD line from M.17.d.0.9. to the BUTTE DE WARLENCOURT as shown on map attached to Right D.A. Group Operation Order No. 64 dated 6/10/16.

   (c) Zero hour will be communicated later.

2. ARTILLERY ACTION.

   (a) Right D.A. Group and four F.A. Brigades of Left D.A. Group will fire as per attached schedule.

   (b) On the 12th. instant during the day, previous to Zero hour each Brigade will detail one battery to search the ground methodically from our trenches up to the GIRD LINE.

   (c) If the S.O.S. Signal is seen fire will be quickened to, or at once opened at, 3 rounds per gun per minute for 5 minutes and then dropped to 1 round per gun per minute till situation clears.

3.   Watches will be again synchronized from 47th. D.A. H.Q. one hour before Zero.

                                            W. Muirhead

H.Q. 47th. D.A.   Major R.A.,
                                            Brigade Major,
11th. October 1916.   Right D.A. Group.

   Copies to :-

         No. 1. War Diary.
              2. File.
              3. 25th. Brigade R.F.A.
              4. 39th. Brigade R.F.A.
              5. 235th. Brigade R.F.A.
              6. 236th. Brigade R.F.A.
              7. 237th. Brigade R.F.A.
              8. 238th. Brigade R.F.A.
              9. 47th. D.A.C.
             10. D.T.M.O. 47th. Division.
             11. IIIrd. Corps R.A.
             12. IIIrd. Corps H.A.
       13 to 23. 9th. Division.
       24 to 28. Left D.A. Group.
             29. 21st. D.A. Group.

S E C R E T.

SCHEDULE OF FIRE --- TABLE "A" --- (To accompany Right D.A. Group Op. Order No. 65).

CREEPING BARRAGE.

UNIT.	TIME.	OBJECTIVE.	PROCEDURE.	REMARKS.
235th. Brigade R.F.A.	Zero to plus 3.	M.17.c.5.3½. to M.16.d.6.2.	Barrage.	At Zero plus 3 starts creeping back by 50 yards per minute till it reaches a line 200 yards beyond the 1st. objective where it remains till zero plus 20.
"	Zero plus 20.	Creeps back by 50 yards per minute till it arrives 200 yards beyond final objective on line M.11.c.3.3½ - M.18.a.0.7½. where it remains till further orders.		
237th. Brigade R.F.A.	Zero to plus 3.	M.17.d.2.4. to M.17.c.5.3½.	Barrage.	As for 235th. Brigade R.F.A.
"	Zero plus 20.	As for 235th. Brigade R.F.A.		
238th. Brigade R.F.A.	Zero to plus 3	M.18.c.0.4. to M.17.d.2.4.	Barrage.	As for 235th. Brigade R.F.A.
	Zero plus 20.	As for 235th. Brigade R.F.A.		

(1) Howitzer Batteries of the Brigades mentioned above will be included in the Creeping barrage but will fire 100 yards beyond the 18-pounders.

(2) On reaching the final line of the Creeping barrage 1 Battery of 237th. Brigade and 1 Battery of 235th. Brigade will sweep the road from WARLENCOURT to the BAPAUME - ALBERT road.

SECRET.

SCHEDULE OF FIRE -- TABLE "B" -- (To accompany Right D.A. Group Op. Order No. 5).

STATIONARY BARRAGE.

UNIT.	TIME.	OBJECTIVE.	PROCEDURE.	REMARKS.
25th. Bde. R.F.A.	Zero to plus 3.	Trench M.18.c.0.4. to M.17.d.5.4.	Barrage.	At plus 3 lifts.
"	Plus 3 to plus 20.	Line M.18.c.0.8. to M.17.b.5.2.	"	At plus 20 lengthens range 100 yards on to GIRD Front line.
"	Plus 20 to plus 26.	GIRD Front line.	"	At plus 26 lifts.
"	Plus 26 to plus 29.	GIRD Support line.	"	At plus 29 lengthens 200 yards and remains on that line till further orders.
39th. Bde. R.F.A.	Zero to plus 3.	M.17.d.5.4. to M.17.d.0.5.	"	At plus 3 lifts.
"	Plus 3 to plus 20.	M.17.b.5.2. to M.17.b.0.4.	"	At plus 20 lengthens range 100 yards on to GIRD Front line.
"	Plus 20 to plus 27.	GIRD Front line.	"	At plus 27 lifts on to Support line.
"	Plus 27 to plus 29.	GIRD Support line.	"	At plus 29 lengthens range 200 yards and remains on that line till further orders.
1 Brigade R.F.A. Left D.A. Group.	Zero to plus 5.	M.17.d.0.5. to M.17.c.5.4½.	"	At plus 5 lifts.
"	Plus 5 to plus 20.	M.17.b.0.4. to M.17.a.5.6.	"	At plus 20 lengthens range 100 yards on to GIRD Front line.
"	Plus 20 to plus 28.	GIRD front line.	"	At plus 28 lifts on to Support line.
"	Plus 28 to plus 29.	GIRD Support line.	"	At plus 29 lengthens range 200 yards and remains on that line till further orders.

P.T.O.

S E C R E T.

TABLE "B" CONTINUED.
****

UNIT.	TIME.	OBJECTIVE.	PROCEDURE.	REMARKS.
1 Brigade R.F.A. Left D.A. Group.	Zero to plus 5.	M.17.c.5.4½. to M.16.d.7.4.	Barrage.	At plus 5 lifts.
	Plus 5 to plus 20.	M.17.a.5.6. to M.17.a.0.6.	"	At plus 20 lengthens range 100 yards on to GIRD Front line.
	Plus 20 to plus 29.	GIRD Front line.	"	At plus 29 lifts on to Support line.
	Plus 29 to plus 30.	GIRD Support line.	"	At plus 30 lengthens range 200 yards and remains on that line till further orders.

SECRET.

SCHEDULE OF FIRE. — TABLE "C". — (To accompany Right D.A. Group Op. Order No. 65).

UNIT.	TIME.	OBJECTIVE.	PROCEDURE.	REMARKS.
1 Brigade R.F.A. Left D.A. Group.	Zero to plus 20.	Rectangle – M.17.c.0.4. – M.17.c.3.4. M.16.b.9.7. – M.17.a.3.7.	Bursts of fire.	At plus 20 lengthens 50 yards per minute until it reaches the line M.17.a.0.6. – M.11.c.4.5. where it will form a barrage and remain till further orders.
1 Brigade R.F.A. Left D.A. Group.	Zero to plus 5.	Enemy machine gun emplacements at – M.17.c.4.5. – M.17.c.3½.7. M.17.c.1½.8.		At plus 5 lengthens 50 yards per minute for 200 yards. At plus 20 lengthens 50 yards per minute until it reaches the line M.17.a.0.6. – M.11.c.4.5. where it will form a barrage and remain till further orders.

RATES OF FIRE.

TABLES "A", "B" and "C".   18-Pounders and Howitzers.

ZERO to plus 6	—	3 rounds per gun and How. per minute.
Plus 6 to plus 20	—	1 round " " " " "
Plus 20 to plus 26	—	3 rounds " " " " "
Plus 26 to plus 30	—	2 rounds " " " " "
Plus 30 onwards	—	1 round " " " " "

S E C R E T.   COPY NO. 14

ADDENDUM NO. 2 TO RIGHT DIVISIONAL ARTILLERY GROUP OPERATION

ORDER NO. 65.

1.   At Zero plus 36, 4.5" Howitzer Batteries will fire on following objectives :-

   D/25 Battery   - Houses about M.10.d.5.9½.
   40th. Battery
    (section)   - House about M.10.b.9.1½.
   D/236 Battery - Cross Roads in M.5.c.
   30th. Battery - (BAPAUME Road at M.11.b.8.5.
                    (Banks in M.11.d., southern portion.
   D/238 Battery - Road between M.11.a.0.3 and M.11.b.6.4

2.   Rates of fire :-

   Final lift off GIRD LINE to plus 1 hour 30 minutes - one round per gun per 6 minutes.

   Plus 1 hour 30 minutes onwards - occasional bursts.

H.Q. 47th. D.A.   Major R.A.,
                                      Brigade Major,
18th. October 1916.   Right D.A. Group.

Issued to all recipients of Right D.A. Group Op. O. No. 65.

Scheme J.

Operation Orders
9th Division

Scheme J.

Addendum No. 2 to 9th Division Operation Order No. 86.
----

1.   Zero hour will be at 5.40 a.m. on 18th October.

2.   A contact aeroplane will fly over the front as soon as light permits. Red flares will be shown by the advanced infantry in reply to aeroplane signals.

3.   Correct time will be distributed by to representatives of infantry and artillery Brigades by a member of the III Corps Staff, at 26th Inf. Bde. Headquarters BAZENTIN le GRAND at 9 p.m. 17th October.

4.   ACKNOWLEDGE by wire.

Lieutenant Colonel,
General Staff,
9th (Scottish) Division.

17th Octr. 1916.

Copies to:-
    Recipients of Operation Order No. 86.

"A" Form
Army Form C. 2121
MESSAGES AND SIGNALS.

Sender's Number.	Day of Month	In reply to Number	AAA
J 832	17/10		

Addendum No. 1 to 9th Division Operation Order No.94 AAA Para five line four for one and a half minutes read two minutes AAA ACKNOWLEDGE AAA Addressed recipients of Operation Order No. 94

From
Place 9th Division.
Time

SECRET.

Copy No _____

9th Division Operation Order No. 86.

16.10.16.

1. The 9th Division will attack the enemy's trenches from
m.18.c.2.5. to m.17.c.0.5. on the 18th inst. in conjunction with
the 50th Division which will attack the enemy's firing and support
lines running S.E. from m.18.c.4.6. and m.18.c.6.8.
    The 15th Division on the left will co-operate by bringing
machine gun fire to bear on the BUTTE de WARLENCOURT and on the
enemy's trenches S. of the BUTTE, both during the attack and during
the consolidation of the position.
    Their Stokes Mortars will also be in action ready to deal
with any hostile machine guns about m.10.d.

2. The dividing line between the 9th and 50th Divisions will be
the sunken road in m.18.c. and m.17.d. exclusive to the 9th Division.

3. The hour of Zero will be notified later.
    It will be two or three hours prior to dawn.

4. The attack will be carried out by the 26th Inf. Bde. on the
right and the S.African Inf. Bde. on the left.
    The dividing line between the Brigades will be a line between
the branding tree in the Quarry just North of the cross roads at
m.23.a.9.4. and a lone tree about m.17.a.9.0. i.e. a North and
South line 50 yards West of the dividing line between m.17.c. and
m.17.d.

5. The attack will be preceded by an artillery barrage on the
enemy's line from Zero to Zero plus 1 minute. The barrage will be
intensified by a Stokes mortar barrage which will be maintained
on the enemy's trench till Zero plus 1½ minutes.
    Where our trench is closest to the enemy at about m.17.d.1.2.
the barrage on the enemy's trench will be entirely Stokes.

6. A smoke barrage will be arranged so as to blind the BUTTE
de WARLENCOURT and the Valley between the BUTTE and LE SARS North of
the line joining m.17.central and m.13.central.

7. The leading wave of the attacking infantry will form up
outside their front trench under cover of darkness and will advance
as close under the barrage as possible, assaulting the enemy's line
as soon as the barrage lifts.

8. As soon as the line is captured the S.African Bd. will send
a party up the trench running N.W. from m.17.c.4.4., and the
26th Inf. Bde. will similarly send a party up the trench running
N.W. from m.17.d.2½.3½. The 26th Inf. Bde. will also co-operate
with the 50th Division by enfilading with rifle and Lewis Gun fire
the trench running N.E. across the sunken road from the right of
their objective at m.18.c.3.5. This will however only be done
provided the 26th Inf. Bde. is not delayed in attaining its
objective. Should the advance of the 26th Inf. Bde. be delayed
fire in this direction will not be opened unless it is clear to
our infantry that the trenches East of them are still in the hands
of the enemy.
    The right of the 26th Bde. will not enter the sunken road
which will be kept under fire by Stokes Mortars of the 50th Division.

2.

9. The enemy's line when captured will be consolidated, strong points being made:-
    (a) Immediately W. of the sunken road)   By
    (b) At trench junction M.17.d.2½.6½   ) 26th Inf. Bde.
    (c) At trench junction M.17.c.4.4.   By S.African Bde.

The trenches running N.W. from M.17.d.2½.6½ and M.17.c.4.4. will be blocked at about M.17.c.8.10 and M.17.c.1.8. respectively with a view to their being joined up on the following night to form a new front line.

10. Each Brigade will open up a communication trench from the present front line to the captured line, 26th Inf. Bde. about M.17.d.5.3. to 5.5. and the S.African Bde. about M.17.c.4.0. to M.17.c.4.4.

11. The following will be attached to each Brigade for the operations:-

To 26th Bde. Half a company (60 strong) 9th Seaforths (Pioneers)
              One Section 63rd Field Coy. R.E.
              A detachment of a Light Trench Mortar Battery
                 of the 15th Division with 4 guns.

To S.A.Bde.   Half a company (60 strong) 9th Seaforths (Pioneers)
              One Section 64th Field Coy. R.E.

12. Red flares will be used by the Infantry to show their positions to contact aeroplane.

13. The programme of artillery action will be issued separately.
    Lieut.Col. Cape, 51st Bde. R.F.A. will act as Artillery Liaison Officer with the 26th and 1st S.African Bdes.

14. A main Divisional receiving station has been established at M.29.d.4.4. which is visible from the whole front to be attacked.
    Brigades will arrange for visual communication to be established with this station from the captured line.

15. Arrangements for evacuation of wounded will be similar to those of the 12th inst.

16. 26th and S.African Bde. Headquarters will be at LAZENTIN le GRAND, S.18.b.5.5.
    9th Division Headquarters will remain at FRICOURT FARM.

                                    Lieutenant Colonel,
                                    General Staff,
Issued at 11.30 p.m.   9th (Scottish) Division.

Copies to:-
No. 1 26th Bde.   10 C.R.E.   20 50th Division.
    2 27th Bde.   11 9/Seaforths   21 O.C.Heavy Sec.
    3 S.African Bde.   12 9th Train   M.G.C.
    4 C.R.A.   13 9/Signals   22 25th Bde. R.F.A.
    5 50th Bde. R.F.A.   14 A.D.M.S.   23 59th Bde. R.F.A.
    6 51st Bde. R.F.A.   15 A.D.V.S.   24 O.C. 4th Spl.Coy.
    7 52nd Bde. R.F.A.   16 A.P.M.   R.E.
    8 O.C.Trench Mortars 17 & 18 III Corps   25 War Diary.
    9 9th Div. Colm.   19 15th Divn.   26 File.

"A" Form.
MESSAGES AND SIGNALS.
Army Form C. 2121.

Prefix......Code......m.	Words	Charge	This message is on a/c of:	Recd. at.............m.
Office of Origin and Service Instructions.				Date..............
Priority	Sent		............Service.	From..............
	At.............m.			
	To..............		(Signature of "Franking Officer.")	By..............
	By..............			

TO { G.H.
     M.A.
     R.T.

| Sender's Number. | Day of Month | In reply to Number | |
| G. 892 | 18th. | | AAA |

Enemy still holds the SWITCH Trench and about 100 yards on each side of its junction with the trench which was our main objective today aaa The Division will hold on to all ground gained & at all costs, the 26th Inf.Bde. joining up with 50th Div. and making a C.T. as ordered, and the S.A.Bde forming two intermediate posts somewhere near the path joining our new front trench to our old front trench between M.17.c.8.5. and M.17.c.6.0. and joining up our old front trench with at least one of these posts by a C.T. before dawn aaa S.A.Bde will place mark on the parados to show our gunners where its left rests in our new line aaa At dawn tomorrow 2" trench mortars will engage the trench junction at M.17.c.4.4. and the SWITCH Trench and the 9.2 will also engage the same target aaa Before the latter begins orders will be issued by Div.H.Q. to withdraw

From
Place
Time

The above may be forwarded as now corrected.   (Z)

Censor.   Signature of Addressor or person authorised to telegraph in his name.
* This line should be erased if not required.

"A" Form.
MESSAGES AND SIGNALS.

Army Form C. 2121.

No. of Message _____

Prefix .... Code .... m.	Words	Charge	*This message is on a/c of:*	Recd. at .... m.
Office of Origin and Service Instructions.				Date ....
....	Sent At .... n.		.... Service.	From ....
....	To By		(Signature of "Franking Officer.")	By ....

TO ....

| Sender's Number. | Day of Month | In reply to Number | **A A A** |

our Infantry to a safe distance aaa When the SWITCH Trench and junction has been thoroughly bombarded the S.A.Bde will clear and occupy the SWITCH Trench as far North as M.17.c.1.8. aaa All arrangements to be made for carrying out this attack by eleven a.m. tomorrow aaa ACKNOWLEDGE aaa Addressed H.A., C.B., and R.T.

From: 9th Division
Place:
Time: 9.10 p.m.

The above may be forwarded as now corrected. (Z)

(Sgd) A.E. McNamara.

Censor. Signature of Addressor or person authorised to telegraph in his name.

* This line should be erased if not required.

"A" Form.
MESSAGES AND SIGNALS.
Army Form C. 2121.

Prefix	Code	m.	Words	Charge	This message is on a/c of:	Recd. at	m.
Office of Origin and Service Instructions.			Sent		Service.	Date	
			At	n.		From	
			To				
			By		(Signature of "Franking Officer.")	By	

TO — M.D.   G.D.S.   A.F.C.   3rd Corps.

Sender's Number.	Day of Month	In reply to Number	AAA
* G893	18/10		

L.D. will relieve N.D. and G.D. on October 19th and night Oct. 19th/20th AAA On morning Oct. 19th L.D. will move one battalion to HIGH WOOD area and one battalion to BAZENTIN area in relief of two battalions of N.D. who will move back to MAMETZ WOOD on relief AAA On completion of this relief the two L.D. battalions will come under the orders of N.D. and the two N.D. battns. under the orders of L.D. AAA Similarly on morning Oct. 19th L.D. will move another battalion to HIGH WOOD area and another to BAZENTIN area in relief of two battns. of G.D. which on relief will move to MAMETZ WOOD AAA On completion this relief the two L.D. battns. will come under orders of G.D. and two G.D. battns. under orders of L.D. AAA On night Oct. 19th/20th L.D. will relieve N.D. and G.D. in front line and in support about FLERS line AAA On relief N.D. and G.D. will each move one battalion to HIGH WOOD area and one battalion to BAZENTIN area AAA On completion of relief on night Oct. 19th/20th B.G.C. L.D. will assume command of front with his headquarters at BAZENTIN le GRAND AAA N.D. will move his headquarters to MAMETZ AAA G.D. headquarters will remain at BAZENTIN AAA All details of relief to be arranged between Brigadiers concerned AAA Completion of relief to be wired to Div.H.Q. AAA ACKNOWLEDGE AAA

From				3rd Corps.
Place				
Time	9.25 p.m.			

SECRET.

Copy No _____

9th Division Operation Order No. 86.

16.10.16.

1. The 9th Division will attack the enemy's trenches from m.18.c.2.5. to m.17.c.0.5. on the 18th inst. in conjunction with the 50th Division which will attack the enemy's firing and support lines running S.E. from m.18.c.4.6. and m.18.c.6.8.

The 15th Division on the left will co-operate by bringing machine gun fire to bear on the BUTTE de WARLENCOURT and on the enemy's trenches E. of the BUTTE, both during the attack and during the consolidation of the position.

Their Stokes Mortars will also be in action ready to deal with any hostile machine guns about m.10.d.

2. The dividing line between the 9th and 50th Divisions will be the sunken road in m.18.c. and m.17.d. exclusive to the 9th Division.

3. The hour of Zero will be notified later.
It will be two or three hours prior to dawn.

4. The attack will be carried out by the 26th Inf. Bde. on the right and the S.African Inf. Bde. on the left.

The dividing line between the Brigades will be a line between the leading tree in the Quarry just North of the cross roads at m.23.a.9.4. and a lone tree about m.17.a.9.0. i.e. a North and South line 50 yards West of the dividing line between m.17.c. and m.17.d.

5. The attack will be preceded by an artillery barrage on the enemy's line from Zero to Zero plus 1 minute. The barrage will be intensified by a Stokes Mortar barrage which will be maintained on the enemy's trench till Zero plus 1½ minutes.

Where our trench is closest to the enemy at about m.17.d.4.2. the barrage on the enemy's trench will be entirely Stokes.

6. A smoke barrage will be arranged so as to blind the BUTTE de WARLENCOURT and the Valley between the BUTTE and LE SARS North of the line joining m.17.central and m.13.central.

7. The leading wave of the attacking infantry will form up outside their front trench under cover of darkness and will advance as close under the barrage as possible, assaulting the enemy's line as soon as the barrage lifts.

8. As soon as the line is captured the S.African Bd. will send a party up the trench running N.W. from m.17.c.4.4., and the 26th Inf. Bde. will similarly send a party up the trench running N.W. from m.17.d.2½.8½. The 26th Inf. Bde. will also co-operate with the 50th Division by enfilading with rifle and Lewis Gun fire the trench running N.E. across the sunken road from the right of their objective at m.18.c.3.5. This will however only be done provided the 26th Inf. Bde. is not delayed in attaining its objective. Should the advance of the 26th Inf. Bde. be delayed fire in this direction will not be opened unless it is clear to our infantry that the trenches East of them are still in the hands of the enemy.

The right of the 26th Bde. will not enter the sunken road which will be kept under fire by Stokes Mortars of the 50th Division.

9/

9. The enemy's line when captured will be consolidated, strong points being made:-
(a) Immediately W. of the sunken road)
(b) At trench junction M.17.d.2½.6½) 26th Inf. Bde.
(c) At trench junction M.17.c.4.4.   ) S.African Bde.

The trenches running N.W. from M.17.d.2½.6½ and M.17.c.4.4. will be blocked at about M.17.c.8.10 and M.17.c.1.8. respectively with a view to their being joined up on the following night to form a new front line.

10. Each Brigade will open up a communication trench from the present front line to the captured line, 26th Inf. Bde. about M.17.d.5.5. to 5.5, and the S.African Bde. about M.17.c.4.0. to M.17.c.4.4.

11. The following will be attached to each Brigade for the operations:-

To 26th Bde.   Half a company (60 strong) 9th Seaforths (Pioneers)
               One Section 63rd Field Coy. R.E.
               A detachment of a Light Trench Mortar Battery
                 of the 15th Division with 4 guns.

To S.A. Bde.   Half a company (60 strong) 9th Seaforths (Pioneers)
               One Section 64th Field Coy. R.E.

12. Red flares will be used by the Infantry to show their positions to contact aeroplane.

13. The programme of artillery action will be issued separately.
Lieut.Col. Cape, 51st Bde. R.F.A. will act as Artillery Liaison Officer with the 26th and 1st S.African Bdes.

14. A main Divisional receiving station has been established at M.29.d.4.4. which is visible from the whole front to be attacked.
Brigades will arrange for visual communication to be established with this station from the captured line.

15. Arrangements for evacuation of wounded will be similar to those of the 12th inst.

16. 26th and S.African Bde. Headquarters will be at MAZENTIN le GRAND, S.15.b.3.5.
9th Division Headquarters will remain at FRICOURT FARM.

Lieutenant Colonel,
General Staff,
9th (Scottish) Division.

Issued at 11.30 p.m.

Copies to:-
No. 1 26th Bde.   10 C.R.E.   20 50th Division.
    2 27th Bde.   11 9/Seaforths   21 O.C.Heavy Sec.
    3 S.African Bde.   12 9th Train   M.G.C.
    4 C.R.A.   13 9/Signals.   22 25th Bde. R.F.A.
    5 50th Bde. R.F.A.   14 A.D.M.S.   23 59th Bde. R.F.A.
    6 51st Bde. R.F.A.   15 A.D.V.S.   24 O.C. 4th Spl.Coy
    7 52nd Bde. R.F.A.   16 A.P.M.   R.E.
    8 O.C.Trench Mortars 17 & 18 III Corps.   25 War Diary.
    9 9th Div. Colm.   19 15th Divn.   26 File.

"A" Form.
MESSAGES AND SIGNALS.
Army Form C. 2121.

TO { 27th Inf. Bde
S. A " "

Sender's Number	Day of Month	In reply to Number	
G.787	12.10.16		A A A

Ref para 11 of O.O. No 85 of 11th instant aaa In case it is found impracticable to establish the R.A. post at M.17.d.2.7. a post will also be established in the hollow road at M.17.d.9.1. aaa.

From 9th Division
Place
Time 6 am

(Sgd) A. E. McNamara

"A" Form. Army Form C. 2121.
MESSAGES AND SIGNALS.   No. of Message _____

Prefix .... Code .... m.	Words	Charge	This message is on a/c of :	Recd. at .... m.
Office of Origin and Service Instructions.				Date ....
	Sent			From ....
	At .... m.		.... Service.	
	To			
	By	(Signature of "Franking Officer.")	By ....

TO { Recipients of OO. 85

Sender's Number	Day of Month	In reply to Number	**AAA**
O min 20	O min 23		

From
Place
Time

The above may be forwarded as now corrected.   (Z)

Censor.   Signature of Addressor or person authorised to telegraph in his name.

* This line should be erased if not required.

SECRET.

Copy No _____

9th Division Operation Order No. 85.

11.10.16.

1.   The French and British forces will continue the attack to-morrow, 12th October.
          The 9th Division will form the left of the attack.
          Objectives.
              1st.   German line in M.17.d. and c.
              Final. German support line from junction of C.T. in
                        M.18.a.0.5. inclusive to LE SARS – BAPAUME Road
                        exclusive.

2.   Attack will be carried out by 26th Inf. Bde. on the right and S.African Bde. on the left.
          Dividing line. – From S.African Post at M.23.a.7.7. to
                            M.17.b.5.7.

3.   At Zero (hour to be named later) the leading waves will line up in the open under cover of our artillery barrage which will remain till 0 plus 3 minutes about 200 yards in front of our front line. The actual distance will vary in accordance with the proximity of the enemy trench (our 1st objective) which will be under our fire for the first three minutes. The barrage will then creep forward at the rate of 50 yards a minute till it is about 200 yards beyond the 1st objective.
          From there it will again creep forward at 0 plus 20 minutes at the same rate until it reaches about 200 yards beyond our final objective.

4.   It is essential that our assaulting infantry shall keep up as close as possible to our own barrage.

5.   Consolidation.
          (a) The BUTTE de WARLENCOURT must be denied to the enemy.

          (b) The final objective will be held by means of machine
                guns and Lewis guns and as thinly as possible as
                regards garrison.

          (c) Our main consolidation will be just S. of the crest of
                the BUTTE SPUR, so as to avoid direct land observation
                on the enemy's part from the LOUPART WOOD high ground.
                The S.African Brigade will swing their left back from
                about M.17.central to join the valley about M.17.c.5.6.
                so as to get cover from the N.W.

          (d) 26th Inf. Bde. will place machine guns to cover –
                (1) the W. face of the spur running from
                      M.18.central to LE BARQUE and
                (2) the W. face of the spur running N. between
                      M.12.c. and M.11.d.,   and
                (3) The E. face of the spur running N.W. from
                      M.17.b.5.7, and
                (4) the N. face of BUTTE Spur.

(e)

(e) S.African Bde. will -
  (1) place machine guns to cover the W. face of the Spur running N.W. from M.17.b.5.7. and
  (2) will place stops to prevent enemy counter attacks up his trenches on the N.W. face of the BUTTE Spur, and
  (3) will place Trench Mortars to cover the BUTTE from S. and E.

(f) Communication Trenches will be made up to our final objective -
  (1) By 26th Inf. Bde. in M.17.d.
  (2) By S.African Bde. in M.17.a. and c.
One company of Pioneers will be attached to each Brigade for this duty.

(g) The exact positions selected for above works to be reported by Brigades to each other and to Divisional Headquarters.

6. Simultaneously with our attack the 15th Division on our left will attack an enemy strong point in Valley near M.16.b.6.3.

7. The 15th Division will arrange for a smoke screen to be maintained on the enemy's positions between LE SARS and WARLENCOURT from Zero to 0 plus 45.
The BUTTE will be kept under smoke by them until our leading Infantry are approaching it about 0 plus 28.

8. A contact aeroplane will fly over the trenches at one hour after Zero and the advanced Infantry will light yellow flares in reply to the aeroplanes signals.

9. All infantry are reminded that next to gaining their own objective their duty is to assist their neighbours to gain theirs.

10. The 26th Inf. Bde. will gain touch with the 30th Division on their right, and the S.African Bde. with the 15th Division on their left by establishing a post in the neighbourhood of road junction M.18.b.9.0.

11. The programme of artillery action is being issued separately.
Lieut. Col. E.C.Massy, 255th Bde. R.F.A. will act as Artillery liaison officer with the 26th and 1st S.African Bdes.
F.O.Os. will be established as early as possible on the final objectives to deal with targets to the North and West.
The R.A. will also establish a post for connection with Infantry at about trench junction M.17.d.2.7.

12. Visual signalling will be established by both the 26th and S.African Bdes.

13. The 63rd Field Coy. R.E. (less 2 sections) will be under the command of the 26th Inf. Bde.
The 84th Field Coy. R.E. (less 2 sections) will be under the command of the S.African Brigade.

14. The Divisional reserve will consist of -
  27th Inf. Bde.
  9th Seaforths (Pioneers) less 2 Coys.
  90th Fld.Coy. R.E. and 2 sections each of the 63rd and 84th Fld.Coys.

5.

15. The line of evacuation for wounded in from collecting post at EAUCOURT L'ABBAYE by railway to W. of HIGH WOOD, thence by Ambulance to Advanced Dressing Station at BAZENTIN LE PETIT.
Walking wounded will be directed along this route.

16. Brigades will submit situation reports to the Division at every clock hour after Zero.

17. Correct time will be distributed to representatives of Infantry and Artillery Brigades and Heavy Artillery Groups by a member of the III Corps Staff at VILLA WOOD, X.12.c.5.7. at 6 hours before Zero.

18. Brigade Headquarters will be at the following places:-
    26th Inf. Bde.   BAZENTIN LE GRAND, S.15.b.5.5.
    1st S.A.Bde.   do   do
    27th Inf. Bde.   X.30.a.5.8.
9th Division Headquarters will remain at FRICOURT FARM.
The Headquarters of Brigades on either flank of the 9th Division are situated as follows:-
    89th I.Bde. of 30th Division at M.30.c.5.1.
    44th I.Bde. of 15th Division at M.27.c.5.0.

                                  Stewart
                                  Lieutenant Colonel,
                                  General Staff,
Issued at 5 p.m.   9th (Scottish) Division.

    Copies to:-
      No. 1 to 26th Inf. Bde.
         2 to 27th Inf. Bde.
         3 to 1st S.African Bde.
         4 to C.R.A. 9th Divn.
      5 - 10 to C.R.A. 47th Divn.
        11 to C.R.E.
        12 to 9th Seaforths.
        13 to 9th Div. Train.
        14 to 9th Signals.
        15 to A.A. & Q.M.G.
        16 to A.D.M.S.
        17 to A.D.V.S.
        18 to A.P.M.
        19 to III Corps.
        20 to   do
        21 to 15th Divn.
        22 to 30th Divn.
        23 to War Diary.
        24 to File.

SECRET.

Copy No _____

9th Division Operation Order No. 85.

11.10.16.

1.   The French and British forces will continue the attack to-morrow, 12th October.
    The 9th Division will form the left of the attack.
    Objectives.
    1st.   German line in M.17.d. and c.
    Final.   German support line from junction of C.T. in M.18.a.0.5. inclusive to LE SARS - BAPAUME Road exclusive.

2.   Attack will be carried out by 26th Inf. Bde. on the right and S.African Bde. on the left.
    Dividing line. - From S.African Post at M.23.a.7.7. to M.17.b.5.7.

3.   At Zero (hour to be named later) the leading waves will line up in the open under cover of our artillery barrage which will remain till 0 plus 3 minutes about 200 yards in front of our front line. The actual distance will vary in accordance with the proximity of the enemy trench (our 1st objective) which will be under our fire for the first three minutes. The barrage will then creep forward at the rate of 50 yards a minute till it is about 200 yards beyond the 1st objective.
    From there it will again creep forward at 0 plus 23 minutes at the same rate until it reaches about 200 yards beyond our final objective.

4.   It is essential that our assaulting infantry shall keep as close as possible to our own barrage.

5.   **Consolidation.**
    (a)   The BUTTE de WARLENCOURT must be denied to the enemy.

    (b)   The final objective will be held by means of machine guns and Lewis guns and as thinly as possible as regards garrison.

    (c)   Our main consolidation will be just S. of the crest of the BUTTE SPUR, so as to avoid direct land observation on the enemy's part from the LOUPART WOOD high ground. The S.African Brigade will swing their left back from about M.17.central to join the valley about M.17.c.5.6. so as to get cover from the N.W.

    (d)   26th Inf. Bde. will place machine guns to cover -
        (1)   the W. face of the spur running from M.18.central to LE BARQUE and
        (2)   the W. face of the Spur running N. between M.12.c. and M.11.d., and
        (3)   The E. face of the spur running N.W. from M.17.b.5.7, and
        (4)   the N. face of BUTTE Spur.

(e)

2.

    (e) S.African Bde. will -
        (1) place machine guns to cover the W. face of the Spur running N.W. from M.17.b.5.7. and
        (2) will place stops to prevent enemy counter attacks up his trenches on the N.W. face of the BUTTE Spur, and
        (3) will place Trench Mortars to cover the BUTTE from S. and E.

    (f) Communication Trenches will be made up to our final objective -
        (1) By 26th Inf. Bde. in M.17.d.
        (2) By S.African Bde. in M.17.a. and c.
One company of Pioneers will be attached to each Brigade for this duty.

    (g) The exact positions selected for above works to be reported by Brigades to each other and to Divisional Headquarters.

6. Simultaneously with our attack the 15th Division on our left will attack an enemy strong point in Valley near M.16.b.8.5.

7. The 15th Division will arrange for a smoke screen to be maintained on the enemy's positions between LE SARS and WARLENCOURT from Zero to 0 plus 45.
    The BUTTE will be kept under smoke by them until our leading Infantry are approaching it about 0 plus 28.

8. A contact aeroplane will fly over the trenches at one hour after Zero and the advanced Infantry will light yellow flares in reply to the aeroplanes signals.

9. All infantry are reminded that next to gaining their own objective their duty is to assist their neighbours to gain theirs.

10. The 26th Inf. Bde. will gain touch with the 50th Division on their right, and the S.African Bde. with the 15th Division on their left by establishing a post in the neighbourhood of road junction M.18.b.9.0.

11. The programme of artillery action is being issued separately.
    Lieut. Col. E.C.Massey, 255th Bde. R.F.A. will act as Artillery liaison officer with the 23th and 1st S.African Bdes.
    F.O.Os. will be established as early as possible on the final objectives to deal with targets to the North and West.
    The R.A. will also establish a post for connection with Infantry at about trench junction M.17.d.2.7.

12. Visual signalling will be established by both the 26th and S.African Bdes.

13. The 63rd Field Coy. R.E. (less 2 sections) will be under the command of the 26th Inf. Bde.
    The 64th Field Coy. R.E. (less 2 sections) will be under the command of the S.African Brigade.

14. The Divisional reserve will consist of -
    27th Inf. Bde.
    9th Seaforths (Pioneers) less 2 Coys.
    90th Fld.Coy. R.E. and 2 sections each of the 63rd and 64th Fld.Coys.

15. The line of evacuation for wounded in from collecting post at EAUCOURT L'ABBAYE by railway to W. of HIGH WOOD, thence by Ambulance to Advanced Dressing Station at BAZENTIN LE PETIT.
Walking wounded will be directed along this route.

16. Brigades will submit situation reports to the Division at every clock hour after Zero.

17. Correct time will be distributed to representatives of Infantry and Artillery Brigades and Heavy Artillery Groups by a member of the III Corps Staff at VILLA WOOD, X.12.c.5.7. at 6 hours before Zero.

18. Brigade Headquarters will be at the following places:-
    26th Inf. Bde.   BAZENTIN LE GRAND, S.15.b.5.5.
    1st S.A.Bde.   do   do
    27th Inf. Bde.   X.30.a.5.8.
9th Division Headquarters will remain at FRICOURT FARM.
    The Headquarters of Brigades on either flank of the
9th Division are situated as follows:-
    89th I.Bde. of 30th Division at M.30.c.5.1.
    44th I.Bde. of 15th Division at M.27.c.5.0.

Stewart
Lieutenant Colonel,
General Staff,
9th (Scottish) Division.

Issued at 5 p.m.

Copies to:-
    No. 1 to 26th Inf. Bde.
        2 to 27th Inf. Bde.
        3 to 1st S.African Bde.
        4 to C.R.A. 9th Divn.
     5 - 10 to C.R.A. 47th Divn.
        11 to C.R.E.
        12 to 9th Seaforths.
        13 to 9th Div. Train.
        14 to 9th Signals.
        15 to A.A. & Q.M.G.
        16 to A.D.M.S.
        17 to A.D.V.S.
        18 to A.P.M.
        19 to III Corps.
        20 to   do
        21 to 15th Divn.
        22 to 30th Divn.
        23 to War Diary.
        24 to File.

Scheme J.

16th Bde. Operation Orders

"C" Form (Original).
MESSAGES AND SIGNALS.

Army Form C. 2123.
(In books of 50's in duplicate.)

No. of Message ....

Prefix...... Code...... Words......	Received From...... Ma	Sent, or sent out At......m. To...... By......	Office Stamp.
Charges to collect	By......		
Service Instructions.			

Handed in at ...... Office 4.20 p.m. Received ...... m.

TO TA

*Sender's Number	Day of Month	In reply to Number	AAA
26/1344	17/10		

Reference	RO49	para	6	line
9	should	read	FLERS	LINE
South	and	DROP	ALLEY	aaa
Last	line	to	read	C?
no	2	aaa	para	7
sub	2	for	ASH	read
BW				

FROM PLACE & TIME Ma 4.7 pm

*This line should be erased if not required.

SECRET.   Copy No......1....

26th INFANTRY BRIGADE, OPERATION ORDER No. 49.

1.   The Brigade will attack on the 18th October at zero hour, with 21st Brigade, 30th Division on the right and S.A. Brigade on the left.

2.   OBJECTIVES.

   9th Division. Hostile line M.18.c.2.5 to M.17.c.0.3.

   30th Division. Hostile firing and support lines running south east from M.18.c.4.6 and M.18.c.6.8.

3.   FRONTAGE OF ATTACK FOR 26th BRIGADE.

   Between the sunken road running from M.17.d.7.0 to M.18.c.2.5 exclusive, and a line running from the bending tree in the quarry just north of the cross roads at M.23.a.9.4 to alone tree about M.17.a.9.0, that is a north and south line 50 yards west of the dividing line between M.17.c. and M.17.d.

4.   DISPOSITIONS.

   (1). 5th Camerons will attack in 4 waves, having 4 Coys in line each on a one platoon frontage.

   (2). One Coy., 8th Black Watch will be in support to and under the orders of the 5th Camerons.

   Brigade Reserve. 8th Black Watch, less One Coy., 10th A. & S. H. and 7th Seaforths.

   (3). Vickers Guns. One section to advance with 4th wave of 5th Camerons. One section to hold original front and support lines. 2 Sections Brigade Reserve.

   (4). 26th T.M.Batty, to form a barrage from present front and support lines and on the objective being captured to be ready to cover the front of it from original front line.

   6 Guns. (5). 27th T.M.Batty.) To assist in forming the initial
   3 Guns.   44th T.M.Batty.) barrage and to be withdrawn at first opportunity on objective being gained.

5.   DIRECTION OF ATTACK, for right Company about 55 degrees magnetic bearing. The remaining 3 Companies magnetic north.

6.   PRELIMINARY DISPOSITIONS.

   5th Camerons, 8 Platoons in front line, 8 platoons in support line. The leading waves of attacking Infantry will form up outside their own front trench under cover of darkness parallel to their objective. Headquarters at about M.23.d.5.9.
   One Coy., 8th Black Watch in C.T. No. 3.
   8th Black Watch, less one Coy., in FLERS LINE and FLERS SWITCH. Headquarters at M.29.b.1.2.
   10th A. & S. H. in FLERS LINE south AND DROP ALLEY, Headquarters at STARFISH M.35.c.6.5.
   7th Seaforths, east of HIGH WOOD.
   26th M.G.Coy., 2 sections front and support line, one section FLERS SWITCH, one section FLERS LINE.
   26th T.M.Batty, front and support line.
   Attached troops.) 63rd R.E., 1 section in Flers line
) with 8th Black Watch.
                   9th Seaforths, Pioneers, ½ Coy., 60 men in C.T. No. 2

(2)

7. **TASKS.**

(i) **5th Camerons**
(a) Capture objective. Gain touch with units on flanks.

(b) 5th Camerons will co-operate with 21st Brigade by enfilading with rifle and Lewis gun fire up to zero + 15 the trench running north east across the Sunken Road from the right of the objective M.18.c.3.5.. This will however only be done providing 26th Infantry Brigade is not delayed in obtaining its objective. Should the advance of the 26th Infantry Brigade be delayed, fire in this direction will not be opened unless it is clear to our infantry that the trenches east of them are in the hands of the enemy. At zero + 15 the heavies will lift from the vicinity of M.18.c.3.5.. Bombers will be pushed forward to gain touch with 21st Brigade.
The Sunken Road will be kept under fire of the Stokes Mortars of the 30th Division.

(c) On objective being gained the 5th Camerons will send a party up the trench running north west from M.17.d.2½.6½. to form a block if this trench still exists at about M.17.c.8.10. This block will be joined up later with a block of the South African Brigade at M.17.c.1.8..

(d) A party will also be sent up a new trench running paralell to the trench in para.7.(i)(c) to clear it and form a block.

(e) Consolidate objectives. The hostile trench itself should be avoided in consolidating. "T" heads constructed about 40 yards in front. Supports being dug in on the south side and under enemy's parapet.

(f) Strong points to be constructed north of the hostile line immediately west of the Sunken Road and near trench junction M.17.d.2½.6½.

(g) South African Brigade will construct strong point at M.17.c.4.4..

(ii) **10th A. & S.Hrs.**
(a) One company under 5th Camerons to hold original line, and be ready to reinforce and counter-attack.
(b) Three companies Brigade Reserve. O.C. Battalion is free to send forward these companies to assist 5th Camerons if required.

(iii) **9th Seaforths (Pioneers)**
(a) Half company 60 strong to dig communication trench from about M.17.d.5.3. to M.17.d.5.5. as soon as possible. It is essential to join up our old line and the objective, although full depth of the trench may not at first be obtained.

(iiii) **Machine Gun Company.**
(a) 4 Guns to work in pairs (one officer to each pair) from positions about the two strong points (para.7.(i)(f).) and 17.d.5.6. and the new trench in para.7.(i)(d).
(b) One section to hold original line.
(c) Two sections Brigade Reserve.

(v) **26th T.M.Battery**
(a) Form a barrage on objective from zero to zero + 2.
(b) Two guns to fire on M.18.c.2.5. from zero + 2, five rounds per gun.
(c) Two guns to fire 100 yards north west of trench junction M.17.d.2½.6½. from zero + 2 to zero + 5..
(d) On objective being gained defensive positions will be taken up covering it from our present front line.
(e) As soon as possible one Stokes gun to be pushed forward towards the right of our objective to fire on the GIRD LINE. O.C., 5th Camerons to give the order.

7.   (6). Tasks 1.1. One section to detail Sappers to assist 2 blocking parties and to assist in the wiring of the objective when gained; the latter Sappers to move with the 4th wave, remainder in reserve, except blockers who move with the attack.

8.   ARTILLERY, will barrage the hostile front line from zero to zero plus one.   Barrage will be intensified by Stokes Mortar barrage which will be maintained until zero plus 2.. See para 7 (5).   At zero plus 2 Artillery will lift 200 yards by creeps of 50 Yards.
(2). It is essential that our assaulting Infantry keep as close as possible to their own barrage, therefore the distance between waves should be about 30 yards.
(3). The S.O.S. Signal is 3 Red Very Lights.
(4). One Red Very Light will be sent up by the Infantry when they require the artillery to lift to establish blocks in the trench running north west from M.17.d.2½.6½ and in the new trench to the west of it.
(5). Green Very Lights if fired may lead the enemy to lift his barrage and should be so employed.

9.   RE-DISTRIBUTION.   On completion of work Pioneers will return to their original positions in BAZENTIN LE GRAND.

10.   COMMUNICATIONS.   The main Divisional Receiving Station has been established at M.29.d.4.4.
Visual and telephone stations M.17.d.5.1 - M.29.d.5.4.
S.5.c.1.3.   Telephone Station - Headquarters front Battalion.
M.23.d.5.9.

11.   MEDICAL ARRANGEMENTS.   Line of evacuation for wounded is from collecting post in EAUCOURT L'ABBE by rail to west of HIGH WOOD, thence by ambulance to advanced DRESSING STATION BAZENTIN LE PETIT.   Walking wounded to be directed along this road.
27th Field Ambulance Dressing Station also at M.28.d.7.1.

12.   DUMPS. (1). Brigade Dump at COUGH DROP at about M.35.a.8.2
(2). Advanced Dump at Junction FLERS SWITCH and LINE M.29.b.1.2.

13.   FLARES. Red Flares will be used by the Infantry to show their position to Contact aeroplane which will fly over as soon as light permits.

14.   PRISONERS OF WAR, to be sent under escort of 15% to BAZENTIN LE PETIT to A.P.M. 9th Division.

15.   SITUATION REPORTS, to be sent as frequently as possible.

16.   WATCHES, will be synchronised under Brigade arrangements.

17.   CO-OPERATION,   When objectives have been gained if assistance is required it should be given at once to Units on either flank.
(2). A Smoke barrage will be arranged to blind the BUTTE and the valley between the BUTTE and LA SARS.

18.   BRIGADE HEADQUARTERS   BAZENTIN LE GRAND with Advanced Station at S.E. corner HIGH WOOD.

19.   ACKNOWLEDGE.

JSDrew. Major,
Brigade Major,
26th Infantry Brigade.

17:10:16.

Copy No. 1. 9th Division.   8. 63rd R.E.
        2. 8th Black Watch.   9. 9th Seaforths Pioneers.
        3. 7th Seaforths.   10.   "   "
        4. 5th Camerons.   11. 27th Field Ambulance.
        5. 10th A. & S. H.   12. C.R.E.
        6. 26th M. G. Co.   13. C.R.A.
        7. 26th T. M. Batty.   14. 21st Brigade.
                                15. S.A.I.B.
                                16. 27th Bde.

Scheme I

SECRET.   Copy No. 1.

26th Infantry Brigade, Operation Order No. 48.
----

1. The Brigade will attack on the 12th October, 1916 at zero hour, with 89th Brigade, 30th Division on the right and S.A.Brigade on the left.

2. OBJECTIVES.

    First. Hostile line M.17.d.10.4 - M.17.c.9½.5.

    Second. Hostile Line M.17.b.9½.0 - M.17.b.2.4.

    Third. M.18.a.½.3 - M.17.b.3.7.

3. DISPOSITIONS.

    (1). 7th Seaforths will attack in 4 waves having 2 Companies in line, each on a 2 platoon front.

    (11). 10th A. & S. H. will support the attack with 2 Companies, keeping 2 Companies in Reserve.

    BRIGADE RESERVE. 5th Camerons and 8th Black Watch.

    (111). VICKERS GUNS. One section to advance in rear of 7th Seaforths. One section to advance in rear of the 2 supporting companies 10th A. & S. Hldrs.
    One section to hold original front and support lines.
    One section Brigade Reserve.

    (1V). 26th T.M.Batty. 4 Guns to advance in rear of supporting companies 10th A. & S. H., as far as first objective.
    4 Guns to be in Brigade Reserve.

4. FRONTAGE OF ATTACK, will be between the xxxxxx line M.17.d.8.0 - M.18.a.1.3 and - M.23.a.7.7 and M.17.b.3.7.

5. ~~DIRECTION OF ATTACK~~, 22½ degrees magnetic bearing.

6. PRELIMINARY DISPOSITIONS. 7th Seaforths, 2 Companies front line, 2 Companies support line, Headquarters about M.23.b.6.9.

    10th A. & S. H., 2 Companies in Communication Trenches between front and support lines, one Company FLERS LINE, One Company FLERS SWITCH, Headquarters about M.29.b.2.2.

        5th Camerons.   FLERS LINE and DROP ALLEY and H.Q. at
                         STARFISH (M.35.c.6.5.).
        8th Black Watch. East of HIGH WOOD.
        26th M. G.Coy., 2 sections front and support lines.
                         One section FLERS SWITCH.
                         One section FLERS LINE.
        26th T.M.Batty. 4 Mortars front and support line.
                         4 Mortars FLERS LINE.

    Attached (63rd Field Co. R.E. 2 sections in FLERS LINE.
    Troops. (9th Seaforths (Pioneers) One Company at Head of 5th Camerons in FLERS LINE.

7. **TASKS.** 7th Seaforths.
(1) (a). First two waves to take first objective where they will be until O+23 in order to allow the Brigade attacking on our right to get up into line.   see para 8.

(b). Second two waves supported by the first two to attack and consolidate the second and third objectives.

(c). Second objective to be held by one platoon and 3 Lewis Guns.

(d). Third objective to be held by 4 Vickers and One Lewis Gun and one battle section.

(e). Patrols to be pushed forward as soon as possible.

(ll) (a). 10th A. & S. H. to clear first objective.
(b). Closely support with 2 waves 7th Seaforths attack on second and third objectives. (c). 4 Lewis Guns to hold original front line and to be reinforced by one Reserve Company, as soon as possible.
(d). One Company with 2 sections R.E. to push forward at first opportunity and dig line of resistance just south of the CREST of BUTTE SPUR M.17.d. so as to avoid direct observation from LOUPART WOOD, finally joining up with Brigade on left.

(lll). 9th Seaforths to dig communication trench from M.17.d.7.1 to M.17.b.8.1 at first opportunity.

(lV). Machine Gun Coy. Four Guns, to be placed in pairs (One Officer to each pair) in positions about M.17.b.8.4 and M.17.b.3.8 to cover west face of SPUR running from M.18.Central to LE BARQUE and west face of SPUR running north between M.12.c. and M.11.d. The east face of SPUR running N.W. from M.17.b.5.7 and the north face of BUTTE SPUR.
One section to hold main line of resistance.
One section to hold original front and support lines.

(V). (a). Trench Mortars. 2 Guns to be ready to cover the right and 2 the left flank. (b). Be ready to advance to support the Infantry attack if required, but do not push further forward than necessary. (c). Take up defensive positions about the first objective ready to deal with counter attacks and finally to main line of resistance.

8. **ARTILLERY.** (1).

At zero hour the leading waves will line up in the open under our Artillery Barrage which will remain until O+3 about 200 yards in front of our front line.   The barrage will then creep forward at the rate of 50 yards per minute till it is about 200 yards beyond first objective, from there it will again creep forward from O+23 minutes at the same rate until it reaches about 200 yards beyond our final objective.

(ll). It is essential that our assaulting Infantry keep as close as possible to their own barrage.

9. **RE-DISTRIBUTION.**

(l). When 7th Seaforths have consolidated second and third objectives as ordered, and the Vickers Guns have been dug in, the Infantry not required for garrison will be systematically withdrawn to the main line of resistance, and to our original front line taking over from 10th A. & S. H. who will withdraw to original support line and FLERS LINE.

(ll). On completion of work R.E. and Pioneers will return to their original positions south of HIGH WOOD and vicinity of BAZENTIN respectively.

Para 18.

The BUTTE will be kept under smoke by them until SA. leading Infantry are approaching it about 0 plus 28.

3.

10. **CONNECTING POST.**

The R.A. will also establish a post for connection with Infantry at about Trench Junction M.17.d.2.7 and at M.23.b.6.9 vicinity.

11. **MEDICAL ARRANGEMENTS.**

Line of evacuation for wounded is from collecting post at EAUCOURT L'ABBE by rail to west of HIGH WOOD thence by Ambulance to advanced dressing Station at BAZENTIN-LE-PETIT. Walking wounded to be directed along this road.

27th Field Ambulance dressing station also at M.28.d.7.1.

12. **DUMPS.** (1). Brigade Dump at COUGH DROP about M.35.a.8.2
(2). Advanced dump will be formed at junction of FLERS SWITCH and FLERS LINE M.29.b.1.2.

13. A contact aeroplane will fly over the trenches at one hour after zero, the advanced Infantry will light flares in reply to Aeroplane signals (see instructions ref. communication with aircraft).

14. **PRISONERS OF WAR,** will be sent down under escort of 15% to BAZENTIN-LE-PETIT and there handed over to A.P.M. 9th Division, the escorts rejoining their units at once.

15. **SITUATION REPORTS.** Situation reports will be sent in as frequently as possible.

16. **WATCHES.**, will be synchronised under Brigade arrangements.

17. **COMMUNICATIONS.** Visual and telephone stations; M.23.b.6.9.
(advanced Battalion Headquarters).
M.29.d.5.4. - S.4.c.1.3.
Police Posts. 5th Camerons will supply Police posts at following junctions.   FLERS SWITCH - FLERS LINE. M.29.b.1.2.
FLERS SWITCH and WILLOW ROAD M.29.a.2.3.

18. **CO-OPERATION.** (1). When objectives have been gained if required assistance should at once be given to the Brigades on our right and left. (11). The 15th Division will arrange for a smoke screen to be maintained on the enemy's positions between LE SARS and WARLENCOURT from zero to 0 plus 28. 45.

19. **BRIGADE HEADQUARTERS,** will be at BAZENTIN-LE-GRAND with advanced station at South East corner HIGH WOOD.

20. ACKNOWLEDGE.

                                 JSDrew Major,
                                 Brigade Major,
12:10:16.   26th Infantry Brigade.

Copy No. 1. 9th Divn.   10. 27th Field Ambn.
2. 8th Black Watch.   11. C.R.E.
3. 7th Seaforths.   12. C.R.A.
4. 5th Camerons.   13. 89th Infantry Brigade.
5. 10th A. & S. H.   14. S.A. Infantry Brigade.
6. 26th M. G. Coy.   15. 6 extra Copies.
7. 26th T.M. Batty.
8. 63rd Field Co. R.E.
9. 9th Seaforths (2 Copies).

W. 15517—M. 141. 250,000. 1/16. L.S.&Co. Forms/W 3091/2.   Army Form W. 3091.

SECRET

Cover for Documents.

Nature of Enclosures.

Scheme J

Notes, or Letters written.

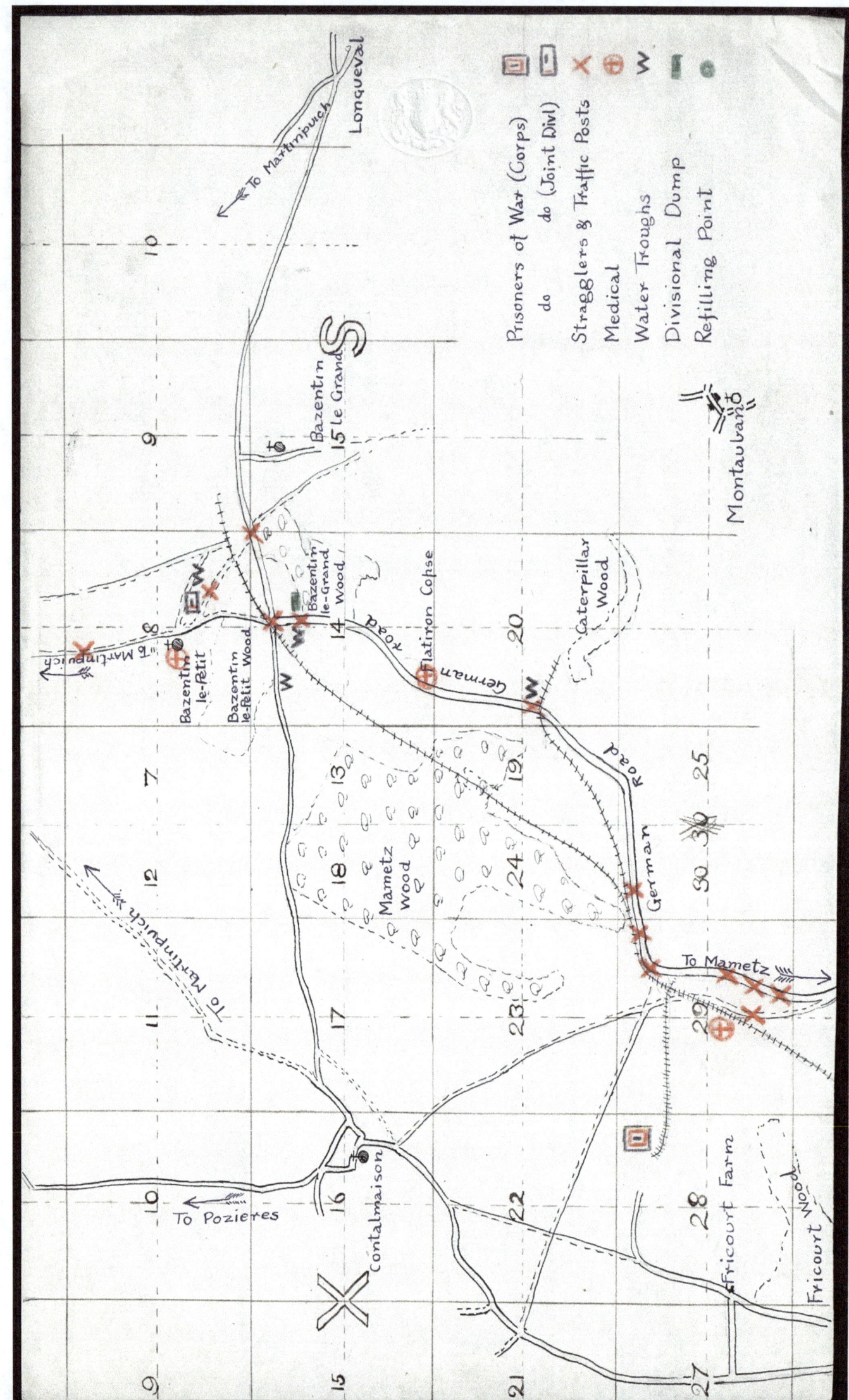

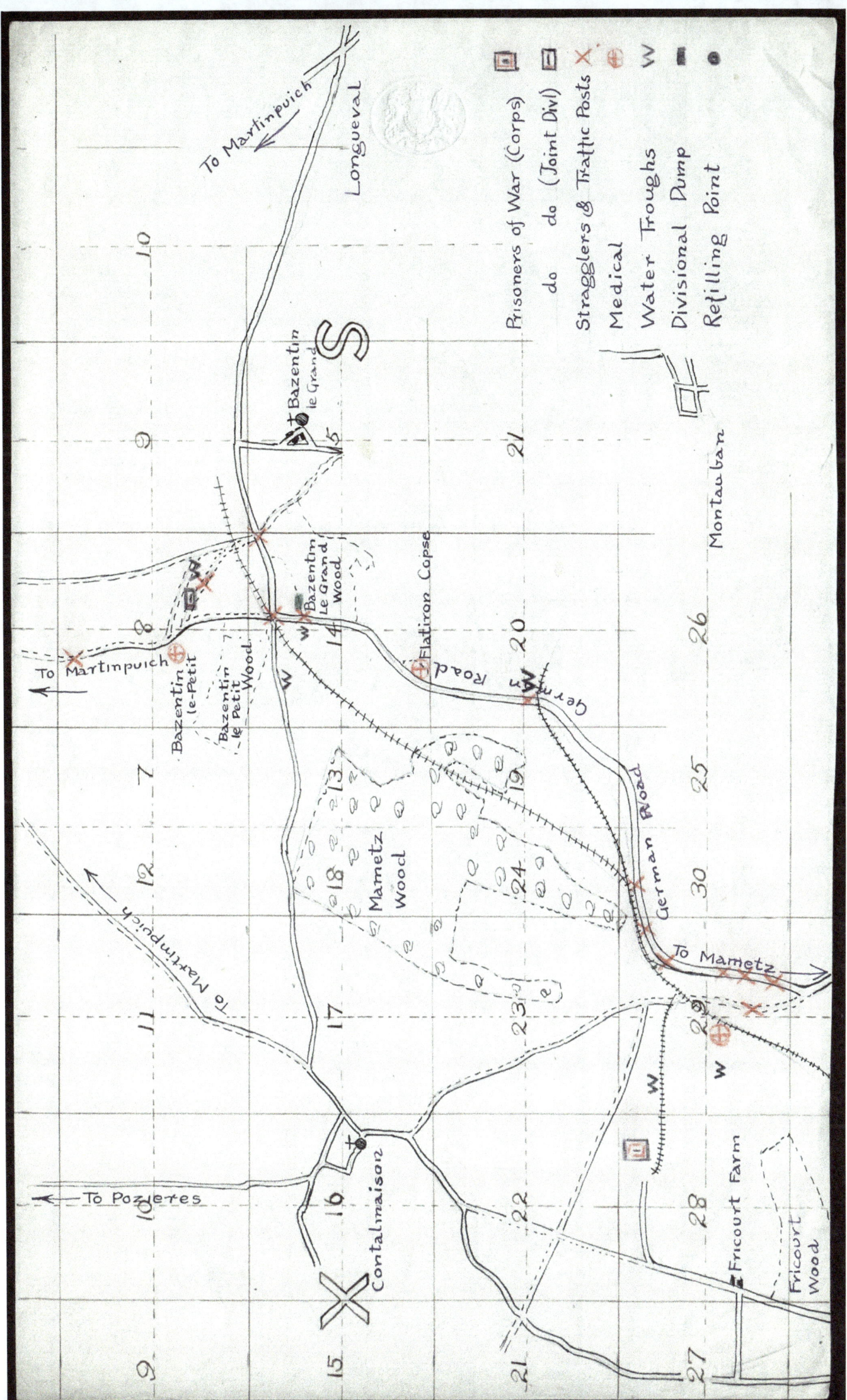

SECRET.

15th Division No. 100(1)/11 G.a.

46th Inf. Bde.

To Inf. Bdes.
& Left Gp.
D.A. only.

Reference 15th Division No. 100/11 G.a.# dated 15.10.16.

The following is an advance copy of a para. which will be included in an Operation Order regarding the co-operation of the Division with the attack of the 9th Division on the 18th inst. (early morning):-

"(1). If the wind is favourable No. 4 Special Company R.E. will place a smoke barrage with the object of -
    (a). blinding the BUTTE de WARLENCOURT and preventing aimed enemy machine gun fire from M.10.c. and d. and M.16.b. being brought to bear on the attacking troops.
    (b). Blinding the WARLENCOURT LINE on the 15th Divisional front to induce the enemy to expect an attack by the 15th Division.

(2). The O.C. Company will place -
    (a). 4 guns in M.16.c. and d. which will drop bombs at varying heights on the slopes in M.17.a., in the bottom in M.16.b. and on the slopes in M.16.a. north east and in M.10.c.9.0. and north east of that point. The cloud is to be thick and at suitable points lachrymatory bombs are to be added to it.
    (b). 3 guns about M.16.a.2.7. to barrage from M.10.d.9.0. to M.9.b.5.0.

(3). Fire to open at zero and to continue for 45 minutes.

(4). No. 4 Special Company R.E. will decide if the wind is favourable for the operation or not.
    Under no circumstances are smoke or lachrymatory bombs to be thrown in such a position as to admit of smoke going south of a line through M.18. - 17 central. - M.16.b.7.0. - M.15.b.1.8. to CHALK PIT.

(5). The 46th Infantry Brigade will assist the Officer Commanding Special Company in every possible way."

                                                    Lieut. Colonel,

16th October, 1916.   General Staff, 15th Division.

Copy to - 44th Inf. Bde.   )
          46th Inf. Bde.   )
          Left Group D.A.   ) For information.
          No.4 Spec.Coy. R.E.)
          9th Division.   )

Secret BM0 20

9th Division

The attached sketch map shows the dividing line agreed on between S.A.I. 2nd Bde and myself. There is an excellent landmark in the shape of a single black tree which is visible from almost any portion of our trenches. Although this is some 50 yards to the west of M 17 central it forms a first rate directing mark and is due north from a single bending tree in the quarry just north of the cross roads at 23 A 9 3

15.10.16   H. _____
             Brigadier General
             Comdg 1st SAI Bde

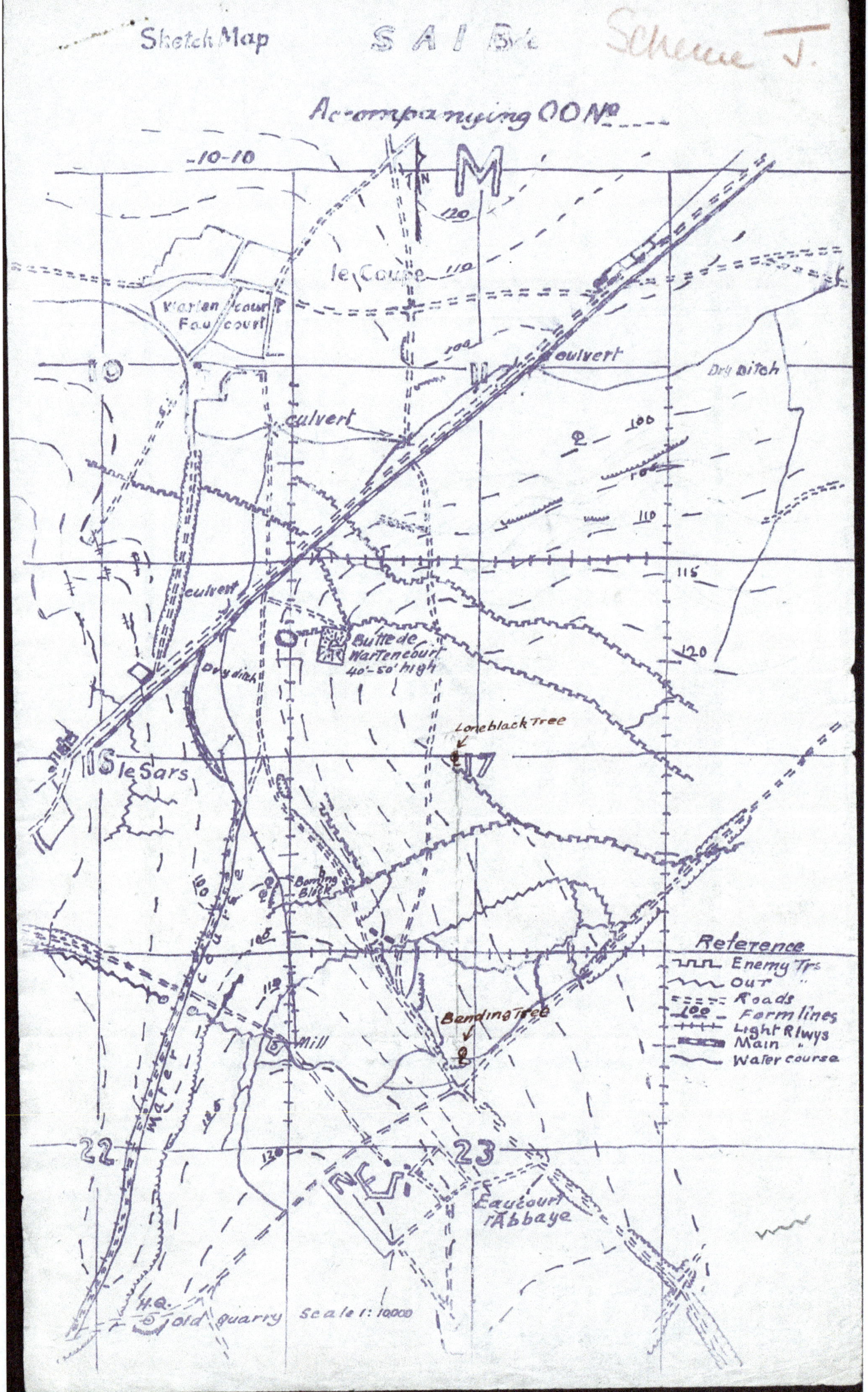
Sketch Map
S A I Bde
Scheme J.
Accompanying O O No ----
M
N
-10-10
120
110
le Coupe
Warlencourt
Faucourt
10
11
100
culvert
culvert
Dry Ditch
culvert
115
120
O
Butte de Warlencourt 40'-50' high
Dry ditch
Lone black Tree
17
S le Sars
Bombing Block
Reference
Enemy Trs
Our "
Roads
100 Form lines
Light Rlwys
Main "
Water course
Bending Tree
Mill
Water course
22
23
125
120
Eaucourt l'Abbaye
H.Q.
5 old quarry
Scale 1: 10000

SECRET.
....
Copy No. 6..

ADDENDUM NO. 1

to

III CORPS OPERATION ORDER NO. 147.   17/10/16.
....

1. ZERO hour will be 3.40 a.m. on the 18th October.

2. A Contact Patrol aeroplane will fly over the front as soon as the light permits. RED flares will be shown by the advanced infantry in reply to the aeroplane signals.

3. Correct time will be distributed to representatives of Infantry and Artillery Brigades and H.A. Groups by a member of 3rd Corps Staff at BAZENTIN-LE-GRAND at 9 p.m. 17th October.

4. ACKNOWLEDGE BY WIRE.

Brigadier-General,
General Staff,
III Corps.

Issued by D.R. at 8.15 a.m.

To all recipients of O.O. 147
    Minus copies 17 and 18.

Done

No 4. Special Company, R.E.

Report on Operations 18.10.1916.

Serial No. 04
Report: 20.
British Front: COURCELETTE to FLERS.
Ry. Map.
Zero Time: 3.40 A.M.

Section and Subsection	Corps & Divn. to which attached	Map Reference	No. of guns in emplacements and spares	Purpose of Operation	Nature of Ammunition	No. of rounds allotted to be fired.	No. of rounds fired.	Reason for Discrepancy (if any)	Casualties Names of Officers Number of Other Ranks	Remarks	Names of Officers i/c operations
"N" Section 3) Subsection	III Corps. 15th Division	M.16.6. and d.	4.	1. Blinding the BUTTE de WARLENCOURT. 2. Preventing observed enemy machine-gun fire from M.16.6. being brought to bear on the attacking troops of the 9th Divn. in the assault on the enemy trenches in M.17.c and M.17.A. 3. In hop lachrymatory bombs in the vicinity of the BUTTE de WARLENCOURT, with the object of causing discomfort and confusion to the enemy.	Smoke and S.K.	120 Smoke, 20 S.K.	137.	3 Rounds shot out of line, owing probably to the extreme net having been affected by the weather.	Nil.	The purpose of the barrage was apparently attained, as reports show that machine gun fire or being barraged position was nil. The barrage was to have been maintained for 145 minutes, but owing to the presence of a very strong wind, it was found impossible to establish a strong smoke-curtain for the whole of this prescribed 145 minutes, but a very efficient barrage was retained for 55 minutes. Considering the extremely bad weather conditions the performance of the detachment is extremely creditable. A copy of this report has been forwarded to 3rd Corps.	2nd Lt. J.E. BENTLEY. Lt. H.G. WISDOM.

15th Division
O.C. 5p. Coy R.E.
A.E. Kent Capt,
O.C., No. 4. Spec. Coy., R.E.

No 4. Special Company, R.E.
Report on Operations 18.10.1916.

Zero Time: 3.40 A.M.

Serial No. of Report	Ref. Map. British Front from COURCELETTE to FLERS	Section and Subsection	Corps & Divn. to which attd.	Map Reference of emplacements	No. of guns in emplacements and spares	Purpose of Operation	Nature of Ammunition	No. of rounds allotted	No. of rounds fired.	Reason for Discrepancy (if any)	Casualties Names of Officers Number of Other Ranks	Remarks	Names of officers i/c operations
a		"N" Section 39 Sub-Section	III Corps. 15th Division	In our trenches — SW9 M 16.a	3.	1. To prevent observed enemy machine gun fire from M.10.C and d. being brought to bear on the retreating troops of the 9th Div. 2. To induce enemy to expect an attack by the 15th Division. 3. To cause discomfort to the enemy.	Livens and S.K.	100.	80 Livens 19. S.K.	1 M.G. fire.	2nd Lt. F. OATES wounded.	Duration of barrage, 44 minutes. Operation:- Successful. Although the weather conditions were extremely bad, the detachment carried out its duties in a very efficient manner. 2nd Lt. F. Oates was wounded when coming out of the trenches, but thought this disinclined himself to walk, before going to the dressing station.	2nd Lt. F. OATES. Lieut. H.G. WISDOM.

A copy of this report has been forwarded to 3rd Corps 15th Div.

A.E. Kent. Capt.,
O.C. No 4. Spec. Coy., R.E.

SECRET.

1st S.African Brigade.

No. X.5/1868/12.   17th October, 1916.

1. The G.O.C. wishes the machine guns posted on the Mound at M.16.a.9.3. to be retained at that post as part of the permanent defences of the new line when it is captured.

2. Every opportunity should also be taken to push forward other Vickers and Lewis guns for the defence of the line.

Lieutenant Colonel,
General Staff,
9th (Scottish) Division.

SECRET.

1st S.African Brigade.

No. X.5/1868/12.   17th October, 1916.

1. The G.O.C. wishes the machine guns posted on the Mound at M.16.a.9.3. to be retained at that post as part of the permanent defences of the new line when it is captured.

2. Every opportunity should also be taken to push forward other Vickers and Lewis guns for the defence of the line.

[signature]
Lieutenant Colonel,
General Staff,
9th (Scottish) Division.

SECRET.

26th Inf. Brigade.
1st S.African Bde.
15th Division.) for information.
30th Division.)

No. X.5/1868/11.   17th October, 1916.

With reference to para 4 of 9th Divisional Artillery Operation Order No. 68 of to-days date, the Signal to be given by the Infantry when they require the artillery to lift so as to establish the blocks in the two trenches running N.W. from the first objective will be ONE RED Very Light.

If the signal has to be repeated there must be an interval of at least 30 seconds between the two.

Lieutenant Colonel,
General Staff,
9th (Scottish) Division.

SECRET.

26th Inf. Brigade.
1st S.African Bde.
15th Division. } for information.
30th Division. }

No. X.5/1868/11. 17th October, 1916.

With reference to para 4 of 9th Divisional Artillery Operation Order No. 68 of to-days date, the Signal to be given by the Infantry when they require the artillery to lift so as to establish the blocks in the two trenches running N.W. from the first objective will be ONE RED Very Light.

If the signal has to be repeated there must be an interval of at least 30 seconds between the two.

Lieutenant Colonel,
General Staff,
9th (Scottish) Division.

26th Inf. Brigade.
30th Division.   } for information
C.R.A.

No. X.5/1868/10.   17th October, 1916.

With reference to para 8 of 9th Division Operation Order No. 86 of 16th inst. and para 7 of 9th Divisional Artillery Operation Order No. 68 of to-days date, when the fire of the artillery lifts off the sunken road M.18.c.4.7. at Zero plus 15 minutes, if the enemy still remains in the trench across the sunken road at M.18.c.3.5. the 26th Inf. Bde. will bomb up this trench to gain touch with the 30th Division.

R. Stewart
Lieutenant Colonel,
General Staff,
9th (Scottish) Division.

S E C R E T.

26th Infantry Brigade.
1st South African Brigade.
15th Division.
30th Division.

No. X.5/1868/9. 17th October, 1916.

A rehearsal bombardment of one minute's duration will be carried out at 4 p.m. to-day on enemy's trenches in M.17.c. and d.

Lieutenant Colonel,
General Staff,
9th (Scottish) Division.

SECRET.

26th Infantry Brigade,
1st S. African Brigade.

No. X/1868/8.   16th October, 1916.

G.O.Cs., 26th and S. African Brigades will observe the conditions of the light at 3 a.m., 4 a.m., and 5 a.m. tomorrow and will report by 7 a.m. what hour they each consider would be suitable for the attack on the morning of the 18th. Consideration should be given to the possibility of the morning of the 18th being cloudy and also to the fact that the moon will be waning.

Lieutenant Colonel,
General Staff,
9th (Scottish) Division.

III Corps.

No. X.5/1868/7.   14th October, 1916.

Reference III Corps No. G.500 of 13th inst.

1.   My desire was -

(a) To obscure the view of the enemy's machine guns which by the contours on the map would almost certainly be placed about M.10.c. firing across the valley against the S.W. face of the BUTTE de WARLENCOURT/RIDGE over which my infantry were to attack.

(b) To keep under smoke the BUTTE itself.

2.   The officer in charge of the operation, Lieut. Thomson, showed me on the map this morning where his guns were placed and where his shells had fallen.

Three mortars were placed about M.16.d.2.9., two of these fired their bombs so as to land just S.W. of the BUTTE and must have carried out thoroughly my intention B.

The third of these three mortars dropped its bombs on the BAPAUME Road about M.16.b.8.8. The smoke from this mortar with the S.Westerly wind would not have done me much good.

3.   The other two mortars placed at M.15.b.9.2. and firing Northwards may have effected my purpose A, though it is possible that the distance the smoke travelled before crossing the enemy machine gun line of fire, and the strength of the wind may have dispersed the smoke cloud somewhat too early, especially as the machine guns

would/

would be placed on considerably lower ground than the points at which these latter smoke bombs would have dropped.

4. There is no question that the short range of these Stokes Mortars affects very adversely the tactical value of these smoke bombs and considering the weight of the mortar itself, as also of the bombs one can hardly imagine a more clumsily uneconomical projector for the purpose.

We shall never have a real test of the tactical value of smoke for blinding the enemy until we are supplied with smoke shells to be fired by our Field Artillery.

Major-General,
Commanding 9th (Scottish) Division.

"A" Form.
MESSAGES AND SIGNALS.
Army Form C. 2121

TO M.A.
    C.B.

Sender's Number: G 628
Day of Month: 13
AAA

Please report soon as possible on smoke barrage employed in attack yesterday AAA Was this entirely successful or otherwise and have you any suggestions to make as to future use AAA Addressed M.A & C.B.

From T A
Time 9.20 PM

"C" Form (Duplicate).
MESSAGES AND SIGNALS.

Army Form C. 2123.
(In books of 50's in duplicate.)

No. of Message ...13.V.16...

fm CFC 44 C60
Steph

Charges to Pay £ s. d.

Office Stamp

Service Instructions.

Handed in at ....C60 (3 Corps)... Office ..5.30... m. Received ..5.38.. m.

TO 9th Div

Sender's Number	Day of Month	In reply to Number	A A A
G.500	13.		

Please report on the smoke barrage employed in the attack yesterday afternoon aaa was this entirely successful from the infantry point of view and have you any suggestions to make for similar operations in future

FROM PLACE & TIME   3rd Corps
5.25 pm

"C" Form (Duplicate). Army Form C. 2123.
MESSAGES AND SIGNALS. (In books of 50's in duplicate.)
No. of Message ....

	Charges to Pay.	Office Stamp.
Service Instructions.	£ s. d.	TA 13 X 16

Handed in at............... Office............ m. Received............ m.

TO

Sender's Number	Day of Month	In reply to Number	A A A

FROM

PLACE & TIME

Wt. 432—M487 500,000 Pads. H W V 5/16 Forms, C.2123.

"C" Form (Original).
MESSAGES AND SIGNALS.

Army Form C. 2123.
(In books of 50's in duplicate.)

No. of Message............

Prefix	Code	Words 36	Received From....	Sent, or sent out At............m. To............ By............	Office Stamp
Charges to collect			By............		
Service Instructions.					

Handed in at............ Office............m. Received............m.

TO: 1st

Sender's Number: 26/1/21 — Day of Month: 13.10 — In reply to Number: 3828 — A A A

gunners to commence about four
minutes before zero and slowly
lead by zero and action
as on alarm signal to every
the own command to fire
by vickers

FROM
PLACE & TIME

Scheme I

CONFERENCE.

Held at S.African Bde. H.Q. at 9 a.m. on
15/10/16.

G.O.C. 9th Division, G.S.O.1 and C.R.A.   ) present.
G.Os.C. Inf. Bde. and their Bde. Majors.   )

1. G.O.C. 26th Bde. states the new front trench had been dug to its junction with the S.African Bde. line but last 150 yards were too shallow yet for occupation.

2. Divisional Commander explained the operations which were to take place on 18th. The objective being the German line which formed the first objective on 12th.

3. 26th Brigade to attack on the right, S.African Bde. on left.

4. The dividing line between Brigades to be the N. and S. line through '17' from present front line Northwards, boundary South of present front line to remain as before.
   Brigadiers to select in conjunction some prominent feature near enemy's line to mark the dividing line.

5. The 26th Bde. to attack due North, through the sunken road is to form the boundary between them and the 30th Division.
   The ground between the N. and S. line joining the 26th right and the sunken road to be kept under artillery fire, till 26th reach the trench when the fire will lift and infantry will work to the right to join up with 30th.

6. 30th Division starting point will be nearly 400 yards S. of 26th starting point.

7. Two tanks allotted to the Division.
   One of these with one allotted to 30th to go up on either side of the sunken road, the other to work up the valley on the S.African Bde. front.

8. Hour of attack to be between 2 a.m. and 6 a.m.

9. S.African post at 16.c.2.6. to make slits to the S.E. for anti-bombardment purposes and for placing machine guns in to enfilade enemy's trench.
   15th Division has been asked to look out for places for machine guns for the same purpose.

10. Artillery barrage to be very short. Stokes guns to be got into position and to register. Half of 27th L.T.M. battery, to be allotted and 26th Inf. Bde. and half to S.African Bde.

11. G.O.C. considers it advisable to put companies on a narrow front.

12. Necessity for reconnaissance by all officers, and of reporting to Divisional Headquarters all suitable places for machine guns etc.

13. Clearing of battle field.

14. Lewis guns to be pushed forward to shell holes to cover the forming up of the Brigades for the attack.

15. Sniping and patrolling to be carried out energetically.

16.   Importance of using flares and ensuring supply of dry flares.

17.   C.R.A. asks for 6 air lines to be put up between Divisional Headquarters and Advanced Centre.

SECRET.

26th Infantry Brigade.
1st South African Brigade.
C.R.E.
9th Seaforths.

No.X.5/1868/6. 14th October, 1916.

1. All work on the front line must be pushed forward with the utmost energy with a view to an attack Northward at a very early date on the enemy's line which was our first objective on the 12th instant.

2. The work on the new trench about M.17.d.1.3. must be pressed on by the 26th Brigade as far as the dividing line between the 26th Brigade and South African Brigade about M.17.c.7.3.

The South African Brigade will join up their present right with the 26th Brigade at this point.

3. The South African Brigade will arrange to occupy the post at M.17.c.0.3. at dusk tonight and dig a trench from the road at M.16.d.6.1. through the post to join up with their front line about M.17.c.3.0.

Lieutenant Colonel,
General Staff,
9th (Scottish) Division.

No 4 Special C.P. Coy. R.E.

Report on Operations 12.10.1916.

Ref: Wyl. Report... **British Front:** COURCELETTE to FLERS. **Zero Time:** 2.5 pm

Serial No.	Section and Subsection	Corps & Divn. to which attd.	Map Reference	No. of guns in emplacements and spares	Purpose of Operation	Nature of Ammunition	No. of rounds allotted	No. of rounds fired	Reason for Discrepancy (if any)	Casualties Names of Officers Number of Other Ranks	Remarks	Names of Officers i/c operations
17	"F" Section 4 Coy. 4th Sect. 15th Divn.	III Corps 15th Divn.	M.16.d.7.9.	3	1. To prevent enemy machine-guns in M.10.C. and A.4. sweeping with their own fire the valley W-S. of the BUTTE de WARLENCOURT. 2. To screen the attack of the 9th Division from enemy observation in and about the BUTTE de WARLENCOURT.	S. smoke	90 87	3 mis-fires	Nil.	Wind:- S.W. The barrage was formed at Zero, lasted 45 minutes, and was very thick. It must have thoroughly obscured enemy observation from all visible points, particularly the BUTTE de WARLENCOURT.	2nd Lt. J. THOMPSON. 2nd Lt. E.N. JONES.
	"P" Section 4 Coy. 4th Sect. 15th Divn.	III Corps 15th Divn.	M.15.c.9.2.	2	1. To place a smoke barrage in front of LITTLE WOOD, to prevent enemy observation and to smother enemy fire to support the attack by the 15th Division.	smoke	40 39	1 mis-fire	Nil.	Wind:- S.W. A thoroughly good barrage was formed. Hostile artillery retaliation was rather severe, which goes to show that purpose of barrage was attained.	2nd Lt. NASH.

A copy of this report has been forwarded to _____ 3rd Division.
J.F. Curtis.
O.C. Special Coys R.E.

A.E.K Emr Capt.
O.C. No 4. Spec. Coy. R.E.

9th Division.

Points affecting the attack on 12th October 1916.

1. **Artillery point of view.**

    Preliminary bombardment insufficient and did not knock out either the infantry trenches or machine guns.

2. **Infantry point of view.**

    The cause of the advance being checked was the Machine Gun fire from front and both flanks.

3. **Barrages.**

    (a) Left Brigade reported our barrage to be very good. Right Brigade consideredcthat at times it was short but this may have been due to the enemy's barrage being mixed with ours.

    (b) Enemy's barrage was not so intense as experienced in July. It was more broken up into localities, viz:-

    > EAUCOURT l'ABBAYE.
    > Sunken Road in M.23.b.
    >   M.23.d.
    > Quarry M.23.a.9.4.
    > Valley M.22.b. and d.

4. **Direction.**

    The extent of the advance was not sufficient for any loss of direction to be felt.

5. **Forming-up and jumping-off trenches.**

    The Right Brigade only had room for 6 companies to form up and would have liked to have had room for another two.

    The advance was made in 6 waves and is reported to have been excellent as regards forming up and alignment and proximity to our own barrage.

    Had there been more trenches the remaining two companies of the second battalion would have been brought forward earlier so as to have avoided an advance through the hostile barrage.

Left

2.

Left Brigade had sufficient room and the waves, 8 in number, went over very well.

6. Position of reserves.

The third and fourth battalions of the two brigades were distributed in depth extending back to HIGH WOOD. This disposition did not militate against the use of the reserves.

7. Flank support.

The battalion on the left of the 30th Division having also failed to obtain its first objective was unable to assist our right flank.

On the left flank arrangements were made with the 15th Division for machine gun fire to be brought to bear on the north of the BUTTE de WARLENCOURT. A smoke barrage was also put up by the 15th Division to cover our left.

8. Communications from Brigade H.Q. to Battalions were maintained satisfactorily but in front of battalion H.Q. wire were immediately broken and visual signalling failed owing in one case to the station being knocked out, and in another case to the dust and smoke of the battle.

Lieut-Colonel,

13.10.16.   General Staff, 9th (Scottish) Division.

9th Division.
Points affecting the attack on 12th October 1916.

1. **Artillery point of view.**

    Preliminary bombardment insufficient and did not knock out either the infantry trenches or machine guns.

2. **Infantry point of view.**

    The cause of the advance being checked was the Machine Gun fire from front and both flanks.

3. **Barrages.**

    (a) Left Brigade reported our barrage to be very good. Right Brigade considered that at times it was short but this may have been due to the enemy's barrage being mixed with ours.

    (b) Enemy's barrage was not so intense as experienced in July. It was more broken up into localities, viz:-

    > EAUCOURT l'ABBAYE.
    > Sunken Road in M.23.b.
    > M.23.d.
    > Quarry M.23.a.9.4.
    > Valley M.23.b. and d.

4. **Direction.**

    The extent of the advance was not sufficient for any loss of direction to be felt.

5. **Forming-up and jumping-off trenches.**

    The Right Brigade only had room for 6 companies to form up and would have liked to have had room for another two.

    The advance was made in 6 waves and is reported to have been excellent as regards forming up and alignment and proximity to our own barrage.

    Had there been more trenches the remaining two companies of the second battalion would have been brought forward earlier so as to have avoided an advance through the hostile barrage.

Left

2.

Left Brigade had sufficient room and the waves, 8 in number, went over very well.

6. **Position of reserves.**

The third and fourth battalions of the two brigades were distributed in depth extending back to HIGH WOOD. This disposition did not militate against the use of the reserves.

7. **Flank support.**

The battalion on the left of the 30th Division having also failed to obtain its objective was unable to assist our right flank.

On the left flank arrangements were made with the 15th Division for machine gun fire to be brought to bear on the north of the BUTTE de WARLENCOURT. A smoke barrage was also put up by the 15th Division to cover our left.

8. Communications from Brigade H.Q. to Battalions were maintained satisfactorily but in front of battalion H.Q. wire were immediately broken and visual signalling failed owing in one case to the station being knocked out, and in another case to the dust and smoke of the battle.

Lieut-Colonel,

13.10.16.   General Staff, 9th (Scottish) Division.

9th Division.

Points affecting the attack on 12th October 1916.

1. **Artillery point of view.**

    Preliminary bombardment insufficient and did not knock out either the infantry trenches or machine guns.

2. **Infantry point of view.**

    The cause of the advance being checked was the Machine Gun fire from front and both flanks.

3. **Barrages.**

    (a) Left Brigade reported our barrage to be very good. Right Brigade considered that at times it was short but this may have been due to the enemy's barrage being mixed with ours.

    (b) Enemy's barrage was not so intense as experienced in July. It was more broken up into localities, viz:-

           EAUCOURT l'ABBAYE.
           Sunken Road in M.23.b.
                         M.23.d.
           Quarry M.23.a.9.4.
           Valley M.22.b. and d.

4. **Direction.**

    The extent of the advance was not sufficient for any loss of direction to be felt.

5. **Forming-up and jumping-off trenches.**

    The Right Brigade only had room for 6 companies to form up and would have liked to have had room for another two.

    The advance was made in 6 waves and is reported to have been excellent as regards forming up and alignment and proximity to our own barrage.

    Had there been more trenches the remaining two companies of the second battalion would have been brought forward earlier so as to have avoided an advance through the hostile barrage.

                                                             Left

Left Brigade had sufficient room and the waves, 8 in number, went over very well.

6. **Position of reserves.**

The third and fourth battalions of the two brigades were distributed in depth extending back to HIGH WOOD. This disposition did not militate against the use of the reserves.

7. **Flank support.**

The battalion on the left of the 30th Division having also failed to obtain its first objective was unable to assist our right flank.

On the left flank arrangements were made with the 15th Division for machine gun fire to be brought to bear on the north of the BUTTE de WARLENCOURT. A smoke barrage was also put up by the 15th Division to cover our left.

8. Communications from Brigade H.Q. to Battalions were maintained satisfactorily but in front of battalion H.Q. wire were immediately broken and visual signalling failed owing in one case to the station being knocked out, and in another case to the dust and smoke of the battle.

Lieut-Colonel,
13.10.16. General Staff, 9th (Scottish) Division.

26th Inf. Bde.
1st S.African Bde.
C.R.A.

No. X.5/1868/5.   12th October, 1916.

The following extract from Air Report
3 p.m. - 4 p.m. on Chinese Attack 11/10/16 is forwarded
for information:-

"VI.   THE GERMAN RETALIATION.
The first hostile fire was observed on the CUTTING S.E.
of LE SARS at 3.16½.

A barrage which included a proportion of 5.9" shells
arrived on GOOSE ALLEY and EAUCOURT L'ABBAYE both at 3.19 p.m.

The EAUCOURT MILL was included in the barrage at
3.25 p.m.

Between 3.20 p.m. and 3.30 p.m. a shrapnel barrage was
put on the FLERS LINE between EAUCOURT L'ABBAYE and the
MARTINPUICH - WARLENCOURT ROAD. It was bursting very high.

By 3.30 p.m. the areas which were under barrage fire
were as follows:-

(1) The valley running N.W. in M.23.a.
(2) EAUCOURT L'ABBAYE and vicinity.
(3) The CUTTING in M.23.d.
(4) The CUTTING S.E. of LE SARS in M.16.c.
(5) The area along the main road in M.16.b. between the
     N.E. end of LE SARS & the cross roads at M.16.b.3.4.
(6) Our support line in M.23.a. & b.

Of the above localities our front and support lines
in M.23.a. and b., EAUCOURT L'ABBAYE and its vicinity and the
cutting S.E. of LE SARS were most consistently and heavily
shelled especially at 3.45 p.m.

There was practically no hostile shelling North of the
BAPAUME ROAD at any time. The hostile fire died down slightly
at 3.35 p.m. but resumed its former proportions after about
5 minutes.

It had died away almost entirely by 4 p.m.

There appeared to be no German counter-battery fire and
no fire outside on our front area except that just before
4 p.m. some shelling of the East side of MARTINPUICH and the
POZIERES - MARTINPUICH ROAD took place.

As a whole the German Artillery retaliation was not
great and their fire seldom amounted to a barrage either in
volume or rapidity.

It appeared to consist mainly of 4.2" and H.E.
The 77 mm. fire was nearly all shrapnel fire.
The percentage of 5.9" shells was very small.
LE SARS was not shelled except slightly with shrapnel.
The most noticeable feature was the almost complete
absence of hostile artillery fire North of the BAPAUME Road.

VII.   GENERAL.
The new German trench in M.17.c. and d. is still in good
condition.

The Gird Line is very badly knocked about by artillery
fire - in places it is unrecognisable. Except for two small
portions of trench viz:-

from M.17.a.2.9. to 99 and from M.17.b.8.4. to M.18.a.1.3.
the support trench does not exist.

SECRET

The portion of the GIRD LINE in 17.a. in the close vicinity of the BUTTE and the main road is almost obliterated. Both the main road and the BUTTE are a mass of shell holes.

The portion of trench in front of LITTLE WOOD from M.9.d.8.6. to 3.5. is almost destroyed, also the portion from M.9.d.1.5. to M.9.c.7.5.

LITTLE WOOD is very much thinned out.

The trench dug round the West and South sides of WARLENCOURT is now continuous.

The communication trench leaving the GIRD LINE at M.10.c.8.6. and going North is now continuous except for 2 small gaps at M.10.c.8.9. and M.10.a.5.2. "

Major,
General Staff
9th (Scottish) Division.

9th Division.
15th Division.
Heavy Artillery.
B.G., R.A.

AIR REPORT 3 P.M. - 4 P.M. ON "CHINESE ATTACK" 11/10/16.

I. <u>3.15 p.m. - 3.20 p.m.</u>

    Our barrage started exactly at 3.15 p.m.
    The Divisional Artillery shells reached their objective about 3.15 9 secs.

(a) The fire of our 4.5" Hows. on the right Divisional Artillery objective viz :-
the trench in M.17.c. & d. was a little over the trench - the fire was very intense.
    The Germans were seen to be occupying this trench but not very strongly.

(b) The fire on the Left Divisional Artillery objective viz :-
the GIRD LINE in front of LITTLE WOOD was a little short at the commencement. This fire was also very intense. The Germans were holding this line very thickly.

(c) The Heavy Artillery fire appeared to be a little late on to its objective, but the fire was excellent, all the shells falling into the GIRD LINE which also appeared strongly held.

II. <u>3.20 p.m. - 3.25 p.m.</u>

(a) The fire of both the Right and Left Divisional Artilleries crept back very regularly - there were no gaps in the barrage. The fire of both was very intense and none of the area covered by the objectives appeared to be left uncovered.

(b) The fire of the Heavy Artillery covered the southern portion of WARLENCOURT mostly though some large shells fell about the centre of the village. A very large explosion was seen at 3.22 - 30 secs.
    Their fire on the SUNKEN ROAD in M.11.a. & b. was not observed till 3.23 when it appeared short of this target. Their fire on their other special objectives was accurate.

III. <u>3.25 p.m. - 3.28 p.m.</u>

(a) It was hard to time the exact moment when the Divisional Artilleries came back to their first objectives, but it appeared to be about 3.26 p.m.
    The fire was very intense and accurate a large percentage of the shells falling actually into the trench most particularly at the trench junction at M.17.d.3.6.

(b) The fire of the Heavy Artillery was very good more especially on the GIRD TRENCH North of the main road and on the vicinity of the BUTTE.

IV..........

IV. 3.28 p.m. - 3.33 p.m.

(a) The fire of both Divisional Artilleries crept back very regularly though it appeared to go back at a greater rate than 50 yards per minute.

(b) The Heavy Artillery continued to fire very accurately on the GIRD LINE - the fire appearing to be very intense & most accurate in that portion in M.17.a. & b. & in the vicinity of the BUTTE.

V. 3.33 p.m. - 3.35 p.m.

At 3.34 p.m. the first salvoes were observed. That of the Right Divisional Royal Artillery being a little in advance of the Left.
Both salvoes were excellent there being a rain of shells bursting simultaneously over the objectives.
The three salvoes took place at intervals of about a minute.
The first of these appeared to be the best.

VI. THE GERMAN RETALIATION.

The first hostile fire was observed on the CUTTING S.E. of LE SARS at 3.16½.
A barrage which included a proportion of 5.9" shells arrived on GOOSE ALLEY & EAUCOURT L'ABBAYE both at 3.19 p.m.
The EAUCOURT MILL was included in the barrage at 3.23 p.m.
Between 3.20 p.m. and 3.30 p.m. a shrapnel barrage was put on the FLERS LINE between EAUCOURT L'ABBAYE and the MARTINPUICH - WARLENCOURT ROAD. It was bursting very high.
By 3.30 p.m. the areas which were under barrage fire were as follows :-

(1) The valley running N.W. in M.23.a.
(2) EAUCOURT L'ABBAYE & vicinity.
(3) The CUTTING in M.23.d.
(4) The CUTTING S.E. of LE SARS in M.16.c.
(5) The area along the main road in M.16.b. between the N.E. end of LE SARS & the cross roads at M.16.b.3.4.
(6) Our support line in M.23.a. & b.

Of the above localities our front and support lines in M.23.a. & b, EAUCOURT L'ABBAYE and its vicinity & the cutting S.E. of LE SARS were most consistently & heavily shelled especially at 3.45 p.m.
There was practically no hostile shelling North of the BAPAUME ROAD at any time. The hostile fire died down slightly at 3.35 p.m. but resumed its former proportions after about 5 minutes.
It had died away almost entirely by 4 p.m..
There appeared to be no German counter-battery fire & no fire outside of our front area except that just before 4 p.m. some shelling of the East side of MARTINPUICH & the POZIERES - MARTINPUICH ROAD took place.
As a whole the German Artillery retaliation was not great and their fire seldom amounted to a barrage either in

volume........

volume or rapidity.

It appeared to consist mainly of 4.2" & H.E.
The 77 mm. fire was nearly all shrapnel fire.
The percentage of 5.9" shells was very small.
LE SARS was not shelled except slightly with ~~shrapnel~~ shrapnel.
The most noticeable feature was the almost complete absence of hostile artillery fire North of the BAPAUME ROAD.

VII. GENERAL.

The new German trench in M.17.c. & d. is still in good condition.

The GIRD LINE is very badly knocked about by artillery fire - in places it is unrecogisable.   Except for two small portions of trench viz :-
  from M.17.a.2.9. to 99 and from M.17.b.8.4. to M.18.a.1.3. the support trench does not exist.

The portion of the GIRD LINE in 17.a. in the close vicinity of the BUTTE & the main road is almost obliterated. Both the main road and the BUTTE are a mass of shell holes.

The portion of trench in front of LITTLE WOOD from M.9.d.8.6. to 3.5. is almost destroyed, also the portion from M.9.d.1.5. to M.9.c.7.5.

LITTLE WOOD is very much thinned out.

The trench dug round the West & South sides of WARLENCOURT is now continuous.

The communication trench leaving the GIRD LINE at M.10.c.8.8. & going North is now continuous except for 2 small gaps at M.10.c.8.9. & M.10.a.5.2.

3rd Corps "I"
11th October, 1916.

SECRET.

Recipients of 9th Division
    Operation Order No. 85.

No. X.5/1868/4.   11th October, 1916.

            Reference para 5 of 9th Division
Operation Order No. 85 of 11th October.

1.   Zero hour will be at 2.5 p.m. on October 12th.

2.   Please acknowledge by wire.

                                        Major,
                                    General Staff
                                9th (Scottish) Division.

Secret

1st S.A. Infantry Brigade.
10th ~~11th~~ October 1916. (midnight)

9th Division,

B.M.O. 20.

With reference to the instructions received by me ~~yesterday~~ to-day from the Divisional Commander - a copy of my notes regarding which is enclosed - I propose to carry out the operation on the 12th instant on the following broad lines.

    A. The Brigade to attack on a one battalion front on a frontage of approximately 250 yards in column of companies.

        My reason for proposing this restricted frontage is to avoid as far as possible direct fire from enemy machine guns in the WARLENCOURT Valley and to take as much advantage as possible of the shoulder of ground running along approximately the bottom of M.17.

    B. Machine guns to be placed in the existing posts at M.22.b.5.8 and M.17.d.9.3. to command the WARLENCOURT Valley.

    C. The 44th Brigade to be asked to assist with Trench Mortar fire on the WARLENCOURT Valley and Machine Gun fire on the BUTTE de WARLENCOURT and on the trench running east therefrom.

    I would suggest that a standing barrage should be placed from the commencement of the bombardment on both objectives. Otherwise enemy's Machine Gun and rifle fire from the second objective would prove most troublesome to our men in the attack on the first objective.

                            Brigadier General.
                 Commanding 1st S.A. Infantry Brigade.

The foregoing was written prior to receipt of patrol reports this morning they do not alter my opinion as to the best manner of dealing with the situation

11/10/16

SECRET.

INSTRUCTIONS RECEIVED BY G.O.C. SOUTH AFRICAN
INFANTRY BRIGADE FROM DIV. COMMANDER 10/10/16.

There will be a Chinese attack tomorrow (11th). Hour to be notified later.

Os.C.Units in forward trenches to be instructed to keep their men under as good cover as possible, as enemy is certain to open a heavy barrage.

Machine Guns to be held in readiness with a view to taking advantage of the enemy manning his parapet, should he do so.

Observers to be at their posts with the object of spotting where the enemy barrage falls.

Attack to be carried out on 12th instant. Two objectives.

BRIGADE'S FIRST OBJECTIVE.
Trench running approximately from M.17.c.3.5 to M.17.c.d.0.8.

BRIGADE'S SECOND OBJECTIVE.
BUTTE de WARLENCOURT and trench running east therefrom as far as M.17.b.0.5.

On the capture of the second objective, strong points to be made at,

(1) M.17.b.0.5. with two lewis guns (to be replaced later by machine guns, and with field of fire N.E. up the valley to cross with guns of 26th Brigade, and

(2) forward slope of the BUTTE de WARLENCOURT with several Lewis guns.

Line to be consolidated to run approximately from M.17.central to M.17.c.2.6. being on the reverse slope from the enemy. Three Stokes' mortar emplacements to be made in that line.

Strong points are to be held by as few men as possible, but there must be an officer in charge of each.

Steps are to be taken to ensure that the BUTTE de WARLENCOURT is absolutely clear of the enemy. (Special parties will be told off for this purpose.)

Communication trench to be dug from the right of our consolidated line to M.17.b.0.5.

ARTILLERY BARRAGES.
There will be two barrages, one a standing barrage, the other a creeping barrage. The standing barrage will be on the Brigade's first objective, whilst the creeping barrage will commence 200 yards in advance of our front line, and after three minutes, will lift 50 yards at a time, at stated intervals, until it comes up to the standing barrage. The standing barrage will then be lifted on to the second objective, and the creeping barrage will again proceed by lifts of 50 yards at a time.

Troops to be reminded of the advantage of advancing close under the barrage.

"A" Form.
MESSAGES AND SIGNALS.

Army Form C. 2121.

TO: M A   C R A
    C B

Sender's Number	Day of Month	In reply to Number	AAA
G 764	Eleventh		

Reference X5/1868/1 of 10/10/16

Para 3 AAA During operation indicated special arrangements will be made today to note when enemy places his barrages and reports as reports sent it me to Div HQ

From: T.A
Place:
Time: 9.40 AM

SECRET.

26th Inf. Brigade.
27th Inf. Brigade.
1st S.African Bde.
C.R.A.
C.R.E.
9th Seaforths.

No. K.S./1988/1.   10th October. 1916.

Reference 9th Division K.S./1988 of 9th Octr.

1. The attack referred to therein will be carried out on the 12th Octr. Detailed orders will be issued later.

2. A bombardment of the objectives to be attacked will be carried out from 7 a.m. to 6 p.m. on October 11th. It will be continued from 7 a.m. till Zero on 12th October.

3. In order to inflict losses on the enemy by inducing him to man his trenches and at the same time to check the accuracy and intensity of our barrage, Chinese attacks will be carried out at 1.30 and 3.15 p.m. October 11th, all along the line.

At this time, the artillery of the Right Divisional Group will place a barrage on its First objective while the artillery of the Left Divisional Group will place a barrage on the German trenches in front of LITTLE WOOD.

At 1.40 and 3.25 p.m. the barrage will cease and the normal bombardment be continued.

Our trenches will be kept as clear of troops as possible during the Chinese attacks.

4. Correct time will be distributed by a Staff Officer of the III Corps at 9 a.m. to-morrow 11th inst. at VILLA WOOD to representatives of Artillery Brigades and Groups.

5. Please acknowledge by wire.

a.r. mchamall.

Lieutenant Colonel,
General Staff,
9th (Scottish) Division.

SECRET.

26th Inf. Brigade.
27th Inf. Brigade.
1st S.African Bde.
C.R.A.
C.R.E.
9th Seaforths.

No. X.5/1848/1.   10th October, 1916.

Reference 9th Division X.5/1848 of 9th Octr.

1.   The attack referred to therein will be carried out on the 12th Octr. Detailed orders will be issued later.

2.   A bombardment of the objectives to be attacked will be carried out from 7 a.m. to 6 p.m. on October 11th. It will be continued from 7 a.m. till Zero on 12th October.

3.   In order to inflict losses on the enemy by inducing him to man his trenches and at the same time to check the accuracy and intensity of our barrage, Chinese attacks will be carried out at 1.30 and 3.15 p.m. October 11th, all along the line.

   At this time, the artillery of the Right Divisional Group will place a barrage on its first objective while the artillery of the Left Divisional Group will place a barrage on the German trenches in front of LITTLE WOOD.

   At 1.40 and 3.30 p.m. the barrage will cease and the normal bombardment be continued.

   Our trenches will be kept as clear of troops as possible during the Chinese attacks.

4.   Correct time will be distributed by a Staff Officer of the III Corps at 9 a.m. tomorrow 11th inst. at VILLA WOOD to representatives of Artillery Brigades and Groups.

5.   Please acknowledge by wire.

                            a r m'namara

                            Lieutenant Colonel,
                            General Staff,
                            9th (Scottish) Division.

SECRET.

26th Inf. Bde.
1st S.African Bde.
C.R.E.
27th Inf. Bde.)
C.R.A.) for information.
9th Seaforths.)

No. X.5/1888.   9th October, 1916.

1. The 9th Division will attack the enemy's position on the high ground between M.17.d.9.9. and the LE SARS - BAPAUME Road.
   The date has not yet been fixed but will probably be the 12th inst.

2. The advanced posts established by the 47th Division will be connected up and made into a continuous line from the sunken road S.17.d.9.1. to the MARTINPUICH - WARLENCOURT Road about M.28.b.5.9. as early as possible.

3. This line will be connected up with the present front line on each Brigade front by at least two communication trenches which are to be sited to take full advantage of any defilade which the lie of the ground may afford.

4. Approach trenches from the rear to the present front line will be opened up under orders of the C.R.E. in consultation with Brigadiers.

5. Emplacements will be prepared for Stokes Mortars wherever it is possible with their limited range to reach the enemy's trenches.

6. Patrolling by night must be constant and bold with a view to fixing definitely the position of any hostile trenches and wire or advanced machine gun emplacements.

7 Acknowledge by wire

Lieutenant Colonel,
General Staff,
9th (Scottish) Division.

Secret   X5/1901

W. 15517—M. 141. 250,000. 1/16. L.S.&Co. Forms/W 3091/2.   Army Form W. 3091.

Cover for Documents.

Nature of Enclosures.

Scheme K.

Notes, or Letters written.

MESSAGES AND SIGNALS.

Army Form C. 2121.

TO: 9th Division

Sender's Number: BM 361
Day of Month: 23
AAA

X 5/1901/3 received

From: 9th DA
Time: 12.25 PM

Signature: J. Rose

SECRET

C.R.A.

No.X.5/1901/3   23rd October, 1916.

The following extract from Addendum No.2 to IIIrd Corps Operation Order No.148 dated 22.10.16 is forwarded for your information.

x x x x x x x x x x x

3. The Field Artillery barrage will at Zero be placed 150 yards in front of the objective. Divisions will arrange the times at which it will begin to rake back according to the distance between their jumping off trench and the objective. The rate at which the barrage rakes back will be 50 yards a minute.

4. In order to agree with the programme of the 15th Corps, the Field Artillery barrage on the right of the 9th Division will begin to rake back at plus 3 minutes.

x x x x x x x x x x x

Major,
General Staff, 9th (Scottish) Division.

26th Infantry Brigade.
27th Infantry Brigade.
1st S.A. Infantry Brigade.
C.R.A.
C.R.E.
A.D.M.S.
"Q"

No.X.5/1901/2   22nd October, 1918.

---

1. The boundary between the 13th and 3rd Corps for the operation on the 25th October will be amended to that shown on attached map C.

2. In view of this alteration the boundary between the 26th and 27th Infantry Brigades will be amended as shown on attached map C.

3. The communication trench running from M.23.b.8.8. to M.17.d.8.2. will be common to the 9th Division and the 5th Australian Division.

4. Maps showing boundaries for this operation previously issued to be cancelled.

5 ACKNOWLEDGE

A L M'Namara

Major,
General Staff, 9th (Scottish) Division.

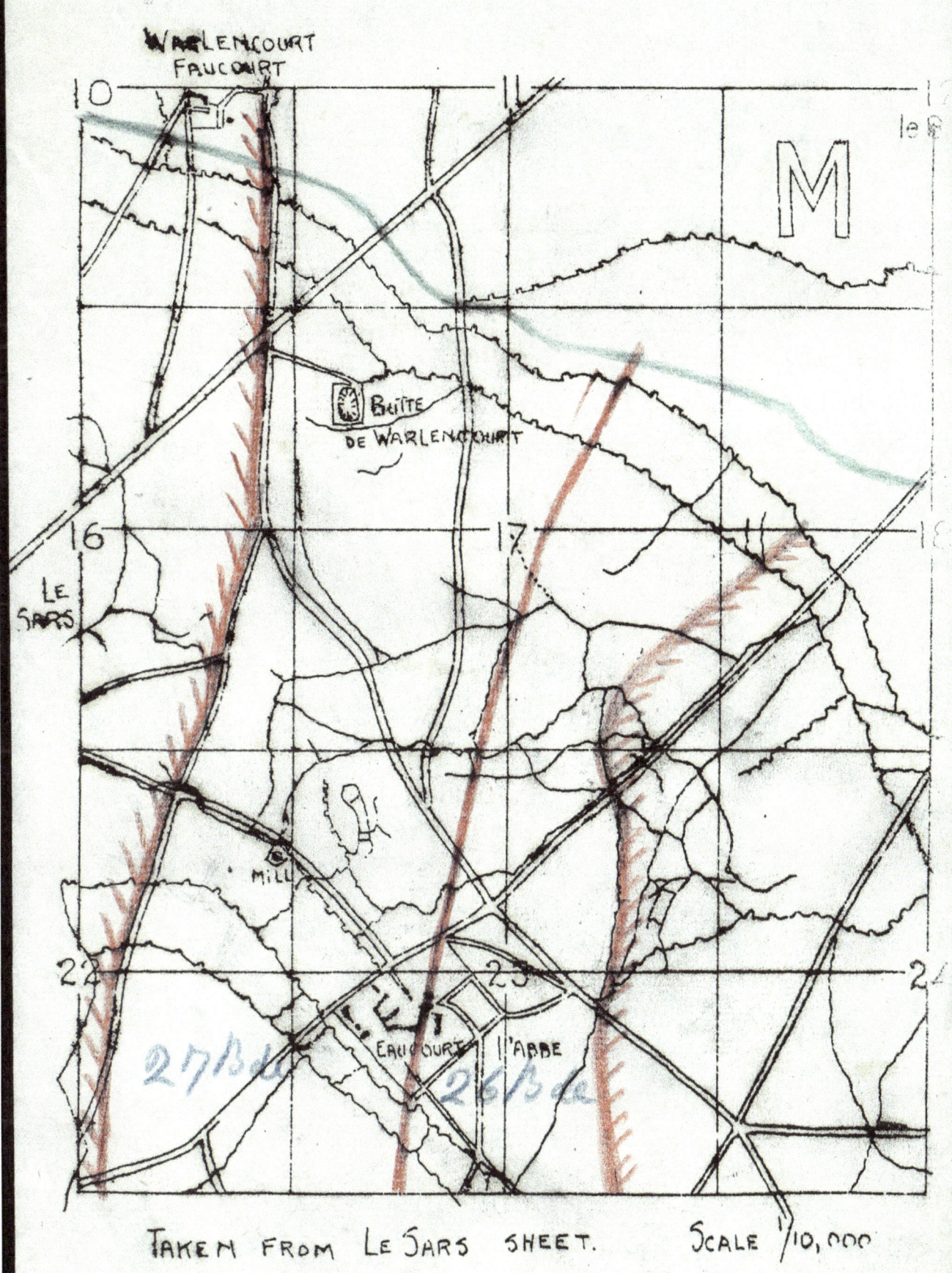

Scheme K.

S.African Brigade,
C. R. A.
C. R. E.
9th Seaforths,
"Q",
A. D. M. S.

No. X.5/1901/1. 22nd October, 1916.

The attached Map should be substituted for that issued with 9th Division Operation Order No. 87 of 20th instant.

The Map previously issued should be destroyed.

Please acknowledge receipt

R Stewart
Lieutenant Colonel,
General Staff,
9th (Scottish) Division.

S.African Brigade,
C. R. A.
C. R. E.
9th Seaforths,
"Q",
A. D. M. S.

extra copy

No. X.5/1901/1. 22nd October, 1916.

The attached Map should be substituted for that issued with 9th Division Operation Order No.87 of 20th instant.

The Map previously issued should be destroyed.

Please acknowledge receipt.

R Stewart
Lieutenant Colonel,
General Staff,
9th (Scottish) Division.

Copies taken
to 26th & 27th
Bdes personally
by Maj McNamara

27/10/16

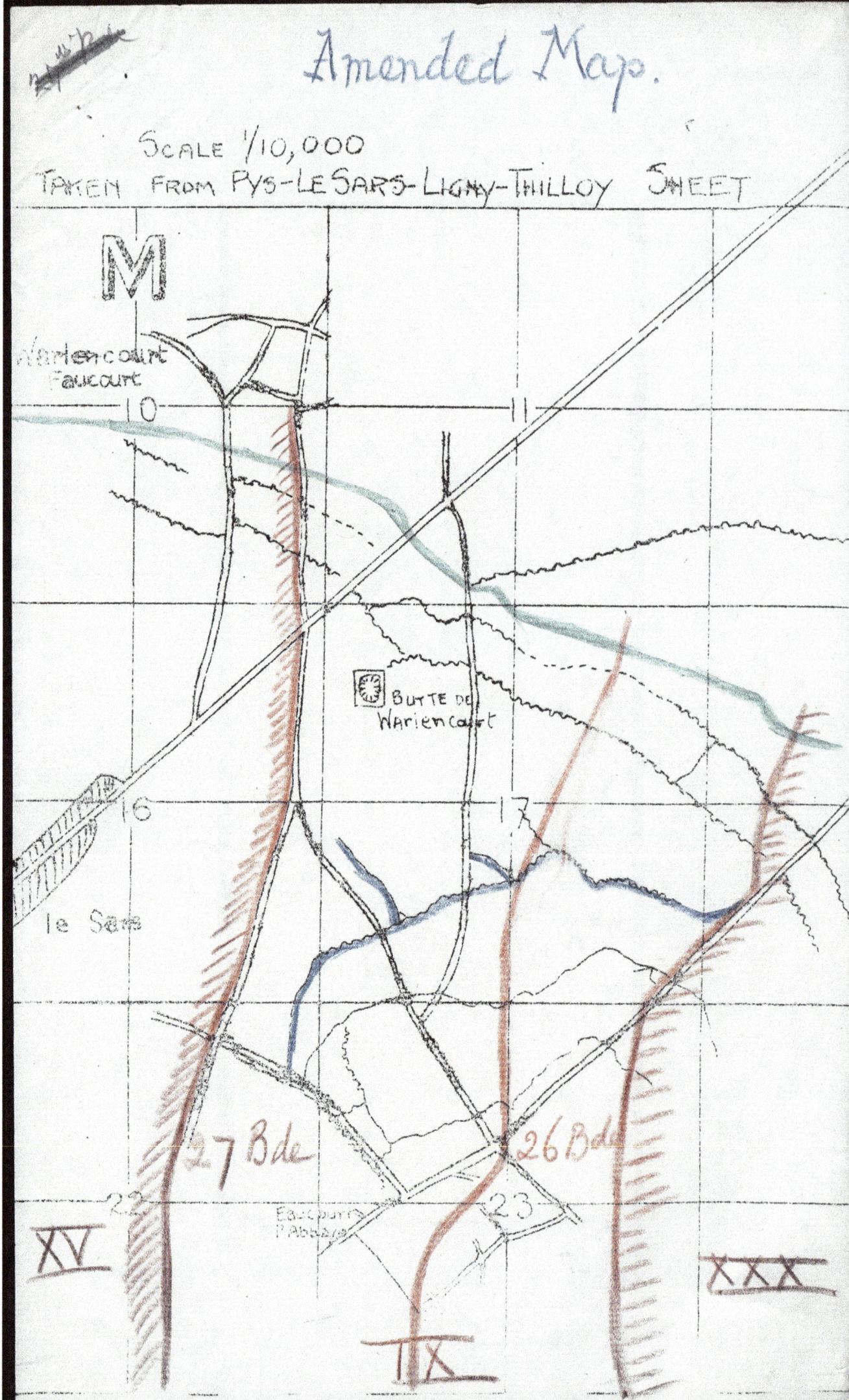

O.C.T.M.

Amended Map

Scale 1/10,000
Taken from Pys-Le Sars-Ligny-Thilloy Sheet

M

Warlencourt Faucourt

Butte de Warlencourt

le Sars

27 Bde   26 Bde

Eaucourt l'Abbaye

XV   IX   XXX

Scheme K.

27th Bde Operation Orders

SECRET.

PRELIMINARY ORDERS.

B.M.3/72.
Headquarters,
27th.Inf.B'de.
22/10/16.

DISPOSITION &
& OBJECTIVE OF
THE DIVISION.
1. The 26th. & 27th. Bdes will attack the GIRD trench and GIRD support at Zero hour on 25th.Oct.
The S.African Bde will be in Div'nl Reserve.

Boundary.
2. The dividing line between 26th.& 27th.Bdes will be the new C.T. dug on night of 21/22 from old front trench to the new one in front of it.
This C.T. will be reserved for the 27th.Inf.Bde.
The dividing line between the 27th.Bde & the Divn on our left will be the MARTINPUICH - WARLENCOURT road.

DISPOSITION
OF
27th.Inf.Bde.
3. Assaulting Battalions -

12th.Royal Scots on the Right.
11th.Royal Scots on the Left.

Supporting Battalion -

9th.Scottish Rifles.

Reserve battalion, to find carrying parties etc -

6th.K.O.S.B's.

The dividing line between the 11th.& 12th.R. Scots will be approximately a point midway between the new C.T. on the Right and the post at M.17.c.1.8.

OBJECTIVES. 4. The Battalion objectives will be notified later.

H.Qrs. 5. The Headquarters of both the 11th.& 12th.R.Scots will be in dug-outs at M.17.c.4.4.
The position of the Support & Reserve Battalions & their H.Q. will be notified later.

6. Brigade Headquarters will be at dug-outs on road at M.22.d.6.0. (Present M.G.Coy H.Q.).

Major,
Brigade Major,
27th. Infantry Brigade.

SECRET.   Copy No...1......

27th. INFANTRY BRIGADE OPERATION ORDER NO.103.

22nd. October 1916.

With reference to Preliminary Order, B.M.X/72 issued to-day, the following reliefs will be carried out on 23rd. October -

1. 12th.R.Scots will side step from their present position and occupy its portion of the Brigade Section under direct arrangements with the 11th.R.Scots.

    The relief to be carried out in the forenoon but in very small bodies, along trenches only.

2. To give 11th.R.Scots & 12th.R.Scots sufficient room (in depth) on this narrow front, the 6th.K.O.S.B. will be moved from their present area back to BAZENTIN LE GRAND & take over the lines to be vacated by the 1st S.African Infantry, 6th.K.O.S.B. to be clear by 11.a.m.

3. The 9th.Sco.Rifles will be relieved by 2 coys 5th Camerons 2 coys 10th A & S during the afternoon, and will move to HIGH WOOD taking over the quarters of the 3rd S.African Infantry. The 9th.Sco.Rifles will make their own arrangemnets for advance parties.

    To enable relief by bns of 26 Bde to be carried out in daylight, the PIONEER Trench must be thoroughly cleared out up to the front line. This will be done by a section of R.E., assisted by as many of 9th.S.Rifles as possible. R.E. Officer will report at H.Q., 9th.S.Rifles at 8.30.A.M. to make necessary arrangements.

4. The guns of 27th.M.G.Coy & the 27th.T.M.Battery at present in the section to be handed over to the 26th. Inf.Bde will be relieved by opposite numbers of the 26th.Bde Details later.

Issued at 8.p.m.
Copy No.1. to 9th.Divn.
         2.   11th.R.S.
         3.   12th.R.S.
         4.   6th.K.O.S.B.
         5.   9th.S.R.
         6.   27th.M.G.Coy,
         7.   27th.T.M.Bty,
         8.   90th.F.Coy.R.E.
         9.   27th.F.Ambce.
10. 106th.Coy.A.S.C. 11. 26th.Inf.Bde.
12 1st.S.A.Bde.   13. / 20 Office.

Major,
Brigade Major,
27th. Infantry Brigade.

Scheme K.
9th Div. Operation Orders.

OPERATION ORDERS IN CONNECTION WITH SCHEME K.

9th Division.

	Operation Order No. 88	of	22-10-16.
Addendum	do. do. No. 87	"	25-10-16.
	do. do. No. 87	"	20-10-16.

3rd Corps.

	Operation Order No. 148	of	19-10-16.
Correction No. 1 to	do. do. " do.	"	do.
Addendum No. 1 to	do. do. " do.	"	22-10-16.
Correction No. 2 to	do. do. " do.	"	20-10-16.
Correction No. 3 to	do. do. " do.	"	22-10-16.
Addendum No. 5 to	do. do. " do.	"	26-10-16.

50th Division.

Operation Order No. G.X.2868/2. of 26-10-16.

15th Division.

Addendum No. 4 to Operation-Odere Order No. 105 of 26-10-16.

27th Inf. Bde.

Operation Order No. 103 of 22-10-16.
Preliminary Order No. B.M.3/72 of 22-10-16.

"A" Form.
MESSAGES AND SIGNALS.

Army Form C.2121 (in pads of 100). No. of Message ....

Prefix .... Code .... m.	Words	Charge	This message is on a/c of:	Recd. at .... m.
Office of Origin and Service Instructions.				Date ....
....	Sent		.... Service.	From ....
....	At .... m.			
....	To			
....	By		(Signature of "Franking Officer.")	By ....

TO	C.B.	L.D.		
	M.A.			

Sender's Number.	Day of Month.	In reply to Number.	A A A
	23/10		

Reference 9th Division O.O. 88 of 22.10.16. para 3 (b) AAA One company of C.B. Regt., at High Wood will NOT be placed at disposal of M.A. AAA The whole of C.B. Regiment at HIGH WOOD will therefore move to BAZENTIN AAA ACKNOWLEDGE AAA Addsd. C.B. reptd. M.A. and L.D.

From L.D.
Place
Time 7.0 am.

The above may be forwarded as now corrected.   (Z) (Sd) A.E.McNamara Major.
.... Censor.   Signature of Addressor or person authorised to telegraph in his name.
* This line should be erased if not required.

SECRET.

Copy No_____

9th Division Operation Order No. 88.

22.10.16.

1. The 14th Inf. Bde., 5th Australian Division will relieve the 27th Inf. Bde. to-morrow in that portion of its front from Sunken Road to M.17.d.8.5. (to which point a new trench will be dug from M.18.c.0.3).

2. The 26th Inf. Bde. (less 8th Black Watch) will relieve the 27th Inf. Bde. on October 23rd and night October 23rd/24th in that portion of its front from new trench junction M.17.d.8.5. to the trench junction at M.17.d.0.7. (exclusive).

3. The 1st S.African Bde. will -
   (a) move its battalion now at BAZENTIN to MAMETZ to the quarters vacated by the 7th Seaforths. To be clear of BAZENTIN by 12 noon.
   (b) move its battalion at HIGH WOOD (less one Coy.) to BAZENTIN to the quarters vacated by the 10th Arg. & Suth. Hlrs. Not to leave HIGH WOOD till 4 p.m.
   One Company of this Battalion will be placed at the disposal of the 26th Inf. Bde. and will move to the FLERS Line under orders to be issued by 26th Inf. Bde.

4. The quarters vacated by the 1st S.African Bde. at HIGH WOOD and BAZENTIN will be at the disposal of the 27th Inf. Bde.

5. The dividing line between the 26th and 27th Inf. Bdes. will be from front line at M.17.d.0.5. to M.17.c.9.0. (leaving C.T. to 27th Bde.) thence M.25.c.5.4., thence southwards to junction SWITCH and WILLOW Road thence to M.54.d.8.0. thence along S.E. edge of HIGH WOOD, thence through centre of BAZENTIN LE GRAND.

6. All details of relief will be arranged direct between Brigadiers concerned.
   Command will pass on completion of relief which will be reported by wire to Divisional Headquarters.

P. Stewart
Lieutenant Colonel,
General Staff,
9th (Scottish) Division.

Issued at 11.30 p.m.

Copies to:-
No. 1 to 26th Inf. Bde.	14 to "Q".
2 to 27th Inf. Bde.	15 to A.D.M.S.
3 to 1st S.African Bde.	16 to A.D.V.S.
4 to C.R.A.	17 to A.P.M.
5 to 50th Bde. R.F.A.	18 to III Corps.
6 to 51st Bde. R.F.A.	19 to III Corps.
7 to 52nd Bde. R.F.A.	20 to 15th Division.
8 to Trench Mortars.	21 to 5th Australian Divn.
9 to Div. Column.	22 to 50th Division.
10 to C.R.E.	23 to 25th Bd. R.F.A.
11 to 9th Seaforths.	24 to 59th Bde. R.F.A.
12 to 9th Div. Train.	25 to War Diary.
13 to 9th Signals.	26 to File.

SECRET.

Copy No _____

ADDENDUM NO. 1 to 9th DIVISION OPERATION ORDER No. 87 d/20/10/

25.10.16.

1.   The position to be consolidated is the system of trenches known as the GIRD Trench and GIRD Support between M.18.c.5.8. and the road (inclusive) at M.10.d.8½.2.
       Posts with machine guns will be established as follows:-
(a) By 26th Inf. Bde.
   1. To cover the W. face of the Spur running from M.18.central to LE BARQUE.
   2. The West face of the Spur running N. between M.12.c. and M.11.d.
   3. The East face of the Spur running N.W. from M.17.b.5.7.
   4. The N. face of the BUTTE Spur

(b) By 27th Inf. Bde.
       To cover the West face of the Spur running N.W. from M.17.b.5.7. and also to enfilade the sunken road running North through M.11.a.

2.   At least one communication trench from the present front line to the objective will be made on each Brigade front.
       One Company of Pioneers will be attached to each Brigade for this purpose.
       The exact positions selected for the above works to be reported by Brigades to each other and to Divisional Headquarters.

3.   The two Tanks allotted to the 9th Division will move to the vicinity of BEAUCOURT l'ABBAYE on the night 24th/25th.
       At Zero hour on the 25th Octr. they will move forward behind the Infantry, one in the direction of the BUTTE de WARLENCOURT and the other in the direction of the new German trench about M.17.d.5.8. They will avail themselves of any opportunity which may occur of assisting the Infantry to obtain their objectives.
       The 1st S.African Bde. will detail an escort of 2 officers and 20 men for the Tanks. This party will report to the O.C. Tanks at BAZENTIN LE GRAND at 12 noon to-morrow October 24th. The O.C. Tanks will give the necessary instructions to this party.

4.   At Zero the artillery will open intense fire all along the enemy's front trenches.
       The leading waves of the infantry will advance at Zero and get as close to our artillery fire as possible, and as the fire lifts will follow it up and assault the enemy's trenches.
       The lifts of the artillery fire will be timed so as to allow one minute for getting out of the trench and forming up, and 1 minute for every 50 yards advance by the infantry.
       In no case will field artillery fire within 200 yards of our own front line.
       Any enemy trench within that distance must be barraged at Zero by Stokes mortars.

2.

5. The Artillery fire after lifting from the GIRD Support will form a close barrage beyond the final objective till Zero plus 2 hours.

The Artillery Liaison Officer with 26th Inf. Bde. will be Lieut. Col. Belcher, D.S.O. 52nd Bde. R.F.A., and with 27th Inf. Capt. Nickle, V.C Battery.

Detailed artillery orders will be issued separately.

6. Brigades after reaching their objectives will be prepared as soon as the lift of our artillery fire permits, to push forward to the North strong patrols to gain touch with the enemy.

7. Every body of men after gaining their own objective will fight to the flanks if necessary to assist their neighbours to reach theirs.

8. Brigades will arrange to establish visual signal communication with the captured line where possible.

9. In the event of the wind being either S. or S.W. a smoke barrage will be formed by the 15th Division with the purpose of blinding the enemy on the Northern face of the BUTTE and the slopes which run down to the LE SARS - BAPAUME Road from that point. No smoke is to be S. of the BUTTE.

10. (a) The Divisional reserve will consist of the 1st S.African Bde., the 64th Field Coy. R.E. and 2 sections each of 63rd and 90th Field Coys. and Pioneer Battalion less 2 Coys.

    (b) The 1st S.African Bde. will be disposed as under:-
2 Battalions (less 2 Coys.)   HIGH WOOD.
2 Coys. in FLERS Line at disposal of G.O.C. 26th Inf. Bde.
S.African Stokes Mortar Battery   HIGH WOOD.
2 Battalions   BAZENTIN
28th Machine Gun Coy.   BAZENTIN.

    (c) The G.O.C. 1st S.African Bde. will move forward is troops into their allotted positions as soon as these positions have been vacated by the troops of the 26th and 27th Inf. Bdes. 26th and 27th Inf. Bdes. will keep G.O.C. S.African Bde. informed of their movements.

11. Two sections 63rd Field Coy. R.E. will be attached to 26th Bde. and two sections 90th Coy. R.E. to the 27th Inf. Bde. during the operations.

One of these sections should be held in reserve by each Brigade.

12. The arrangements for the evacuation of wounded will be similar to those of the 18th inst.

13. Position of Headquarters :-

9th Division   FRICOURT FARM.
26th Inf. Bde.   BAZENTIN LE GRAND.
27th Inf. Bde.   Adv. H.Q. at M.22.d.3.2.
S.African Bde.   X.30.a.5.8.

Lieutenant Colonel,
General Staff,
9th (Scottish) Division.

Issued at 6 p.m.

Copies to Recipients of Operation Order No. 87 of 20/7/16.

SECRET.

Correction No. 1 to 9th Division Operation
Order No. 87.

1. In para 1 (a) for 24th read 25th.

2. Please acknowledge by wire.

21.10.18.

Major,
General Staff
9th (Scottish) Division.

Copies to recipients of Operation Order No. 87.

SECRET.

Copy No _____

9th Division Operation Order No. 87.

20.10.16.

Reference 1/10,000 map P/S - LE SARS - LIGNY THILLOY d/13.10.16.

1. (a) The III Corps will continue the attack on   inst.
   (b) The 15th Corps is to capture the GIRD Line and GIRD Support on the immediate right of the 9th Division.
   (c) The 15th Division is to capture the GALLWITZ Trench on the left of the 9th Division.

2. The attack on the 9th Division front will be carried out by the 26th Inf. Bde. on the right and the 27th Inf. Bde. on the left.

3. The attached map shows the objectives, the boundaries between the 9th Division and 15th Corps, and the 9th Division and 15th Division and between the 26th and 27th Inf. Bdes.

4. The 27th Inf. Bde. will establish jumping off trenches for the assault of the objectives as early as possible and will join up the left of their front line with the 15th Division right at M.16.d.7½.7½ by a continuous trench.

5. Zero time will be issued later.

6. The preliminary bombardment will begin at once.

7. Two tanks are placed at the disposal of the Division for the attack.

8. Orders regarding the display of flares and the distribution of them will be issued later.

Lieutenant Colonel,
General Staff,
9th (Scottish) Division.

Issued at 7 a.m.

Copies to:-
No. 1 to 26th Inf. Bde.
    2 to 27th Inf. Bde.
    3 to S.African Bde.
    4 to C.R.A.
    5 to 50th Bde. R.F.A.
    6 to 51st Bde. R.F.A.
    7 to 52nd Bde. R.F.A.
    8 to O.C. T.Mortars.
    9 to 9th Div. Coln.
   10 to C.R.E.
   11 to 9th Seaforths.
   12 to 9th Div. Train.
   13 to 9th Signals.

No. 14 to A.A. & Q.M.G.
   15 to A.D.M.S.
   16 to A.D.V.S.
   17 to A.P.M.
   18 to III Corps
   19 to III Corps
   20 to 15th Division.
   21 to 50th Division.
   22 to 50th Division.
   23 to 25th Bde. R.F.A.
   24 to 59th Bde. R.F.A.
   25   War Diary
   26   File

Map issued to Nos. 1, 2, 3, 4, 10, 11, 14, and 15.

Amended Map.

Scale 1/10,000
Taken from Pys-Le Sars-Ligny-Thilloy Sheet

M

Warlencourt
Eaucourt

Butte de Warlencourt

le Sars

27 Bde   26 Bde

Eaucourt l'Abbaye

XV   IX   XXX

Scheme K.

3rd Corps Operation Order

SECRET

Copy No. 6

ADDENDUM NO. 5

to

III CORPS OPERATION ORDER NO. 148.   26.10.16.

1. The Operations which were to have taken place on the 28th. (Vide Addendum No. 4) are postponed till October 30th.

2. ACKNOWLEDGE ON ATTACHED SLIP.

Issued by D.R. at 11.30 a.m.

To all recipients of O.O.148.
  PLUS :- Copy No. 28 to 48th. Division.

Brigadier-General,
General Staff,
III Corps.

SECRET

Copy No. 7

ADDENDUM NO. 5

to

III CORPS OPERATION ORDER NO. 148.   26.10.16.

1. The Operations which were to have taken place on the 28th. (Vide Addendum No. 4) are postponed till October 30th.

2. ACKNOWLEDGE ON ATTACHED SLIP.

Issued by D.R. at 11.30 a.m.

To all recipients of O.O.148.
   PLUS :- Copy No. 28 to 48th. Division.

Brigadier-General,
General Staff,
III Corps.

"C" Form (Original).
MESSAGES AND SIGNALS.

Army Form C. 2123.
(In books of 50's in duplicate.)

No. of Message ....

Prefix	Code	Words	Received	Sent, or sent out	Office Stamp.
			From	At .... m.	
Charges to collect			By	To	
Service Instructions.				By	

Priority

Handed in at BCO (3 Corps) Office .... m. Received .... m.

TO: 9th Div

Sender's Number	Day of Month	In reply to Number	AAA
G624	22		

CORRECTION no 3 to 3rd Corps OO. no 148 begins aaa Reference addendum no 1 aaa In para 1 of addendum no 1 for BAZENTIN LE PETIT read CONTALMAISON aaa Both Bdes will de-bus at CONTALMAISON and march on to BAZENTIN LE PETIT aaa Busses will move eastward via Boisselle and return by FRICOURT aaa Speed of busses from BOISELLE onwards is not to exceed 4 to 5 mph aaa addsd 9th and 50th Div Reptd apm and Q 3rd Corps

FROM: 3rd Corps

PLACE & TIME: 6/50 pm

SECRET.

CORRECTION No. 3   Copy No...6...

to

III CORPS OPERATION ORDER No. 148.   22.10.16.
....

Reference Addendum No. 1 :-

In Para. 1 of Addendum No. 1 for "BAZENTIN LE PETIT" read "CONTALMAISON".

Both Battalions will de-bus at CONTALMAISON and march on to BAZENTIN LE PETIT.

Busses will move Eastward via BOISSELLE and return by FRICOURT.

Speed of Busses from BOISSELLE onwards is not to exceed 4 to 5 Miles per hour.

Issued by D.R. at 7.15 p.m.

To all recipients of Addendum No. 1.   Brigadier-General,
                                              General Staff,
                                                 III Corps.

Wired "PRIORITY" at 6.50 p.m. to :
    9th. Div.
    50th. Div.
    A.P.M. 3rd. Corps.
    "Q" 3rd. Corps.

acknowledged my wire

SECRET.

CORRECTION No. 3   Copy No...7...

to

III CORPS OPERATION ORDER No. 148.   22.10.16.

Reference Addendum No. 1 :-

In Para. 1 of Addendum No. 1 for "BAZENTIN LE PETIT" read "CONTALMAISON".

Both Battalions will de-bus at CONTALMAISON and march on to BAZENTIN LE PETIT.

Busses will move Eastward via BOISSELLE and return by FRICOURT.

Speed of Busses from BOISSELLE onwards is not to exceed 4 to 5 Miles per hour.

Issued by D.R. at 7.15 p.m.

To all recipients of Addendum No. 1.

                                      Brigadier-General,
                                      General Staff,
                                      III Corps.

Wired "PRIORITY" at 6.50 p.m. to :
    9th. Div.
    50th. Div.
    A.P.M. 3rd. Corps.
    "Q" 3rd. Corps.

SECRET.

CORRECTION NO. 2　　　　　Copy No. 6

to

III CORPS OPERATION ORDER NO. 148.　　20th. Octr. 1916.

1. Correction No. 1 is cancelled.

2. In para. 1 :-

   FOR　23rd.　　READ　25th.

3. ACKNOWLEDGE BY WIRE. Done HS

Issued by D.R. at 7.30 p.m.
To all recipients of O.O.148.

for Brigadier-General,
General Staff,
III Corps.

                                                    S E C R E T.
                                                    ....

                    CORRECTION NO. 2   Copy No. 7...

                                  to

                    III CORPS OPERATION ORDER NO. 148.   20th, Octr.1916.
....

1.   Correction No. 1 is cancelled.

2.   In para. 1 :-

                    FOR   23rd.   READ   25th.

3.   ACKNOWLEDGE BY WIRE.

....

    Issued by D.R. at 7.30 p.m.
    To all recipients of O.O.148.

                                                signature
                                            for Brigadier-General,
                                                 General Staff,
                                                 III Corps.

Identification Trace for use with Artillery Maps.

Trace No 15/A to accompany Add No 2 to O.O. No 48 dated 22/10/16.

17

M

23

Trace as before

NOTE.—(1). These traces are intended to facilitate the communication of information as to the position of targets, which have been located on a squared map.
(2). The squares on this trace are 500 yards in length on the 1/10,000 scale, 1,000 yards in length on the 1/20,000 scale, and 2,000 yards in length on the 1/40,000 scale.
(3). The squares on the trace are fitted to the squares of the map showing the targets, which are then drawn on the trace. Sufficient letters and numbers must also be added to enable the recipient to place the trace in the correct position on his own map. A little detail may also be traced, but this is not essential. The name and scale of the map to which the trace refers must be always given. The trace can be used for the 1/10,000, 1/20,000, or 1/40,000 scale.

G.S.G.S. 3023.

Tracing taken from Sheet GUEUDECOUR

of the 1/20,000 map of

Signature   Date

"A" Form.
MESSAGES AND SIGNALS.

Army Form C.2121 (in pads of 100).

TO { 9th Division
     50th Division }

Sender's Number: G.617
Day of Month: 22
AAA

ADDENDUM NO. 1 to Operation Order 148 begins.
Para 1 AAA 50th Division Infantry Brigades will move to-morrow to area MILLENCOURT - ALBERT - BECOURT - tail of column to be clear of HENENCOURT by 1 p.m. after which hour road is required by Second Corps. AAA

Para. 2 AAA Two battalions of 50th Division will move by bus under arrangements to be made by 3rd Corps Q to BAZENTIN LE PETIT to-morrow the 23rd instant - move to be complete by 12 noon - and be placed at disposal of 9th Division for work to-morrow night in the front line AAA Both battalions together to provide a sum total digging party of not less than 800 diggers with proper proportion of Officers and N.C.Os etc AAA They will take rations for 24th instant with them after which they will be rationed by 9th Division AAA These two battalions will return to the FLERS LINE after completion of work, where they will remain under orders of the 9th Division, who will provide bivouacing accommodation for two battalions with first line transport AAA Add Acknowledge AAA Added 50th and 9th Divisions AAA

From Place: 3rd Corps
Time: 3.40 p.m.

SECRET.

COPY NO. 6

ADDENDUM NO.1

to

III CORPS OPERATION ORDER NO.148.

22nd October, 1916.

1. 50th Division Infantry Brigades will move to-morrow to area HILLENCOURT - ALBERT - BECOURT - tail of column to be clear of HENENCOURT by 1 p.m., after which hour road is required by II Corps.

2. Two battalions of 50th Division will move by bus (under arrangements to be made by III Corps Q) to BAZENTIN LE PETIT to-morrow, 23rd instant - move to be complete by 12 noon - and be placed at disposal of 9th Division for work to-morrow night in the front line. Both battalions together to provide a sum total digging party of not less than 800 diggers, with proper proportion of Officers and N.C.Os etc. They will take rations for 24th instant with them, after which they will be rationed by 9th Division. These two battalions will return to the FLERS LINE after completion of work, where they will remain under orders of the 9th Division, who will provide bivouacing accommodation for two battalions with first line transport.

3. ACKNOWLEDGE ON ATTACHED SLIP.

Brigadier-General,
General Staff,
III CORPS.

Issued by D.R. at 5.15 p.m.

To recipients of O.O.148,
   MINUS :- Copies 4-5
              12-16
              17-22
              25

Despatched by S.D.R. at 3.40 p.m.
   to 9th and 50th Divisions,
   (III Corps G.617)

SECRET.

COPY NO. 7

ADDENDUM NO.1

to

III CORPS OPERATION ORDER NO.148.

22nd October, 1916.

1. 50th Division Infantry Brigades will move to-morrow to area HILLENCOURT – ALBERT – BECOURT – tail of column to be clear of HENENCOURT by 1 p.m., after which hour road is required by II Corps.

2. Two battalions of 50th Division will move by bus (under arrangements to be made by III Corps Q) to BAZENTIN LE PETIT to-morrow, 23rd instant – move to be complete by 12 noon – and be placed at disposal of 9th Division for work to-morrow night in the front line. Both battalions together to provide a sum total digging party of not less than 800 diggers, with proper proportion of Officers and N.C.Os etc. They will take rations for 24th instant with them, after which they will be rationed by 9th Division. These two battalions will return to the FLERS LINE after completion of work, where they will remain under orders of the 9th Division, who will provide bivouacing accommodation for two battalions with first line transport.

3. ACKNOWLEDGE ON ATTACHED SLIP.

Brigadier-General,
General Staff,
III CORPS.

Issued by D.R. at 5.15 p.m.

To recipients of O.O.148,
   MINUS :- Copies 4-5
              12-16
              17-22
              25

Despatched by S.D.R. at 3.40 p.m.
   to 9th and 50th Divisions,
   (III Corps G.617)

SECRET.

COPY NO......7......

CORRECTION NO.1
to
III CORPS OPERATION ORDER NO. 148.

19th Oct.1916.

In para.1 :-

    <u>For</u> 23rd,

    <u>Read</u> 24th,   → *done*

ACKNOWLEDGE BY WIRE.

Issued by D.R. at 5 p.m.
To all recipients of O.O.148.

Brigadier-General,
General Staff,
III CORPS.

S E C R E T.

COPY NO. 6

CORRECTION NO.1
to
III CORPS OPERATION ORDER NO. 148.

19th Oct. 1916.

In para.1 :-

    For 23rd,

    Read 24th,

ACKNOWLEDGE BY WIRE.

Issued by D.R. at 5 p.m.

To all recipients of O.O.148.

Brigadier-General,
General Staff,
III CORPS.

SECRET.
....
COPY NO..7..

III CORPS OPERATION ORDER NO. 148.   19th October, 1916.

Reference:- 1/10,000 Map PYS-LE SARS-LIGNY-THILLOY dated 18/10/16.

1. The Fourth Army is continuing the attack on the 23rd inst.

The 15th Corps is to capture the Gird Line and Gird Support on the immediate right of the 9th Division.

The 4th Canadian Division (2nd Corps) is to capture the Quadrilateral and the Gallwitz Trench on the left of the 15th Division.

2. The attack on the 3rd Corps front will be carried out by the 9th Division on the right and 15th Division on the Left.

3. The attached Map (No.18) shows the objectives and the boundaries between Divisions.

4. ZERO time will be issued later.

5. The preliminary bombardment of objectives will begin at once.

6. Two tanks are placed at the disposal of the 9th Division for the attack.

7. The 9th Division will capture the remainder of Snag Trench and the Tail at the earliest possible date and will establish a jumping-off trench for the assault of their objective. The 15th Division will arrange to join up with the Left of the 9th Division by a continuous trench.

8. Orders regarding the display of flares and the distribution of time will be issued later.

9. Acknowledge by wire.

Brigadier-General,
General Staff,
III Corps.

Issued by D.R. at 11 a.m.

As per Standard List (2nd Corps replacing Can.Corps)
    Plus Copy No. 27 to O.C. Tanks, 3rd Corps.
    Minus Copies 4 & 5.
*Map No.18 issued to Nos. 6, 8, 10, 12, 14, 19, 20, 21, 27.

SECRET.
....
COPY NO. 6.

III CORPS OPERATION ORDER NO. 148.   19th October, 1916.

Reference:- 1/10,000 Map PYS-LE SARS-LIGNY-THILLOY dated 16/10/16.

1. The Fourth Army is continuing the attack on the 23rd inst.

The 15th Corps is to capture the Gird Line and Gird Support on the immediate right of the 9th Division.

The 4th Canadian Division (2nd Corps) is to capture the Quadrilateral and the Gallwitz Trench on the left of the 15th Division.

2. The attack on the 3rd Corps front will be carried out by the 9th Division on the right and 15th Division on the Left.

3. The attached Map (No.18) shows the objectives and the boundaries between Divisions.

4. ZERO time will be issued later.

5. The preliminary bombardment of objectives will begin at once.

6. Two tanks are placed at the disposal of the 9th Division for the attack.

7. The 9th Division will capture the remainder of Snag Trench and the Tail at the earliest possible date and will establish a jumping-off trench for the assault of their objective. The 15th Division will arrange to join up with the Left of the 9th Division by a continuous trench.

8. Orders regarding the display of flares and the distribution of time will be issued later.

9. Acknowledge by wire.

Brigadier-General,
General Staff,
III Corps.

Issued by D.R. at 11 a.m.

As per Standard List (2nd Corps replacing Can.Corps)
    Plus Copy No. 27 to O.C. Tanks, 3rd Corps.
    Minus Copies 4 & 5.
*Map No.18 issued to Nos. 6, 8, 10, 12, 14, 19, 20, 21, 27.

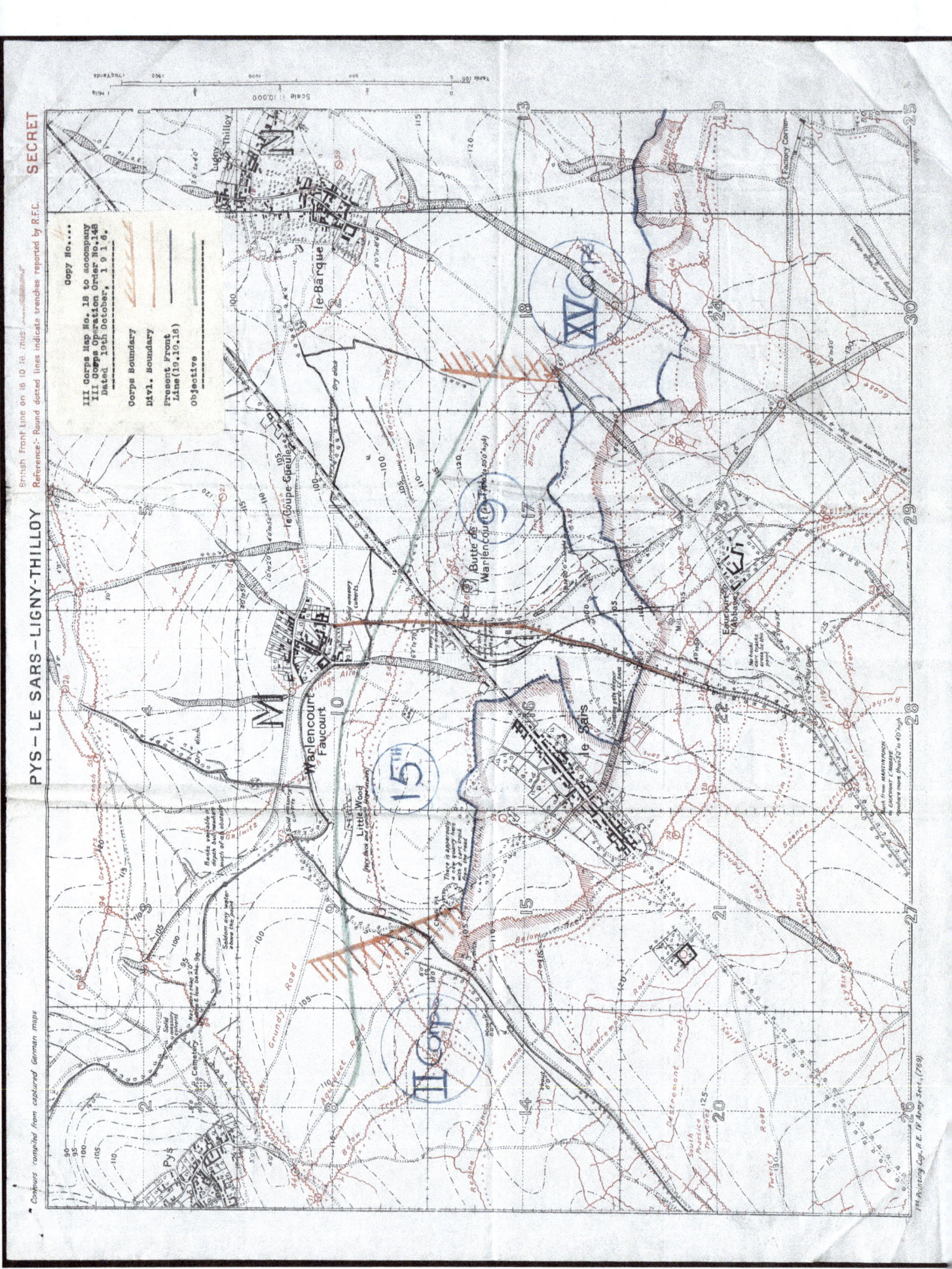

Acknowledged

9th Division

SECRET.
Copy No. 15.

50th. Divn.
G.X.2868/2.

The Operation mentioned in 50th Division Operation Order No. 60 dated 26th October 1916 is postponed two days, and will take place on Monday, 30th October instead of 28th October.

H.W.B. Thorp, Major.
for
Lt.-Col,
General Staff,
50th. Division.

26th. October 1916.

Issued at 4.0 P.M.

Copy No. 1. - 149th Infantry Brigade.
2. - 150th " "
3. - 151st " "
4. - C. R. A. Right Group.
5. - C. R. E.
6. - 7th D.L.I. Pioneers.
7. - Div. Signal Coy.
8. - A. D. M. S.
9. - Div. Train A.S.C.
10. - A. P. M.
11. - Div. T. M. Officer.
12. - "Q" Office.
13. - III Corps.
14. - III Corps.
15. - 9th Division.
16. - 15th Division.
17. - 5th Australian Division.
18. - III Corps Heavy Artillery.
19. - 34th Squadron A.F.C.
20. - Camp Commandant, 50th. Division.
21. - War Diary.
22. - Office.
23. - Office.

SECRET.   Copy No. 6

Addendum No. 4.

to

15th Division Operation Order No. 105.

Headquarters,
15th Division.
26th October, 1916.

Handed over to 50th Div

1. Operations are now postponed till the 30th inst.

2. Reference Addendum No. 3 - para. 2.

The battalions of the 46th Infantry Brigade which have been placed at the disposal of Brigades in line will remain with them until the night of the 28th/29th October, when they will rejoin the 46th Infantry Brigade.

3. The C.R.E. will arrange for the 74th Field Company R.E. to relieve the 73rd Field Company R.E. in line on the night of the 26th/27th inst. Work is not to be interrupted.

H. Knox
Lieut. Colonel,
Issued at 3.15 p.m.   General Staff, 15th Division.

to :-   Copy No.

III Corps.	1 & 2.
III Corps Arty.	3.
III Corps H.Arty.	4.
4th Canadian Div.	5.
9th Division.	6.
50th Division.	7.
44th Inf. Bde.	8.
45th Inf. Bde.	9.
46th Inf. Bde.	10.
9th Gordons.	11.
15th Signals	12.
Left Group D.A.	13.
C.R.E.	14.
A.D.M.S.	15.
"A" & "Q".	16.
A.D.V.S.	17.
15th Train.	18.
No. 4 Special Coy. R.E.	19.
War Diary.	20.
File.	21.
A.P.M.	22.
48th Division.	23.

www.ingramcontent.com/pod-product-compliance
Lightning Source LLC
Chambersburg PA
CBHW080920230426
43668CB00014B/2166